MW01294105

Transforming Schooling for Second Language Learners

A volume in
Research in Second Language Learning
Bogum Yoon, *Series Editor*

Transforming Schooling for Second Language Learners

Theoretical Insights, Policies, Pedagogies, and Practices

edited by

Mariana Pacheco
University of Wisconsin–Madison

P. Zitlali Morales
University of Illinois at Chicago

Colleen Hamilton
University of Wisconsin–Madison

INFORMATION AGE PUBLISHING, INC.
Charlotte, NC • www.infoagepub.com

Library of Congress Cataloging-in-Publication Data

A CIP record for this book is available from the Library of Congress
http://www.loc.gov

ISBN: 978-1-64113-507-8 (Paperback)
        978-1-64113-508-5 (Hardcover)
        978-1-64113-509-2 (ebook)

CONTENTS

SECTION III

TRANSFORMATIVE PEDAGOGIES

SECTION IV

TRANSFORMATIVE PRACTICES

SECTION V

CONCLUSION

ACKNOWLEDGMENTS

Primeramente, queremos agradecer a nuestros papás y familias. Thank you for raising us bilingually and supporting our educational paths. Gracias desde el fondo de nuestros corazones.

We also wish to thank the children, youth, parents, families, community members, teachers, support staff, administrators, critical allies, and educational leaders and activists who have made the contributions to this volume possible. We hope that the insights we share here contribute to our collective understanding about how to realize the academic potential and long-term outcomes of emergent bilingual students more equitably.

Transforming Schooling for Second Language Learners, page ix
Copyright © 2019 by Information Age Publishing

CHAPTER 1

INTRODUCTION AND OVERVIEW

Mariana Pacheco, P. Zitlali Morales, and Colleen Hamilton

In this introduction, we articulate the themes addressed by this edited volume as well as its primary focus and rationale. We provide a brief overview of the four sections of the volume and emphasize the major insights and arguments made in each individual chapter, as well as how individual chapters cohere around broader claims related to the potentially powerful ways that transformative schooling (broadly and diversely defined) could be realized across policies, pedagogies, and practices.

The purpose of this edited volume is to bring together educational researchers and practitioners who have implemented, documented, or examined policies, pedagogies, and practices in and out of classrooms and in real and virtual contexts that are in some way transforming what we know about the extent to which *emergent bilinguals* (EBs) learn and achieve in educational settings. In the following chapters, scholars and researchers identify both (a) the current state of schooling for EBs, from their perspective; and (b) the particular ways that policies, pedagogies, and/or practices transform schooling as it currently exists for EBs in discernible ways based on their scholarship and research.

Transforming Schooling for Second Language Learners, pages 1–17
Copyright © 2019 by Information Age Publishing

For our purposes, the term "emergent bilinguals" will emphasize that "a meaningful education will turn these English language learners not only into English proficient students, but more significantly, also into bilingual students and adults" (García & Kleifgen, 2010, p. 3). Contributing authors to this volume use the terms *emergent bilinguals, linguistically minoritized students, translinguals, bilingual youth, English learners,* and *immigrant and emergent bilingual students.* These terms reflect the following types of student experiences: (a) students that have been labeled English language learners (ELLs) and who hence speak non-English home/first languages, (b) students that participate in educational programs that teach second/additional languages (e.g., English as a second language, bilingual education, etc.), (c) students who have been reclassified as Fluent English Proficient and no longer receive services, and (d) students that have been labeled as ELLs but whose parents/guardians declined services for the student.

Our diverse usage of terms, on the one hand, reflects the varied categories that have been created by educational policymakers, researchers, and practitioners to address the participation of ethnolinguistic minorities in U.S. schools. On the other hand, these terms reflect the diverse conceptual, theoretical, political, and epistemological orientations that have informed attempts to resolve the enduring issues and dilemmas EBs face, such as overcrowded schools, language-based and ability tracking, subtractive approaches, racial/ethnic segregation, inappropriate disability identification, and under resourced schools (Callahan, 2005; Donovan & Cross, 2002; Gándara, Rumberger, Maxwell-Jolly, & Callahan, 2003; Pacheco, 2010a). For example, terms using "trans" and "multi" assert that we must transform the ways we conceptualize the linguistic (and other) backgrounds, experiences, and knowledge that students bring to the classroom, thus transforming narrow and static notions of what counts as language.

Drawing on current and seminal research in fields including second language acquisition, applied linguistics, sociolinguistics, and educational linguistics, contributing authors draw on complementary theoretical, methodological, and philosophical frameworks that attend to the social, cultural, political, and ideological dimensions of being and becoming bi/multilingual and bi/multiliterate in schools and in the United States. In sum, we are deeply committed to asserting hope, possibility, and potential to discussions and discourses about bi/multilingual students. We value the urgency around improving the conditions, experiences, and circumstances in which they are learning languages and academic content (Flores & Rosa, 2015; Gándara & Contreras, 2009; Gutiérrez et al., 2002; Martínez, 2017; Pacheco, 2010b, 2015; Valdés, 1998). Our aim is to highlight perspectives, conceptualizations, orientations, and ideologies that disrupt and contest legacies of deficit thinking, linguistic purism, language standardization, and racism and the racialization of ethnolinguistic minorities. Following Freire (1998),

Hope is something shared between teachers and students. The hope that we can learn together, teach together, be curiously impatient together, produce something together, and resist together the obstacles that prevent the flowering of our joy. In truth, from the point of view of the human condition, hope is an essential component. (p. 69)

Our emphasis on transformation in this volume is inspired by our essential need as educators to speak from a place of hope and hopefulness that the educational plight and crisis for EBs—particularly those from minoritized ethnolinguistic communities of color—can and will be transformed.

Of significance, the present cultural-historical moment is racially-, politically-, and ideologically-charged as nativist and populist rhetoric has renewed and intensified anti-immigrant sentiment and backlash. EBs (and children and youth of color), then, are by and large learning, growing, and developing in contentious circumstances and contexts that vehemently reject and denigrate their backgrounds, experiences, and knowledge and hence position them as Other (Gitlin, Buendía, Crosland, & Doumbia, 2003; Villenas & Deyhle, 1999; Walker, Shafer, & Iiams, 2004). While the majority of EBs are U.S.-born (85% of pre-K to fifth graders and 62% of sixth to twelfth graders; Ruiz Soto, Hooker, & Batalova, 2015), they are nevertheless racialized and constructed as non-native, immigrant Others across sociocultural contexts of learning and development. We believe that a focus on educational transformation for EBs is incredibly timely and relevant, if not of utmost urgency. Language educators must broaden their reach: We must also ensure that the marginalized immigrant communities where EBs are learning, growing, and developing have the tools to thrive and flourish as we support their integration and mobility.

This volume is aimed at language and literacy researchers, practitioners, and policymakers who are committed to enhancing the schooling experiences and educational outcomes of second language learners that have changed the face of school populations across the country. It is also aimed at educators and educational policymakers more broadly who are engaged in policy- and decision-making processes related to second language teaching and learning at the level of districts, schools, classrooms, communities, and states. More often than not, educational policies and reforms for immigrant and bi/multilingual students result in "top-down" approaches that, as several of the contributing authors to this volume demonstrate, contend with political, ideological, and civic debates about the role of language minoritized students and language in learning, schooling, and education in a democratic society (Bartolomé, 2004; Pacheco, 2010b).

For our international colleagues and allies—language researchers, practitioners, and policymakers—we believe this volume has conceptual, theoretical, and epistemological relevance to those that seek to realize 21st century language and education. UNESCO (2003) has articulated the following principles to guide language education globally:

1. UNESCO supports *mother tongue instruction* as a means of improving educational quality by building upon the knowledge and experience of the learners and teachers.
2. UNESCO supports *bilingual and/or multilingual education* at all levels of education as a means of promoting both social and gender equality and as a key element of linguistically diverse societies.
3. UNESCO supports language as an essential component of *intercultural education* in order to encourage understanding between different population groups and ensure respect for fundamental rights. (p. 30)

In this view, social progress and transformation is inextricably linked with equality, mutual understanding, and fundamental rights. Global educators understand that mother tongue instruction in service of bi/multilingual and intercultural education must fundamentally value the experiential knowledge of students and teachers as one way to promote equality and equity across social, cultural, religious, gender, and linguistic difference. Our reading of these principles is that the backgrounds, experiences, and knowledge individuals bring to the education table must form the fundamental basis of learning and language education. The United States, much like the global community, is becoming increasingly and undeniably racially, ethnically, culturally, and linguistically diverse and must not only embrace this diversity but understand that White English monolingualism is no longer tenable (see Ricento, 2000).

This volume focuses on the U.S. context. Research spans traditional gateway communities in Texas, California, New York, and Chicago, Illinois as well as parts of the New Latino Diaspora (Hamann & Harklau, 2010) in Wisconsin and the Mid-Atlantic region. Thus, this volume captures the fundamental diversity in the experiences of students who are being and becoming bi/multilingual and bi/multiliterate in incredibly diverse programs, contexts, and educational settings that may or may not value their languages, their immigrant backgrounds and experiences, their contributions to local communities and economic, and the assets, strengths, and resources they bring to the learning and schooling process.

OUR COLLECTIVE COMMITMENTS

Our collective overarching concerns have to do with addressing and transforming the educational outcomes and schooling experiences of EBs as well as their parents', families', and communities' well-being and mobility. We begin this volume with contributions that articulate theoretical insights about the potential inherent to our particular cultural–historical moment. Global xenophobia and the role of language in public life and discourse have intensified with the rise of Donald Trump's populism and nationalist "Make America Great Again" mantra, which has served to vehemently re-center Whiteness and White superiority and the privileges that come with it. While xenophobic and nationalist rhetoric is not new, it has certainly raised the stakes of reimagining, reenvisioning, reinventing, re-forming, and renewing our intentionality and purpose as equity-oriented research-ers, practitioners, scholars, and public intellectuals (Bartolomé, 2004; Flores & Rosa, 2015; Patel, 2015).

Collectively, we in this volume draw on research and practice related to official and *de facto* policies that affect the structures, practices, and educational possibilities for EBs; pedagogical approaches to the teaching and learning of second languages with EBs; how educators might envision broader equitable and transformative goals. We articulate theoretical and philosophical frameworks that illuminate policies, pedagogies, and prac-tices that create new possibilities for EBs and that might also generate new theoretical constructs, educational approaches, and curriculum practices.

We agree as well on several major points. First, we emphatically uphold stu-dents' home language varieties as essential and fundamental to their learn-ing, development, and subjectivities across their lifetimes but particularly as they attempt to learn second/additional languages (Anzaldúa, 2007; García, 2009; González, 2001; Orellana, 2009; Zentella, 2005). In this regard, we be-lieve that home languages have social, cultural, intellectual, personal, emo-tional, and relational significance for students and their social and familial networks and that to deny these students their right to their home languages is dehumanizing, oppressive, and inequitable and yet a marker of neocolo-nialism in the United States (Cook, 2016; Darder, 1991; Macedo, 2000). Sec-ond, we recognize that the majority of EBs experience subtractive schooling (Callahan, 2005; Ochoa, 2013; Valenzuela, 1999). In particular, subtractive schooling for the majority of EBs includes participation in school contexts that are informed by monolingual biases and ideologies, driven by English-only imperatives and goals, promoting monolingualism (in English), and privileging dominant-group native English-speaking students.

Finally, we agree that the schooling experiences and educational out-comes of EBs in the United States are *always-already* situated within politi-cal and ideological macro contexts that are oppressive, dehumanizing, and part of a neocolonial project (Flores, 2013; González, 2005; Gutierrez et al., 2002; Macedo, 2000; Pacheco, 2010b; Zentella, 1995). At times, these politi-cal and ideological contexts engender overtly discriminatory and harmful policies, such as English-only, anti-bilingual education policies that have taken shape in different states. Often, however, processes of oppression, dehumanization, and neocolonialism are enacted and embodied in micro-level practices, interactions, and activities. As Moll (2003) articulated,

> For Latinos, as for African-American children, particularly those in the work-ing-class, ambiguity and contradiction, not to mention symbolic and even physical violence, are always a backdrop to their language socialization and development, especially in relation to schooling.

Inequitable and symbolically vicious macro contexts, therefore, always-al-ready inform our understanding and conceptualization of what it means to learn and live in U.S. schools, particular for EBs from Chicano and Latino and modest-income backgrounds.

Nevertheless, in developing this edited volume, we were particularly in-spired by the idea of *transformation* for students who are in the process of be-coming bi/multilingual within educational systems and contexts that have a legacy of deficit thinking and exclusion, marginalization, and oppression, particular for EBs from lower-income and Chicano and Latino communi-ties that constitute the majority of EBs (Gándara & Contreras, 2009; Valen-cia & Solórzano, 2004).

We look to scholars such as bell hooks (1994) that speak to the power and potential for education to help transgress and transform schooling in radical, just, and equitable ways. She eloquently argues for a transformation of education as the practice of freedom, particularly through teaching and learning practices:

> Urging all of us to open our minds and hearts so that we can know beyond the boundaries of what is acceptable, so that we can think and rethink, so that we can create new visions, I celebrate teaching that enables transgressions—a movement against and beyond boundaries...which makes education the practice of freedom. (hooks, 1994, p. 12)

Collectively, we highlight scholarship that challenges the persistent pat-terns of educational achievement among EBs in U.S. schools and explores how educational researchers and practitioners transform schooling for these students, who are seemingly bounded by language ideologies, labels, categorizations, and structures that constrain their potential.

In the main, research demonstrates that consistently and across genera-tions of EBs, they do not read, write, and learn content area knowledge at the same rates as native speakers of English (August & Shanahan, 2008). Time and again, research has demonstrated that language minorities, ELLs, and EBs from modest-income backgrounds tend to drop out (or are pushed out) of middle and high school disproportionately and have lower rates of college attainment and socioeconomic mobility despite the fact that the majority of them learn English or have at least attained a functional level of English language proficiency (Callahan, 2005; Gándara & Contreras, 2009).

We believe that our approaches to EBs and language learning and development in K–12 schools affect these outcomes. Thus, this edited volume establishes not only that particular social, socioeconomic, and educational outcomes have persisted for decades, but that specific openings and possibilities exist in schooling and educational spaces that can be—and indeed are being—exploited to alter and transform the landscape and outcomes for EBs. Following hooks (1994), we explore the notion that classrooms— and we would add out-of-school, alternative, and after-school contexts— hold the possibility of teaching and learning for freedom. In these "fields of possibility," she argues,

> We have the opportunity to labor for freedom, to demand of ourselves and our comrades, an openness of mind and heart that allows us to face reality even as we collectively imagine ways to move beyond boundaries, to transgress. This is education as the practice of freedom. (hooks, 1994, p. 207)

As established language researchers, we are deeply concerned that the schooling of EBs has been afflicted by a legacy of deficit perspectives, nationalist and xenophobic English-only language ideologies, underfunded and poorly resourced schools, undertrained and under-qualified teachers, consistent tracking into low-quality and ineffective programs, and a growing emphasis on academic language in English and non-English languages.

Given these circumstances, we highlight research and practices that seek to defy these challenges at different levels of school structures (i.e., classrooms, after-school programs, assessment practices, etc.). We believe this edited volume is both timely and relevant to language researchers, classroom teachers, parents, administrators, and policymakers who seek to transform the ways in which education in effect disenfranchises EBs. Contributing authors focus particularly on the U.S. educational context in which language diversity is both a material but contested reality wherein bi/multilingualism is celebrated for some student populations yet regulated for others (i.e., language minorities). As mentioned earlier, since these circumstances are not unique to the U.S. context, we believe this volume will be similarly timely and relevant to international scholars.

The chapters emphasize the social, cultural, political, and ideological processes that *shape* and are *shaped by* everyday practices in classrooms and schools, as well as learning contexts outside of school. We believe that there is minimal focus on the extent to which schooling and education for EBs is affecting their social, economic, and political mobility. Currently, the overwhelming focus of scholarship in language education policy has called on bilingualism and/or multilingualism/plurilingual-ism *for all* to defy monolingual standards and biases and English-only ideologies (García, 2009; Macedo, 2000). Language pedagogies have centered on leveraging EBs' everyday language practices and meeting the needs of EBs in classrooms (García & Kleifgen, 2010; Wright, 2010). Finally, classroom studies have documented key instructional strategies and activities that seek to accomplish preestablished goals for EBs, such as academic achievement, college readiness, and even reclassification/re-designation to Fluent English Proficient. This edited volume explores these issues in depth. Below we describe in greater detail the chapters included in the respective sections and the contributions they make to our understanding about how to transform schooling for EBs and their families and communities.

ORGANIZATION OF THE VOLUME

This edited volume is divided into four major sections: Section I: Theoretical Insights, Section II: Transformative Policies, Section III: Transformative Pedagogies, and Section IV: Transformative Practices.

Theoretical Insights

In Section I: Theoretical Insights, Aria Razfar begins the volume with a conceptual framework that, rather than reify reductionist and hegemonic approaches to language diversity and difference, pushes us to rethink this national moment as an opportunity to disrupt monolingual rationales and ideologies by re-centering our polyglot realities. By exploring the way that scholars, pundits, and news commentators responded to Donald Trump's discourse and rhetoric, Razfar's conceptual framework emphasizes the identities, ideologies, and affinities that shape solidarity and ultimately give force to the deeper meanings and connections social actors seek. That is, he urges a shift from *language as code* to *language as identity/solidarity*. He uses students and teachers' musings during classroom discussions about Donald and Melania Trump—a formerly "undocumented" immigrant herself who speaks with a thick accent—to argue that the failure to engage deeply in critical interrogations of how language functions to create affinities and connections delimits a polylingual society and propagates EBs' vulnerabilities by focusing on language and deficits rather than deeper meanings, identities, and solidarities.

Donaldo Macedo and Lilia Bartolomé similarly highlight that the current cultural–historical moment presents unparalleled opportunities to engage teachers and educators in processes of linguistic and cultural decolonization.

They focus specifically on dual language education (DLE) programs where native speakers of two languages are grouped. These programs purposely seek to protect minoritized students and sustain and develop their languages from further disenfranchisement, marginalization, and oppression. They draw on Bartolomé's (1994, 2004) conceptualization of *political clarity,* or the extent to which individuals develop a critical consciousness about the sociopolitical and socioeconomic inequities that affect their lives as well as their potential to transform these conditions. This consciousness includes understanding the links between macro-level systems and structures and micro-level practices and experiences in educational institutions. Macedo and Bartolomé argue that decolonization through political clarity can lead to humanizing schooling experiences. Specifically, DLE teachers who promote bilingualism, biliteracy, and biculturalism and work at the intersection of minority (e.g., Korean, Spanish) and majority languages (i.e., English) with White students and students of color from different socioeconomic backgrounds are uniquely positioned to humanize and democratize learning, schooling, and education, and in the process, transform the lives and social trajectories of oppressed students and their communities.

Transformative Policies

Contributors in Section II: Transformative Policies highlight explicit and *de facto* policies that are in effect transforming schooling experiences and possibilities for EB students. This research addresses policymaking processes at the national, state, district, and school levels as well as how particular policies and *de facto* policies challenge narrow English-only language ideologies, academic achievement outcomes, and dominant notions of what it means for EBs to succeed in schools. To be clear, we intend to avoid overlap with recent but important collections that focus on the policy implementation process. For example, Menken & García (2010) focus on "the negotiation of language education policies in schools around the world and to provide educators with deeper understandings of this process to guide their implementation of language policies in schools and classrooms" (pp. 1–2). We, in particular, are interested in actual and *de facto* policies, policymaking processes, and teachers' and students' "policymaking" in the classroom that evidently transform schooling as it currently exists for EBs.

Communities across the United States are responding to demographic shifts that include newcomer immigrants and political refugees, as well as their emergent bilingual children who likewise affect school demographics. Megan Hopkins and Kristina Brezicha focus on a northeastern community that was outright hostile and xenophobic of its growing immigrant population and to the extent to which community-based organizations and community activists—conceptualized as *boundary spanners*—effectively promoted and shaped equity-oriented educational policies. They analyze the policy response in one school district that had to contend with the local community's hostile and xenophobic views as part of the policy- and decision-making processes. They highlight the efforts of equity-minded community members who mediated dialogue between district leaders and community members that, over time, came to shape equitable policies for their growing EB population. Hopkins and Brezicha argue that coalition building across political and ideological difference is necessary if we are to transform the schooling experiences and academic potential of EB students by advancing inclusive and robust school cultures and enhancing student, parent, and family engagement.

Ursula Aldana and Danny Martínez similarly highlight the political struggles undertaken by numerous policymakers, researchers, and interest groups in California to overturn Proposition 227, which in effect eliminated bilingual education for millions of EB students in the state. In particular, they draw on Ruiz's (1984) language policy framework to examine how these key social actors substantively shifted the orientation of *language as problem* to *language as right/resource* to enable the passage of Proposition 58 (The Non English Languages Allowed in Public Education Act) in 2016. They demonstrate that the work of transformative schooling for EBs requires consciousness raising, coalition building, and sustained political and ideological struggle to advance the transformative pedagogies and practices needed to realize transformative educational policies.

Shifting the focus from a community context to a school context, Jamy Stillman investigates how the Common Core State Standards in English Language Arts were mediated through school-level policies and practices at a high-performing dual language immersion school near the U.S.-Mexico border. Drawing on a multi-year ethnographic study, she analyzes the ways that school leaders and teachers mitigated the potentially negative effects of restrictive and reductive educational policies. Specifically, she analyzes the practices and discourses around the organization of teacher autonomy and professionalism as well as the deliberate promotion of asset-oriented and strength-based teaching and learning for EBs. Stillman argues that macro-level educational policies and mandates were mediated powerfully by school-level instantiations that promoted the humanizing, equitable, and ethical pedagogical approaches teachers collectively believed could transform EBs' access to rigorous, responsive teaching and learning.

Transformative Pedagogies

Section III: Transformative Pedagogies includes chapters that address pedagogical approaches to teaching, learning, and curriculum for EBs, as well as the philosophical and theoretical principles that inform and inspire them. These authors focus on additive and asset-based orientations to realizing the social, academic, and personal potential of EBs in various educational settings, including traditional classrooms, and articulate principles of teaching, learning, and curriculum that transform outcomes for EBs. Much of this work focuses on students' everyday home–community language practices, which are leveraged to transform educational experiences and positioning of EBs in school contexts. Recent scholarship has begun to emphasize and demand critical approaches that consider seriously the need to reconcile inequitable circumstances and conditions that characterize schooling for EBs. This section highlights research and scholarship that seeks to "transform the curriculum so that it does not reflect or reinforce systems of domination" by envisioning engaged pedagogies that make "teaching practices a site of resistance" (hooks, 1994, p. 21).

Building on equity-oriented scholarship on social design experiments for EB students, Arturo Córtez and Kris Gutiérrez conceptualize *socio-spatial repertoires* that include linguistic, cultural, spatial, and political tools and practices youth employ to negotiate the everyday demands of tensions that emerge from spatial production and reproduction. Through their analysis of an illustrative example of how translingual youth strategically negotiated a dispute about rights to community space, the authors argue that these experiences incited new literacies, language practices, and stances. Based on their theorizing about the importance of understanding the everyday resistance efforts of translingual youth of color and the repertoires they develop, the authors also analyze the challenges and critical shifts preservice teachers began to enact and embody as they transformed pedagogical spaces and practices for EB students in schools.

Building on Marjorie Orellana's (2016) conceptualization of a "pedagogy of heart," Orellana and her colleagues outline six foundational principles of what they theorize as a transcultural pedagogy of heart and mind that has guided their pedagogical practices in an after-school program that serves immigrant and multilingual students. They draw on sociocultural theories of learning that emphasize the fundamental value of students' linguistic and cultural experiences and knowledge in the service of collaborative literacy learning. For these authors, the "heart" captures the social and relational dimensions of joint, collaborative learning among a community of learners. In the context of an after-school program (B-Club) in Los Angeles that is modeled on the Fifth Dimension programs (Cole and the Distributed Literacy Consortium, 2005), a transcultural pedagogy centers embodied forms of learning and knowing as well as the their affective and spiritual dimensions. They draw on examples from B-Club to illustrate the six principles. The authors argue powerfully that this pedagogical approach has the potential to transform dominant pedagogical approaches that marginalize multicultural, multilingual immigrant students and their families and communities.

Christine Malsbary and her colleague, Jordan Wolf, take up the opportunities afforded by exceptionally diverse high school classrooms that serve multilingual, multicultural, and multiethnic students who are learning science in English, their second language. Malsbary (2016) has theorized these contexts as "hyper-diverse" because rather than suppress diversity, students and their teachers develop resilient and robust practices that capitalize on and leverage cultural and linguistic diversity in ways that promote collaborative learning and meaning making. Building on their experiences in classrooms, they elaborate a set of pedagogical principles for practitioners and researchers who work in hyper-diverse contexts. Next, Wolf describes the ways that these pedagogical principles inform his curriculum design, planning, and implementation in his high school biology classroom. These examples illustrate clearly the ways that language educators can transform schooling for bi/multilingual students and promote transformative pedagogical approaches in the science classroom.

Transformative Practices

Chapters in Section IV: Transformative Practices feature the work of scholars examining the languages and literacy practices of youth and adults/teachers in both in- and out-of-school settings that are often overlooked or undervalued due to the focus on standardized curriculum and narrow academic outcomes. Children and youth have extensive linguistic repertoires and exercise linguistic dexterity (Pacheco, 2015; Paris, 2009; Rymes, 2010). They develop these abilities and insights in practice to navigate their surroundings and develop communicative competence in diverse contexts, from their homes to their interethnic neighborhoods to academic settings. Researchers illustrate the types of practices as well as those dynamic, moment-to-moment, discursive processes that affect how EBs experience classrooms and schooling in ways that affect their access to learning and meaning making.

The first chapter by Ramón Martínez, Michiko Hikida, and Leah Durán focuses on translanguaging practices in the everyday life of the classroom and the concomitant social interactions generated therein. The authors conceptualize *translanguaging* as the flexible ways that EBs employ their full linguistic repertoires across Spanish and English to transform classroom contexts and spaces that create arbitrary but immutable linguistic boundaries, using illustrative examples of classroom discourse to analyze the ways that EB students—and teachers—not only create learning opportunities but develop important peer relationships. This research challenges reductive and narrow constructions of what counts as language and urges researchers and practitioners to challenge the corresponding boundaries of skills, abilities, learning, and achievement that together duplicate EB students' educational vulnerabilities and disenfranchisement.

Colleen Hamilton and Mariana Pacheco draw on in-depth interviews with bilingual youth to analyze how they leveraged their available social networks of family members, teachers, mentors, and counselors in their Spanish and English social worlds to enhance the availability of key resources and access as they sought a postsecondary education. Oftentimes, for example, they needed these networks to help them surmount restrictive and limiting educational practices—such as tracking by language and/or ability, placement in English as a second language classes, and so on—to improve their opportunities for educational mobility. Second, these youth humanized stories of bilingual difference by articulating a "formula for success" that included a college-bound mindset and the ability to design opportunities toward imagined social futures (Gutiérrez, 2008, 2016; Gutiérrez & Jurow, 2016). Finally, they intended to reciprocate the individuals that had supported them across their educational trajectory. This scholarship reminds us that it takes networks and collectives of individuals to undermine discriminatory and subtractive schooling structures, practices, and ideologies to improve EBs' social futures.

The last two chapters in this section focus on the socioemotional meanings and understandings that imbue everyday language and literacy practices across in- and after-school contexts. Lucila D. Ek, Armanda Garza, and Adriana García conceptualize biliteracy as emotional practice in an after-school technology program. In particular, they analyze the language and literacy practices between children and El Maga (a cyber-being who presides over the club) that help foster friendly, positive, and caring relationships by leveraging their full linguistic repertoire, which included Spanish and English. The participants' digital literacy practices included the strategic use of the Spanish lexicon, use of humor (e.g., *dichos y refranes, adivinanzas, y bromas humorísticas,* or cultural sayings, riddles, and humorous jokes), and multimodal texts. This critical analysis compels researchers and practitioners to re-center the social, cultural, personal, and emotional dimensions of language and literacy activity that can come to incite deep and novel engagement and learning opportunities for EBs.

Finally, P. Zitlali Morales and Lydia A. Saravia take up the notion of *cariño*, which invokes cultural ideas that comprise *educación* [education] in Spanish-speaking and bilingual classrooms (Bartolomé, 2008; Curry, 2016; Duncan-Andrade, 2006; Nieto, 2000). They further conceptualize *cariño* as a teacher's deep understanding of EBs' sociopolitical, material, and racialized experiences through enacted and embodied forms of affection for their students and their students' families and communities as demonstrated through high academic expectations and advocacy. Drawing on two qualitative studies of bilingual classrooms in the United States and Guatemala, the authors analyze the Spanish-language and Mayan indigenous-language practices between teachers and students during instruction to illustrate how these teachers enacted and embodied *cariño* in their distinct sociocultural, sociopolitical contexts. This research has implications for how language educators reconceptualize effective and powerful learning for EBs that extends beyond learning goals and outcomes and realize humanizing approaches.

In the conclusion, Chapter 14: "Implications and Future Directions" revisits the contributions each chapter has made to our collective thinking about potential ways to transform outcomes for EBs. It includes specific recommendations for future policies, pedagogies, and practices that could help realize this potential and the promise of an equal *and* equitable educational opportunity for all students in ways that elevate and privilege the social, cultural, socioeconomic, and linguistic backgrounds of EB students and their families and communities.

REFERENCES

Anzaldúa, G. (2007). Borderlands/la frontera: The new mestiza (3rd ed.). San Francisco, CA: Aunt Lute Books.

August, D., & Shanahan, T. (2008). *Developing reading and writing in second language learners*. New York, NY: Routledge.

Bartolomé, L. (1994). Beyond the methods fetish: Toward a humanizing pedagogy. *Harvard Educational Review, 64*(2), 173–194.

Bartolomé, L. (2004). Critical pedagogy and teacher education: Radicalizing prospective teachers. *Teacher Education Quarterly, 31*(1), 97–122.

Bartolomé, L. I. (2008). Authentic cariño and respect in minority education: The political and ideological dimensions of love. *International Journal of Critical Pedagogy, 1*(1), 1–17.

Callahan, R. M. (2005). Tracking and high school English learners: Limiting opportunity to learn. *American Educational Research Journal, 42*(2), 305–328.

Cook, V. (2016). Where is the native speaker now? *TESOL Quarterly, 50*(1), 186–189. https://doi.org/10.1002/tesq.286

Cole, M., & the Distributed Literacy Consortium. (2006). *The fifth dimension: An after-school program built on diversity*. New York, NY: Russell Sage.

Curry, M. W. (2016). Will you stand for me? Authentic cariño and transformative rites of passage in an urban high school. *American Educational Research Journal, 53*(4), 883–918.

Darder, A. (1991). *Culture and power in the classroom: A critical foundation for bicultural education*. Santa Barbara, CA: Greenwood.

Donovan, S., & Cross, C. (2002). Minority students in special and gifted education. Washington, DC: National Academy Press.

Duncan-Andrade, J. M. R. (2006). Utilizing cariño in the development of research methodologies. In J. L. Kincheloe, K. Hayes, K. Rose, & P. M. Anderson (Eds.), *The Praeger handbook of urban education* (Vol. 2, pp. 451–460). Westport, CT: Greenwood.

Flores, N. (2013). Silencing the subaltern: Nation-State/Colonial governmentality and bilingual education in the United States. *Critical Inquiry in Language Studies, 10*(4), 263–287. https://doi.org/10.1080/15427587.2013.846210

Flores, N., & Rosa, J. (2015). Undoing appropriateness: Raciolinguistic ideologies and language diversity in education. *Harvard Educational Review, 85*, 149–171.

Freire, P. (1998). *Pedagogy of freedom: Ethics, democracy, and civic courage.* New York, NY: Rowman & Littlefield.

Gándara, P., & Contreras, F. (2009). *The Latino education crisis: The consequences of failed social policies.* Cambridge, MA: Harvard University Press.

Gándara, P., Rumberger, R., Maxwell-Jolly, J., & Callahan, R. (2003, October 7). English learners in California schools: Unequal resources, unequal outcomes. *Education Policy Analysis Archives, 11*(36). http://dx.doi.org/10.14507/epaa.v11n36.2003

García, O. (2009). *Bilingual education in the 21st century: A global perspective.* Malden, MA: Wiley-Blackwell.

Garcia, O., & Kleifgen, J. A. (2010). *Educating emergent bilinguals: Policies, programs, and practices for English language learners.* New York, NY: Teachers College Press.

Gitlin, A., Buendía, E., Crosland, K., & Doumbia, F. (2003). The production of margin and center: Welcoming–unwelcoming of immigrant students. *American Educational Research Journal, 40*(1), 91–122.

González, N. (2001). I am my language: Discourses of women and children in the borderlands. Tucson, AZ: University of Arizona Press.

González, N. (2005). Children in the eye of the storm: Language socialization and language ideologies in a dual-language school. In A. C. Zentella (Ed.), *Building on strength: language and literacy in Latino families and communities* (pp. 162–174). New York, NY: Teachers College Press.

Gutiérrez, K. D. (2008). Developing a sociocritical literacy in the third space. *Reading Research Quarterly, 43*(2), 148–164. https://doi.org/10.1598/RRQ.43.2.3

Gutiérrez, K. D. (2016). 2011 AERA presidential address: Designing resilient ecologies: Social design experiments and a new social imagination. *Educational Researcher, 45*(3), 187–196. https://doi.org/10.3102/0013189X16645430

Gutiérrez, K. D., Asato, J., Pacheco, M., Moll, L. C., Olson, K., Horng, E. L., ... McCarty, T. L. (2002). "Sounding American": The consequences of new reforms on English language learners. *Reading Research Quarterly, 37*(3), 328–343. doi:10.1598/RRQ.37.3.4

Gutiérrez, K. D., & Jurow, A. S. (2016). Social design experiments: Toward equity by design. *Journal of the Learning Sciences, 25*(4), 565–598. https://doi.org/10.1080/10508406.2016.1204548

Hamann, E. T., & Harklau, L. (2010). Education in the new Latino diaspora. In E. G. Murillo, Jr., Villenas, S. A., Galván, R. T., Muñoz, J. S., Martinez, C., & Machado-Casas, M. (Eds.), *Handbook of Latinos and education: Theory, research, and practice* (pp. 157–169). New York, NY: Routledge.

hooks, b. (1994). *Teaching to transgress: Education as the practice of freedom.* New York, NY: Routledge.

Macedo, D. (2000). The colonialism of the English only movement. *Education Researcher, 29*(3), 15–24.

Malsbary, C. B. (2016). Youth and schools' practices in hyper-diverse contexts. *American Education Research Journal, 53*(6), 1491–1521.

Martínez, R. A. (2017). 'Are you gonna show this to White people?': Chicana/o and Latina/o students' counter-narratives on race, place, and representation. *Race Ethnicity and Education, 20*(1), 101–116.

Menken, K., & García, O. (Eds.). (2010). Negotiating language policies in schools: Educators as policymakers. New York, NY: Routledge.

Moll, L. (2003, April 24). Contemporary issues in the schooling of Latino students: Considering educational sovereignty. Paper presented at the Symposium on National Latino/a Education Research Agenda Project: Imagining New Possibilities for Latino/a Communities. Annual meeting of the American Educational Research Association, Chicago, Il.

Nieto, S. (2000). Puerto Rican students in U.S. schools: A brief history. In S. Nieto (Ed.), *Puerto Rican students in U.S. schools* (pp. 5–38). Mahwah, NJ: Erlbaum.

Ochoa, G. L. (2013). *Academic Profiling: Latinos, Asian Americans, and the Achievement Gap.* Minneapolis: University of Minnesota Press.

Orellana, M. F. (2009). *Translating childhoods: Immigrant youth, language, and culture.* Piscataway, NJ: Rutgers University Press.

Orellana, M. F. (2016). *Immigrant children in transcultural spaces: Language, learning, and love.* New York, NY: Routledge.

Pacheco, M. (2010a). English learners' reading achievement: Dialectical relationships between policy and practices in meaning-making opportunities. *Reading Research Quarterly, 45*(3), 292–317.

Pacheco, M. (2010b). Performativity in the bilingual classroom: The plight of English learners in the current reform context. *Anthropology & Education Quarterly, 41*(1), 75–93.

Pacheco, M. (2015). Bilingualism-as-participation: Examining adolescents' bi(multi) lingual literacies across out-of-school and online contexts. In D. Molle, E. Sato, T. Boals, & C. Hedgespeth (Eds.), *Multilingual learners and academic literacies: Sociocultural contexts of literacy development in adolescents* (pp. 135–165). New York, NY: Routledge.

Paris, D. (2009). "They're in my culture, they speak the same way": African American language in multiethnic high schools. *Harvard Educational Review, 79*, 428–447.

Patel, L. (2015). *Decolonizing educational research: From ownership to answerability.* New York, NY: Routledge.

Ricento, T. (Ed.). (2000). *Ideology, politics, and language policies: Focus on English.* Philadelphia, PA: John Benjamins.

Ruiz, R. (1984). Orientations in language planning. *NABE Journal, 8*(2), 15–34.

Ruiz Soto, A. G., Hooker, S., & Batalova, J. (2015). *States and districts with the highest number and share of English language learners.* Washington, DC: Migration Policy Institute.

Rymes, B. (2010). Communicative repertoires and English language learners. In M. Shatz & L. C. Wilinson (Eds.), *The education of English language learners* (pp. 177–197). New York, NY: Guilford Press.

UNESCO (2003). *Education in a multilingual world.* Paris, France: UNESCO.

Valdés, G. (1998). The world outside and inside schools: Language and immigrant children. *Educational Researcher, 27*(6), 4–18. https://doi.org/10.2307/1176090

Valencia, R. R., & Solórzano, D. (2004). Today's deficit thinking about the education of minority students. In O. Sant Ana (Ed.), Tongue-tied: The lives of multilingual children in public education (pp. 124–133). New York, NY: Rowman & Littlefield.

Valenzuela, A. (1999). *Subtractive schooling: U.S.-Mexican youth and the politics of caring.* Albany: State University of New York.

Villenas, S., & Deyhle, D. (1999). Critical race theory and ethnographies challenging the stereotypes: Latino families, schooling, resilience and resistance. *Curriculum Inquiry, 29,* 413–445. doi:10.1111/0362-6784.00140

Walker, A., Shafer, J., & Iiams, M. (2004). "Not in my classroom": Teacher attitudes towards English language learners in the mainstream classroom. *NABE Journal of Research and Practice, 2*(1), 130–160.

Wright, W. E. (2010). *Foundations for teaching English language learners: Research, theory, policy, and practice.* Philadelphia, PA: Caslon Incorporated.

Zentella, A. C. (1995, April 5–7). The "Chiquitafication" of U.S. Latinos and their languages, or why we need an anthropolitical linguistics. In *SALSA III: Proceedings of the Third Annual Symposium About Language and Society,* Austin, Texas.

Zentella, A. C. (Ed.). (2005). *Building on strength: Language and literacy in Latino families and communities.* New York, NY: Teachers College Press.

SECTION I

THEORETICAL INSIGHTS

CHAPTER 2

SPINNING TRUMP'S LANGUAGE

Cracking the Code and Transforming Identities and Ideologies

Aria Razfar
University of Illinois at Chicago

ABSTRACT

This chapter critiques reductionist and hegemonic approaches to language difference by reframing this national moment as an opportunity to engage with *language as identity/solidarity* beyond *language as code*. It analyzes students' and teachers' reactions to language used by political figures, highlighting the deeper meanings, identities, and solidarities sought by social actors. In this sense, we are now presented with the opportunity to shift from a monoglot ethos to a national discourse of polylingualism. Failure to consider language as a means of social connection may serve to perpetuate monolingual ideologies, rather than seizing this moment to build solidarity across language difference.

In the late nineties, businessman Ron Unz led a movement to eliminate bilingual education that provided some form of home language support

Transforming Schooling for Second Language Learners, pages 21–42
Copyright © 2019 by Information Age Publishing
21

for emergent bilinguals throughout the United States. (Ryan, 2002). Anti-immigrant sentiments and backlash politics led to a number of propositions being passed that severely hampered bilingual education in several states (e.g., Arizona, California, and Massachusetts). In some states, like Colorado, this movement was resisted and voters successfully prevented such measures from carrying the weight of law. However, the movement was particularly successful in other states, like Arizona and California, with the largest immigrant, bilingual population (mostly Spanish-speaking Latino/as). In 1998, California voters elected to restrict and effectively eliminate bilingual education across the state only to vote it back almost 20 years later through Proposition 58, which has the potential to transform the schooling experiences and educational potential of emergent bilingual students.

This cycle of events follows a predictable albeit paradoxical pattern of linguistic restrictivism and weak models of transitional bilingualism (Crawford, 1998; Hartman, 1948). On the one hand, linguistic *restrictivism* severely limits or *restricts* the use of languages other than English in public spaces and this is generally enabled through legislation and/or institutional policies. On the other hand, transitional bilingualism provides tacit recognition of nondominant languages; however, the function of bilingualism is primarily private and a tool toward acquiring the dominant language, in this case English. This oscillation between linguistic restrictivism and transitional bilingualism has effectively sustained the phenomena of a *monoglot ethos* (Silverstein, 1996). While the history of multilingualism in the United States has been a cycle of conflict and concessions, one thing has remained constant: the dominance of monolingual cultural norms, pedagogy, and policy.

The election of Donald Trump may seem like it is signaling a dramatic swing of the pendulum toward linguistic restrictivism and a nativist backlash. However, a closer examination of narrative events and everyday interactions across the nation may suggest a language ideological shift toward polylingualism in our national discourse. This shift is noticeable particularly when it comes to questions about the nature, function, and purpose of language in our society.

For our nation's emergent bilingual population, linguistic restrictivism leads to fear, uncertainty, and a toxic climate. However, it could be transformative for our national conversation to reposition nonstandard varieties, non-English languages, and their speakers at the center of who we imagine ourselves to be. It is essential to examine the current climate with a sociocultural and critical lens of language and learning. In this chapter, I provide a conceptual framework for analyzing the impending episode of an emergent national conversation that moves us toward a *polyglot reality*. It is a perspective grounded in my research and collaborations with educators who are immersed in the urban realities of polylingualism and emergent bilinguals' lives. In contrast to multilingualism where languages are viewed as separate, I use the term *polylingualism* to emphasize the interconnected-ness and simultaneity of all languages. Similar to the term *plurilingualism* adopted by the Council of Europe (2008) to refer to the repertoire and varieties of languages used by individuals, *polylingual* individuals use whatever linguistic features are at their disposal for communicative purposes (Jør-gensen, 2008). I argue that a narrow conception of language, focusing on its formal properties, serves to reify reductive views of emergent bilinguals, positioning them and their families in deficit ways, and far from resisting oppressive practices, it reinvigorates linguistic and cultural hegemony. Finally, I discuss implications for educators, researchers, and broader society working with emergent bilinguals.

FROM MONOGLOTISM TOWARD A POLYLINGUAL CONSCIOUSNESS

In its least reductive formulation, monoglotism holds that languages other than English serve a utilitarian function within the broader assimilationist objectives that ultimately relinquish public and private sovereignty to English use. For example, a teacher may use Spanish in the classroom to clarify or translate in support of learning English, but reject its use as the main code of the classroom. At its worst, authoritarian and ultra-nationalist sentiments galvanize English-only movements in the name of preserving national cohesion and identity. In a nation where 4.5 million (1 out 10) students are classified as English learners, nearly 20% of the population consider themselves bilingual, and transnational migrants are defining the everyday landscape of the United States, it is somewhat understandable why mono-glots are feeling uncertain about their place in an emergent polylingual America. Nevertheless, unlike previous immigrant waves, who by and large lost their connection to their heritage, language, and culture, the communication landscape for recent arrivals has become increasingly polylingual as speakers simultaneously use multiple codes in interwoven ways (Shin & Kominski, 2010). Over the last decade, technology has dramatically shifted people's access to transnational literacies such that migrant literacies have become normative (Razfar & Maravilla-Cano, 2017).

In 2012, President Obama declared, "You should be thinking...how can your child become bilingual? We should have every child speaking more than one language" (Grosjean, 2012, para. 10). This was a dramatic ideological shift coming from the highest office. For most of U.S. history, being American was synonymous with being an English monolingual (Hartman, 1948). A recent Pew research study showed that the majority of survey respondents agreed that to truly be considered American, "it is very or somewhat important that a person speak English" (Stokes, 2017, p. 25).

Debates about language have fueled the American paradox where the push for unity and reductive formations of identity are in constant tension with diversity and emergent polylingual realities (Gillon, 2012). Thus, English proficiency continues to be a strong indicator of allegiance, national purity, and belonging.

Throughout the 2016 campaign, team Trump tapped into these "populist" tropes in order to galvanize an electoral base, mostly monolingual and White, who has grown unsure of its standing in the new America. Nonetheless, as Aldana and Martinez (see Chapter 5) demonstrate, policymakers, researchers, and bilingual education advocates can counter English-only ideologies, as evidenced by the passage of Proposition 58 in California. Over the last twenty years of Proposition 227, bilingual teachers, administrators, and district leaders have resisted English-only legislation and provided necessary primary language support for emergent bilingual students. While their advocacy culminated in the passage of Proposition 58, was this policy a fundamental shift toward a polyglot stance?

I posit that a more robust national conversation about language could disrupt the inertia of monoglotism and move us closer toward a polylingual consciousness which will benefit the lived realities of not only bilingual children but all children. Perhaps the Trump era will generate a fundamentally different conversation about how we think about language and move beyond linguistic restrictivism. The following section articulates a framework for engaging educators and emergent bilinguals who might be feeling unease in the age of rising populism and authoritarian discourses following the election of President Trump.

PRESIDENTIAL DISCOURSE AND RHETORIC

Scholars of language, communication, and rhetoric have long been interested in the speech acts of politicians. In particular, they have sought to understand how politicians strategically use language to align themselves with the hopes, dreams, worries, and fears of their constituents. Presidential candidates in particular play a critical role in representing the prevailing mood of a nation and constructing a cohesive national narrative. Specifically, analyses of presidential discourse have focused on pronunciation irregularities, syntactic miscues, innovative lexical choice, rhetorical eloquence, or style shifting and hence provided a window into the prevailing sentiments, political stances, and ideological tensions within nation states.

Political rhetoric and the language use or misuse of presidents have been the subject of analysis for decades. For many experts, the apparent decline in grammar, syntax, and logical constructions over the course of many presidencies coupled with a paradigm of linguistic oversimplification have produced a culture wherein intellectuals have become "the piñatas" of public life (Lim, 2012). Lim's analysis of inaugural addresses and interviews with presidential speech writers dating back to Harding focused on average sentence length and reading level by grade. His focus on form led to the conclusion that there is a massive campaign of linguistic simplification that emphasizes style over substance, leading to a hostile environment for intellectuals in public spaces. Thus, intellectual discourse has been framed as complicated, convoluted, and inauthentic.

While intellectual talk is characterized through a focus on complex sentence structures and vocabulary, authenticity has been positioned as its polar opposite. The appeal to form and linguistic code have played a significant role in determining who is authentically American enough to be president. Still, according to the polls, President George W. Bush was considered one of the worst offenders of syntactic gaffes and his "mangled English" was viewed as a bad influence on future generations (AFP Daily Telegraph, 2009, para. 1). In 1998, President Clinton's use of the word "is" was one of the key factors in determining whether he was guilty of perjury (Starr, 1998). Ultimately, President Clinton relied on "literal notions of language" and "an appeal to form to save his presidency" (Culpeper & Haugh, 2014, p. 105). In the 2008 campaign, candidate Obama's "ostentatiously exotic" pronunciation of "Pah-kih-stan" was the subject of controversy in conservative circles (Levenson, 2014, para. 6). While his pronunciation was more authentically Pakistani, it signaled a lack of allegiance for conservatives.

Alim and Smitherman (2012) examined the style shifting of Barack Obama and how he leveraged Black language styles in rich ways to create solidarity with various segments of his supporters and obviously alienate his nativist opponents. While they make the case for the vitality of Black language styles and attempt to legitimize them more broadly through the practices of a U.S. president, they lament that teachers continue to hear "what's not said" and view this language through a monoglot gaze and its speakers through a deficit lens. Too often, linguists neglect to examine the function of a language by focusing on its form (Lakoff, 1985). This short-sightedness has been demonstrated in critical analyses of presidential discourse as well as debates about bilingualism. In the weeks leading up to the election, University of Chicago anthropologist Michael Silverstein was asked about the speaking style of candidate Trump. He stated, "Mr. Trump's delivery has long been a cross between stand-up comedy and the kind of thing one hears in the neighborhood bars: no full sentences with clear assertions, but only a stream of phrases" (Daileda, 2016, para. 7). Whether it was President Clinton's use of "is," President Bush's syntax, or President Obama's pronunciation of "Pakistan" or adept style shifting, the focus on form—and that which can be transcribed—has limited our understanding of the personal, sociocultural, and sociopolitical factors impacting meaning making.

CONCEPTUAL FRAMEWORK

Historically, the dominant paradigm in language study has focused on what was thought to be its more objective, scientific properties: phonology, morphology, syntax, and to some degree, semantics. For the purposes of language analysis, these features of language constitute the first layer known as *the code.* Over time, sociolinguists and applied linguists began to stretch the scope of linguistic analysis within academic circles by focusing on prosodic elements such as tone, intonation, stress, and vowel elongation (Halliday, 1967). Since the 1960s, linguistic anthropologists have expanded their focus to the social dimensions of language by analyzing interactions, contexts, and meanings (Hymes, 1964). This expansion was a stark departure from focusing on *the code* as the primary unit of analysis.

Over the last four decades, linguistic anthropologists have argued for the need to go beyond linguistic code (i.e., what is said) and prosody (i.e., how it is said) to better understand how people make sense of their life-worlds across time and space (Ahearn, 2011; Duranti, 2001; Hymes, 1964). The need to focus our analysis on the semiotic and the ideological dimensions of language have never been greater. In fact, to emphasize this broader analysis, educational linguists emphasized the term "discourse" as opposed to "language," given the formal assumptions underlying language (Gee, 2015). Discourse analysis aimed to go beyond the apparent form of language by focusing on the process of shared meaning-making, values, affective dispositions, and intersubjectivity. Specifically, identity(s) and ideology(s) were foregrounded in addition to formalistic features of language. Identity(s) and ideology(s) were conceived as products of discursive functions whether they be grounded in nature (biological identity), institutions (conversational analysis), or interpersonal interactions (affinity; Gee, 2015; Schegloff, 2007).

The NIDALS framework of discourse analysis also integrates learner and solidarity identities across vertical and horizontal learning spaces (Razfar & Rumenapp, 2013). In this framework, *N* reflects natural/biological processes, *I* reflects institutional processes, *D* reflects discursive processes, *A* reflects affinity/affective alignment, *L* reflects expert and novice learners, and *S* reflects solidarity and semiotic struggle with the "other" (see Figure 2.1). In this framework, learner identities are constructed along a continuum of informal (horizontal) and formal (vertical) learning environments. Solidarity identities are the product of "semiotic struggle" with an ideological "other." An ideological other can be polar opposite stances and/or moral positions (e.g., globalism vs. isolationism). This process is generally filled with contestation and even conflict as interlocutors strive to achieve shared understanding. Another key component of this framework are the technologies that mediate analyses of language use. In other words, the medium of language is just as important as the formal properties of

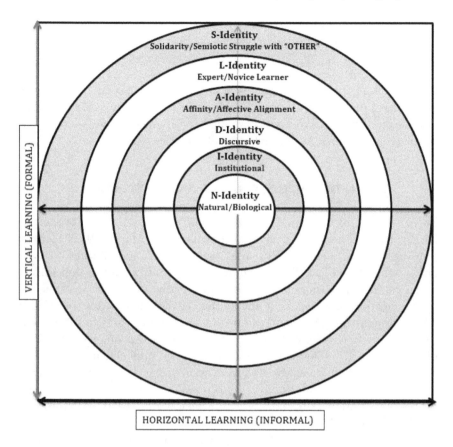

Figure 2.1 Learning through Identities.

language. In the current era, social media, especially synchronic platforms such as *Twitter*, are particularly salient.

In the next section, I situate this NIDALS framework in the context of classroom discourse related to some of Trump's controversial statements and practices. I then demonstrate how the Trump campaign effectively leveraged all four dimensions of language, especially those appealing to identity and ideology. In addition, I discuss the shortcomings of literalist approaches to languages and learners undergirding the critique of Trump's linguistic miscues. My analysis of "Trumpism" and its impact on student–learner identities, including emergent bilingual identities, draws on this framework. The following four questions are the foundation of this type of discourse analysis:

1. Code: What is said?
2. Prosody: How is it said?

3. Semantics: What is meant?
4. Ideology: What underlying values, beliefs, and frameworks mediate meaning?

When we move beyond an analysis of code in isolated speech events, the questions of meaning and values become more prominent. This requires a multifaceted approach to understanding how language frames identity and ideology in discourse, both synchronically and diachronically.

NATIONAL DISSONANCE AND DYSTOPIA

To get a sense of the tenor of our national discourse, it is important to harken back to how we felt on the morning of November 9, 2016 from polylingual centers such as Los Angeles, New York, and Chicago to rural and monoglot America. That morning, Americans from across the conventional political spectrum of liberal and conservative ideologies were shaken by the election of a politically inexperienced billionaire who speaks at a fourth-grade reading level and campaigned to "build a wall." In subsequent weeks, many were asking, "What happened? How did this happen? Why did this happen?" Television pundits and public intellectuals were visibly shocked because their analyses were proven wrong. Polls, statistical models, data analytics, conventional transcript analysis, and "fact-checking" approaches misunderstood the stances of a seemingly evasive electorate during the 2016 presidential campaign.

Similar to Ron Unz, one of the most recent champions of anti-bilingual education, Donald Trump was also a political "outsider" who became the catalyst of a populist, nativist movement. While the rise of Trump may not have been a surprise for long-time liberal advocates of bilingualism, a Trump victory seemed impossible. The national and global shock waves fostered a state of dystopia where everything was imagined to be unpleasant, degraded, and moving toward authoritarianism. The election of President Trump placed a metaphorical question mark on virtually every dimension of our democracy from governance, healthcare, and security to education, language policy, housing, and jurisprudence.

To date, the 2016 campaign and election has unleashed a revived wave of symbolic and physical violence. From taunts of "Build that Wall!" to violent White supremacist rallies in Charlottesville, Virginia, communities of color are feeling under siege. Symbolic and physical violence has been directed at immigrant children across the United States. There are daily reports of children using verbatim presidential quotes to harass and bully others (Samaha, Hayes, & Ansari, 2017). The emergence of White identity politics and the *alt-right* discourse have left many wondering about the state of our democracy and civil society.

The name "Donald Trump" as a signifier provokes intense feelings of anger, rage, and disbelief. Even his star on the Hollywood walk of fame has become a site of protest, rage, and regular vandalism (Rousselle, 2017). During my professional development work in classrooms, an emergent bilingual elementary-aged student who had vacationed in California reported being "shocked" after seeing a man walk by President Trump's Hollywood star, spit on it, and yell "Pendejo!" (Spanish for "stupid"). This action was then followed by a cascade of cheering and booing of Trump, which illustrates the raw evocative nature of our current national moment.

To understand the implications of this "dystopian" reality on language, learning, and policy, we need to go beyond spin and engage in deeper *languaging* about the state of our lived realities. In the remaining sections, I examine the ways we can crack the code of this discourse that has particularly left immigrants, emergent bilinguals, and others living in urban centers wondering about their place in President Trump's "*Merika!*"

PROCESSING "THE TRUMP": BEYOND CODE

In my work, preparing educators to work in linguistically diverse environments, we employ discourse analysis to productively organize for language and STEM learning (Razfar et al., 2015). As stated earlier, four questions are the foundation of discourse analysis that goes beyond literalism, form, and code (Razfar, 2012). Of import, questions about semantics (i.e., what is meant) and ideology (i.e., what underlying values, beliefs, and frameworks mediate meaning) move us beyond isolated events and transcripts and into the homes and communities where our learners and their families live.

Over the last year, I have employed this framework to process *the Trump* in educational spaces and broader society (Razfar, 2017). In the fall of 2016, for example, I visited one of our participating teachers' fifth-grade classroom during language arts instruction. The school had a majority Latina/o student population; one-third qualified for free or reduced lunch and one-fourth were English learners. The class included emergent bilinguals from various parts of the world, including White/Caucasian students, who were recently transitioned to English-only instruction. The teacher self-identified as "female, White, and bilingual Spanish" and regularly facilitated current events discussions at the beginning of the school day based on the articles her students selected.

During one discussion, a student shared an online article about how the host of *The Tonight Show Starring Jimmy Fallon* playfully ran his hands through candidate Trump's hair and as a result "humanized" him. A spirited discussion ensued. One blond-haired student stated, "I would vote for him!" Given that this comment came on the heels of candidate Trump's vile and graphic "locker room" talk episode where he disclosed that his celebrity status gave him the freedom to grope women's genitals (Fahrenthold, 2016), the students and the teacher were visibly startled. The teacher then asked, "How come?" to which the student responded, "He has cool hair!" Since his hair resembled Donald Trump's hair, his support for candidate Trump revealed the invisible factors mitigating voter behavior that the NIDALS framework highlights: a fundamental need to feel connected and foster relational affinity (Razfar & Rumenapp, 2013). This same student later explained that his father "was voting for Hillary *but* his mom was voting for Trump." This was counterintuitive for many of the students and this student was aware of the shock on the face of his peers and the teacher. These examples revealed the hidden semiotic processes that often escape polls and other public "politically correct" displays of ideology, where *what is said* by the speaker obscures *what is meant* rather than directly representing meaning.

TWEETER IN CHIEF

Decades of research in communication has shown that in addition to linguistic form, the medium of communication is a critical barometer for understanding the nature, function, and purpose of language (Mehrabian, 1972; Ottenheimer, 2007). Specifically, electronic-mediated communication has played a significant role in scaling up and distorting reality through language (Garrett, 2011). The ascension of populism in the first half of the 20th century, which ultimately metastasized into global fascism, is an enduring example of the role of language and technology. In the aftermath of WWII, George Orwell's *1984* pointed to the oppressive potential of the nexus between technology and language to foster mind control on a grand scale (Orwell, 1949). Years later, the power of television emerged during The Nixon/Kennedy debates of the early sixties. In 2008, the rise of social media during election season produced the first *Facebook* president who also happened to be the first Black president. The election cycle of 2016 produced the first *Tweeter* in chief, President Donald J. Trump.

Despite shifts in the media of communication, many public intellectuals and political pundits continue to focus on linguistic code (what is said) and prosody (how it is said). As an example, literal approaches to the Constitution demonstrate that the overreliance on linguistic code can obscure the cultural shifts that are taking place. During his first months in office, President Trump fired numerous staff members. While the firings of top administrators, such as Director of the Federal Bureau of Investigation James Comey and Attorney General Susan Yates, signaled a crisis for many constitutional experts, other constitutional literalists argued that President Trump was completely within constitutional bounds in doing what he did (Friedman, 2017). We have had several consecutive national episodes since the disputed elections of 2000 that have stretched the bounds of our constitution's code; however, we have a tendency to overuse the term "crisis" (Levinson & Balkin, 2009). Critiques of politicians or policies based on linguistic code have been limited in helping us understand how the language of identity and ideology shape political processes. That is, narrow analysis of the code and, at times, prosody are more convenient and typical approaches to understanding political action and strategy, but the analysis is incomplete without identity and ideology.

The more that liberals and left-leaning commentators attacked team Trump's linguistic form, the more committed his followers became (Lakoff, 2016). What is said and how it is said does not matter as much as where the talk is perceived to be coming from: a place of authenticity or a place of malice (Lakoff, 2004). The 2016 election cycle was populist in the sense that people wanted to shake up the status quo and go beyond linguistic form. They were probing for deeper meaning, connections, and alignment with their values. Any attempts to silence on the basis of form only fostered greater resentment toward cultural elites who dominate the media and educational institutions. Hence, Trump continued(s) to attack the media and positions them as the untrustworthy enemy. He dismisses the media as "fake news" and provides "other facts" as reported by White House spokesperson Kellyanne Conway (Borchers, 2017, para. 61, 66). This election cycle represented a fundamental cultural, linguistic, and social shift. Millennials were "feeling the Bern" and older, White voters yearned to "Make America Great Again," a slogan that was trademarked in 2011 by Trump. These sentiments had long been brewing and had been cultivated in what were considered "fringe" social media spaces until they became mainstream in 2016.

MEANING: STRIVING FOR AUTHENTICITY

The concept of authenticity has been the subject of interest in various disciplines from psychology to anthropology. One of the ways it is metaphorically constructed in the United States is the notion of "being yourself" and the privileging of uniqueness. Authenticity is viewed by some as the key to happiness even if there may be negative consequences in the short term (Seligman & Csikszentmihalyi, 2014). In linguistic anthropology, the concept of authenticity is complicated by the multiplicity of contexts and a general objection to the notion of a singular authentic self (Theodossopoulos, 2013). Some linguistic anthropologists have argued for the simultaneous coexistence of multiple and contradictory authenticities. Despite these dilemmas and a lack of consensus on the construct, authenticity is still considered a critical component of understanding human meaning-making, communication, and language.

According to Jones (2015), the concern for authenticity in political discourse represents a virtue of representative democracy. Authenticity is not about always being right, it is about "being real." Ultimately, it allowed Bill Clinton to escape impeachment, despite his linguistic gymnastics with the meaning of the word "is." Furthermore, first lady Hillary Clinton was expected to stand by him to project "authentic woman-hood," protect the American presidency, and uphold a patriarchal value system that perceives that "boys will be boys, and presidents will be presidents" (Parry-Giles, 2014, p. 121). Ironically, the 2016 election cycle positioned her as an *un*-authentic representation of "authentic American womanhood"; Hillary Clinton would later state that indeed "misogyny played a role" in her defeat (Greenwood, 2017, para. 1).

One way authenticity is instantiated in political discourse is through the public display of contrition and redemption. The issue of authenticity and understanding the process of authentic meaning making points to the semiotic and ideological questions of a more robust approach to language (Razfar & Rumenapp, 2013). For example, when Melania Trump's speech at the Republican National Convention was verified to have plagiarized parts of Michelle Obama's speech at the Democratic National Convention in 2012, liberal pundits, politicians, and even conservative allies believed adamantly that this mistake was "the nail in the coffin" for the Trump campaign (Nelson et al., 2016). After all, on the level of code, plagiarism represents an inauthentic move. However, within the frame of American political discourse, the public display of contrition has proven to be an even higher measure of authenticity. Those fixated on code and "factual" displays of language errors—including blatant displays of plagiarism—had underestimated how authenticity functions on the levels of affinity, identity, and ideological solidarity (see Figure 2.1). Trump's televised response the following Sunday earned him "authenticity" points with his electoral base as he explained, "She just made a mistake, and I think it was terrific how she came forward and just said, 'Look, it was a mistake that I made'" (Services, 2016, para. 4). The Trump campaign gained ground relative to other Republican candidates, gained momentum, secured the nomination, and ultimately won the presidency.

The new first lady's linguistic profile as an English learner, undocumented immigrant, and polylingual represents a novel opportunity for a new national conversation about language and emergent bilinguals in the United States. Much like 43 million multilingual Americans, Melania Trump is a first-generation immigrant who speaks English "with an accent." During a classroom discussion, one student reported that his mother was "angry" at the media for attacking the first lady's accent. The following vignette was reported by one of our teachers working with a class of emergent bilinguals:

> **Student:** I like Melania. She talks like my mom.
> **Teacher:** What do you mean?
> **Student:** She speaks with an accent, and my mom likes her.

Like the previous example where a student felt affinity with Trump's blonde hair, this emergent bilingual student expressed an affinity with Melania Trump's status as an immigrant as marked by her accent. Ironically, her accent can serve to legitimize nonstandard varieties of English on an unprecedented macroscale. It has the potential to give members of nondominant groups (i.e., language minority and immigrant students) a viable way to project themselves into the American grand narrative. This includes her immigrant status. That is, it has come to light that in 1996, Melania Trump engaged in work while having violated the terms of her tourist visa (England, 2017). This issue resonates with many immigrant and DACA (Deferred Action for Childhood Arrivals) students who feel under siege.

Further, while discussing the initial wave of executive orders imposing a travel ban on members of seven Muslim-majority nations as well as deportation hearings primarily targeting members of the immigrant and Latina/o community, a student stated, "How come Melania wasn't deported?" This was an open, bold, and courageous question in a context where children of immigrants and undocumented parents feel threatened. The inherent contradiction between these anti-immigrant policies and the policies of a president who is married to formerly undocumented Melania Trump has become visible and accessible to a wider audience. The possibility of leveraging an iconic figure, such as the first lady, to argue for polylingualism and immigration status within the broader American narrative can give immigrant and Latina/o children a renewed sense of belonging. It can potentially diminish their sense of voicelessness to foster a move from the margins to society's mainstream. With Melania Trump in the White House, polylingualism as well as immigrant status became mainstream issues that could not easily be erased and marginalized. Yet, immigrant and/or undocumented parents and children continue to live with palpable fear and unease. A recent Southern Poverty Law Center survey revealed that many children are scared that their parents will be deported and that Trump is "racist and against blacks, Mexicans, women, and Muslims" (Southern Poverty Law Center, 2016, p. 185).

As we navigate the contentious possibilities of the Trump era for emergent bilinguals, it is important to consider how language functions to generate and sustain populist discourses. Populism emerges in a climate of uncertainty and dystopia. Populists speak to deeply seeded sentiments that are often outside the purview of socially desirable expectations and modes of expression. Gaining access to these deeper levels of meaning have always been challenging for formal linguists, social scientists, and public pundits. Populists position themselves as being the "voice" of the voiceless such that they necessarily understand how language creates relational affinity, trust, and a deeper sense of authenticity. They understand the heart of language. Since the 2016 election campaign, social media has played a significant role in invoking the heart of language and at the same time provided a way to discuss empirically the less tangible aspects of language.

TWITTER AND THE HEART OF LANGUAGE

Twitter was the first large-scale medium to provide real-time, synchronous communication to wide-ranging and diverse audiences across racialized, classed, gendered, and regional and geographic boundaries. The Arab Spring of 2011 demonstrated the power of social media, and in particular Twitter, in fostering populist movements and toppling authoritarian regimes (Howard et al., 2011). *Twitter* engenders the perception of direct access and a sense of greater authenticity, or "being real." Clearly, what was being said by Trump during the campaign, and how it was being said, was not enough to dissuade voters. Authenticity, meaning, and shared world-views, or *the heart of language* mattered more. While the Clinton campaign outspent Team Trump 6:1, employed 60 statisticians, and developed a sophisticated algorithm model named *Ada* to process polling data, they invested in conventional media such as television ads and did not leverage effectively synchronous communication platforms such as *Twitter.*

In July 2016, *Twitter* was one of the few sources that predicted the possibility of a Trump victory (Perez, 2016). Even after the inauguration, Trump continued to use his "authentic" Twitter handle @realDonaldTrump. Every hashtag (#) that is created on a seemingly daily basis generates public discussion. Effective branding is accomplished through consistent talk and discourse that seeks to connect with people's sense of self and identity (Brinkman, 2017). The electorate, whether for or against his message, demanded this type of heartfelt conversation. Even when repulsed by some of his remarks in isolation, Trump's discourse created a sense of "at least I know where he stands." This sense of reassurance reflects a deep sense of affinity and affiliation that is built across the long term and can only be understood by exploring the heart of language that extends well beyond the literal and formal to highlight the deeper meanings, identities, and solidarities sought by social actors.

On election night, CNN commentator Van Jones declared, "This was a white-lash against a changing country. It was a white-lash against a Black president, in part" (Ryan, 2016, para. 5). While this may have been partially true, it did not explain the 83 electoral votes that twice elected a Black President only to swing toward Trump. Speaking at the "anti-inauguration," scholar Keeanga-Yamahtta Taylor argued that far from an imagined racist backlash, the election of Trump signaled the death of neoliberalism and its policies, ethos, and language (Taylor, 2016). While race and gender have always been a factor in American identity politics, their intersection should be understood in relation to broader economic and ideological considerations. According to Taylor, the neoliberal economic policies initiated by President Clinton in the nineties and continued by President Obama laid the groundwork for Trump's rise, especially in swing states. People were seeking a message and messenger that deviated from conventional politics and responded to their concerns.

For his part, President Trump's inauguration speech was extremely populist, isolationist, and anti-establishment, promising to strip Washington elites of their power and return it "to you, the people" (Fabian, 2017, para. 3). He immediately put a portrait of Andrew Jackson in the oval office, aligning himself symbolically with another anti-establishment populist/ nativist, removed all non-English links to the White House, and gave the most "American" address in the history of inaugurations, using the word "America" and "great" more than any other president in history (Midgley, 2017). In a rapidly changing world where a sense of dystopia has taken root, Trump's language, discourse, and use of Twitter offered an elusive sense of stability and affinity vis-à-vis identity and ideology for a segment of the population that was feeling displaced. Symbols and metaphors transcend time and space and reveal the heart of language, highlighting authentic semiotic and ideological processes in real time. They also leave a historical record to be revisited, reviewed, and revised by future interlocutors. In a world were synchronous communication has become global, shared identities and ideologies are being communicated through media such as Twitter: @realDonaldTrump is the first president to effectively leverage these functions of language through Twitter.

DISCUSSION AND IMPLICATIONS

Throughout U.S. history, our nation's sense of self has been intertwined with questions about the nature, function, and purpose of language. "Standard" English has been the dominant code of our national imagination and discourse. English hegemony is sustained and legitimized in relation to those forms of meaning making it has erased generation after generation even as this hegemony has been met with resistance. With every wave of immigration, every new colonial venture, every act of enslavement, and every transnational linguistic act, our national identity, or more aptly our national *language* has been changed and challenged. With every challenging episode to our national identity, we have generally chosen to restrict and/or erase access to nonstandard English codes. This has been our default script. Whether it was Ron Unz in the late nineties or Donald Trump in 2016, the appeal to the monoglot ethos is a powerful tool of fomenting national solidarity at the expense of nondominant ways of speaking, being, knowing, and feeling.

I have sought to demonstrate throughout this chapter that language is more than what is said or how it is said, especially when it comes to understanding political action and discourse. Language is more than code and prosody; it is simultaneously identity and ideology. The emergence of Trump and his election to the presidency makes the power of identities and ideologies more vivid on a wider scale, even as these have become more fluid, contentious, and situated. Social media has created a semiotic world were traditional physical and metaphorical borders have been blurred. The categories through which people made sense of their own lived narratives and identities are in flux. The heart of language, which is marked by a sense of shared meaning, histories, and values, has become more accessible, scalable, and visible in real time through media like Twitter. It is as if we have a greater window into broader processes of authentic meaning making. While the heart of language has always been more mysterious and elusive, it is indeed a semiotic world familiar to emergent bilinguals, transnationals, immigrants, and polylingual speakers. It is less familiar to those accustomed to the benefits and privileges of a singular code. Both those traditionally in power alongside those who have historically been dominated and disempowered have access to similar media and can communicate in real time. This shift in language practices fosters a sense of dissonance that is uncomfortable, yet tempered by our sense of continuity and stability.

Mocking Trump's grammatical errors, run-ons, sentence fragments, his fourth-grade speaking level, or acts of blatant plagiarism simply did not work. At these rudimentary levels, these analyses did not lessen Trump's appeal to his supporters, much less strengthen the opposition. Moreover—and this is an important point I wish to emphasize—attacks on President Trump's idiosyncratic language practices can also be perceived as an attack on emergent bilinguals who are keenly aware of this linguicism and attacks on their language and hence their person. After all, Trump speaks like his electoral base and they understand him better than other candidates, thus creating a sense of affinity. During the election cycle, false quotes attributed to Trump were circulated and ultimately taken up on social media to then draw parallels to Nazi propaganda techniques. The fact-checker site snopes.com dismissed this discourse as literally false ("Three Times a Liar," 2017). However, these reductive attacks on code did not seem to interrupt the momentum of Trump's campaign. Under the liberal radar, Trump had been "closing the deal" on people's hearts, a move which was realized after the election (Trump & Schwartz, 1987). Furthermore, those who identified with the Trump discourse did not reflect a singular, homogenous demographic. A *GQ* magazine article titled "The Cult of Trump" highlighted the narratives of people from diverse socioeconomic, racial/ethnic, gender, and linguistic backgrounds swearing they were saved by "Trumpism" (Nelson, 2016). In sum, Trump's campaign understood language on all four levels of code, prosody, semiotics, and ideology to propel Trump, Inc. into the American grand narrative. Whether real or imagined, they aimed for the heart of language and built a populist American campaign that went beyond the transcript and focused on meaning, symbolism, shared histories, and worldviews.

For teachers with progressive and transformative views about language, bilingualism, and emergent bilinguals, it may appear that our national discourse has become dangerously regressive regarding the educational potential of immigrant and emergent bilingual students. Despite these perceived tensions and challenges, I argue that we must capitalize on opportunities to engage in dialogues that shift the predominant language ideological landscape. Here, I offer six recommendations for practitioners that seek to take up deeper meanings and the heart of language with their students to begin to reveal the identities and ideologies at play:

1. *Discuss Trump's multilingualism.* Discuss multilingualism in the Trump family and issues pertaining to immigration status. It is important to leverage iconography that aligns with nondominant populations.
2. *Engage in critical languaging.* Critical languaging about the history of immigration, slavery, and colonialism will help teachers and students develop a consciousness that allows them to understand the current climate not as an aberration or an anomaly of history but rather a predictable outgrowth of monoglot hegemony. Polylingualism is the future and our bilingual children will make it happen (Lankiewicz & Wąsikiewicz-Firlej, 2014).
3. *Nurture solidarity.* In times of unease, it is important for educators to assure children of immigrants and bilinguals that they are not only "one of us" but also "they are us."
4. *Discuss Trump's language and its effects on others.* Many of the skills and techniques utilized by Team Trump displayed a consciousness of linguistic functions that bilingual children already possess. In sum, language is more than code.
5. *Critique neoliberal approaches to emergent bilinguals, immigrants, and polylingualism.* Historically, liberal multiculturalism has failed

polylingual learners. Subtractive bilingualism and assimilationist models are disempowering stances and reproduce a failing cycle of displacement and marginalization.

6. *Foster radical empathy (and discuss its limitations).* While it is difficult to imagine engaging the ideological "other," especially in a climate of intense polarization, calls for "radical empathy" need to be amplified across our society (Oxley, 2011). At the same time, it is important to discuss its limitations and practical strategies (e.g., Kloss, 2014). Empathy should not be reduced to a feeling that substitutes for concrete actions.

ADDENDUM

This addendum addresses several significant changes that have occurred since data collection for as this research began shortly after the Presidential elections of 2016. These changes confirm many of the predictions laid out in earlier findings, namely the emergence of a constitutional crisis, the elimination of the Office of English Language Acquisition (OELA), and creating the creation of a hostile environment for children of immigrants and non-dominant populations. First, a growing consensus is emerging that the constitutional crisis that was debated in the immediate aftermath of the elections has indeed arrived (e.g., Abramsky, 2018). Second, efforts to dismantle the Department of Education's Office of English Language Acquisition (OELA) by bypassing Ccongress are "real" and have gained significant momentum (Mitchell, 2018). Finally, the federal government shutdown of January 2019 that was a direct result of President Trump's failure to obtain funding at the appropriate levels for his "Build the Wall" campaign has further exacerbated an already burgeoning hostile climate. The circumvention of Congress in all instances are more evidence of a real constitutional crisis facing the nation.

REFERENCES

Abramsky, S. (2018, November). *Trump is provoking a full-blown constitutional crisis.* Retrieved from https://www.thenation.com/article/trump-is-provoking-a-full-blown-constitutional-crisis/

Ahearn, L. M. (2011). *Living language: An introduction to linguistic anthropology.* Malden, MA: Wiley-Blackwell.

AFP Daily Telegraph. (2009, September 14). George W. Bush's mangled syntax begins its echo down the generations. Retrieved from http://www.telegraph.co

.uk/expat/6163503/George-W-Bushs-mangled-syntax-begins-its-echo-down -the-generations.html

Alim, H. S., & Smitherman, G. (2012). *Articulate while Black: Barack Obama, language, and race in the U.S.* New York, NY: Oxford University Press.

Borchers, C. (2017, February 08). *Kellyanne Conway vs. Jake Tapper, annotated.* Retrieved from https://www.washingtonpost.com/news/the-fix/wp/2017/02/08/ kellyanne-conway-vs-jake-tapper-annotated/?utm_term=.708aa78422a7

Brinkman, A. (2017, September 13). *The power of consistent branding that tells a story.* Retrieved from https://www.forbes.com/sites/forbescommunicationscouncil/ 2017/02/15/the-power-of-consistent-branding-that-tells-a-story/#1b08 170f1302

Council of Europe. (2008, May 7). *White paper on intercultural dialogue: "Living together as equals in dignity."* Council of Europe, Ministers of Foreign Affairs at their 118th Ministerial Session. Strasbourg, France. Retrieved from http://www. coe.int/t/dg4/intercultural/source/white%20paper_final_revised_en.pdf

Crawford, J. (1998). Language politics in the U.S.A.: The paradox of bilingual education. *Social Justice, 25*(3), 50–69.

Culpeper, J., & Haugh, M. (2014). *Pragmatics and the English language.* Basingstoke, England: Palgrave.

Daileda, C. (2016, August 12). *We asked linguists if Donald Trump speaks like that on purpose.* Retrieved from http://mashable.com/2016/08/12/donald-trump -linguists-language-/

Duranti, A. (2001). *Linguistic anthropology: A reader.* Malden, MA: Blackwell.

England, C. (2017, February 24). *Melania Trump would have been priority for deportation under new immigration rules.* Retrieved from http://www.independent .co.uk/news/world/americas/melania-trump-first-lady-deportation-priority -donald-immigration-rules-modelling-work-visa-us-a7597221.html

Fabian, J. (2017, January 20). *Trump: We're giving power back to the people.* Retrieved from http://thehill.com/homenews/administration/315275-trump-were-giving -power-back-to-the-people

Fahrenthold, D. A. (2016, October 08). *Trump recorded having extremely lewd conversation about women in 2005.* Retrieved from https://www.washingtonpost.com/ politics/trump-recorded-having-extremely-lewd-conversation-about-women -in-2005/2016/10/07/3b9ce776-8cb4-11e6-bf8a-3d26847eeed4_story.html? utm_term=.a15e9eab8d17

Friedman, U. (2017, May 11). *America isn't having a constitutional crisis.* Retrieved from https://www.theatlantic.com/politics/archive/2017/05/constitutional -crisis-trump-comey/526089/

Garrett, R. K. (2011). Troubling consequences of online political rumoring. *Human Communications Research, 37*(2), 255–274.

Gee, J. P. (2015). *Social linguistics and literacies* (5th ed.). New York, NY: Routledge Press.

Gillon, S. (2012). *The American paradox: A history of the United States since 1945* (3rd ed.). Boston, MA: Cengage Learning.

Greenwood, M. (2017, April 06). *Clinton: 'Misogyny played a role' in 2016.* Retrieved from http://thehill.com/blogs/blog-briefing-room/news/327706-clinton -misogyny-played-a-role-in-2016-election

Grosjean, F. (2012, May 20). *Bilinguals in the U.S.* Retrieved from https://www.psychologytoday.com/blog/life-bilingual/201205/bilinguals-in-the-united-states

Halliday, M. A. K. (1967). *Intonation and grammar in British English.* The Hague, Netherlands: Mouton.

Hartman, E. G. (1948). *The movement to Americanize the immigrant.* New York, NY: Columbia University Press.

Howard, P. N., Duffy, A., Freelon, D., Hussain, M. M., Mari, W., & Maziad, M. (2011). *Opening closed regimes: What was the role of social media during the Arab spring?* Available at SSRN: https://ssrn.com/abstract=2595096 or http://dx.doi.org/10.2139/ssrn.2595096

Hymes, D. (1964). *Language in culture and society.* New York, NY: Harper and Row.

Jones, B. (2015). Authenticity in political discourse. *Ethical theory and moral practice, 19*(2), 489–504.

Jørgensen, J. N. (2008). Poly-lingual languaging: Evidence from Turkish-speaking youth. In V. Lytra & J. Norman Jørgensen (Eds.), *Multilingualism and identities across contexts cross-disciplinary perspectives on Turkish-speaking youth in Europe* (Vol. 45, pp. 129–150). Copenhagen, Denmark: University of Copenhagen.

Kloss, J. (2014). On the limits of empathy. *The Art Bulletin, 88*(1), 139–157.

Lakoff, G. (2004). *Don't think of an elephant!: Know your values and frame the debate— The essential guide for progressives.* Berkeley, CA: Chelsea Green.

Lakoff, G. (2016, August 19). *Understanding Trump.* Retrieved from https://georgelakoff.com/2016/07/23/understanding-trump-2/

Lakoff, R. (1985). *The Politics of language.* Pittsburgh, PA: Maurice and Laura Falk Foundation.

Lankiewicz, H., & Wąsikiewicz-Firlej, E. (2014). *Languaging experiences: Learning and teaching revisited.* Newcastle, England: Cambridge Scholars.

Levenson, E. (2014, June 05). *A roundup of Obama's most un-American pronunciations.* Retrieved from https://www.theatlantic.com/entertainment/archive/2014/06/a-roundup-of-obamas-most-un-american-pronunciations/372248/

Levinson, S., & Balkin, J. M. (2009). Constitutional crisis. *University of Pennsylvania Law Review, 157*(3), 707–753.

Lim, E. (2012). *The anti-intellectual presidency: The decline of presidential rhetoric from George Washington to George W. Bush.* Oxford, England: Oxford University Press.

Mehrabian, A. (1972). *Nonverbal communication.* New Brunswick, NJ: Aldine Transaction.

Mickey, R., Levitsky, S., & Way, L. A. (2017, September 08). *Is America still safe for democracy?* Retrieved from https://www.foreignaffairs.com/articles/united-states/2017-04-17/america-still-safe-democracy

Midgley, P. S. (2017, January 20). *Donald Trump delivered the most 'American' inauguration speech ever.* Retrieved from http://www.telegraph.co.uk/news/2017/01/20/donald-trump-just-delivered-american-inauguration-speech-ever/

Mitchell, C. (2018, August). *DeVos may bypass congress to get rid of the office for English-learners. Can she?* Retrieved from http://blogs.edweek.org/edweek/learning-the-language/2018/08/could_devos_scrap_the_federal_ELL_office.html

Nelson, L., Gass, N., Hoffman, M., Hasen, R., Troy, T., & Trickey, E. (2016, July 19). Trump campaign does damage control after Melania plagiarism charges. Retrieved from http://www.politico.com/story/2016/07/melania-trump-speech-michelle-obama-225794

Nelson, R. (2016, August 31). The Cult of Trump. Retrieved from https://www.gq.com/story/the-cult-of-trump

Orwell, G. (1949). *1984*. London, England: Secker and Warburg.

Ottenheimer, H. J. (2007). *The anthropology of language: An introduction to linguistic anthropology*. Belmont, CA: Wadsworth.

Oxley, J. (2011). *The moral dimensions of empathy: Limits and applications in ethical theory*. New York, NY: Springer.

Parry-Giles, S. J. (2014). *Hillary Clinton in the news: Gender and authenticity in American politics*. Urbana: University of Illinois Press.

Perez, S. (2016, November 10). Analysis of social media did a better job at predicting Trump's win than the polls. Retrieved from https://techcrunch.com/2016/11/10/social-media-did-a-better-job-at-predicting-trumps-win-than-the-polls/

Razfar, A. (2012). Discoursing mathematics: Using discourse analysis to develop a sociocultural & critical perspective of mathematics education. *The Mathematics Educator, 22*(1), 39–62.

Razfar, A. (2017, May 18). *Process the Trump*. Retrieved from https://anthrosource.onlinelibrary.wiley.com/doi/abs/10.1111/AN.460

Razfar, A., & Maravilla-Cano, J. (2017). Migrants and out-of-school learning. In K. Peppler (Ed.), *The SAGE encyclopedia of out-of-school learning* (Vol. 2, pp. 488–490). Thousand Oaks, CA: SAGE.

Razfar, A., & Rumenapp, J. C. (2013). *Applying linguistics in the classroom: A sociocultural approach*. New York, NY: Routledge Press.

Razfar, A., Troiano, B., Nasir, A., Yang, E., Rumenapp, J. C., & Torres, Z. (2015). Teachers' language ideologies in classroom practices: Using English learners' linguistic capital to socially re-organize learning. In P. Smith (Ed.), *Handbook of Research on Cross-Cultural Approaches to Language and Literacy Development* (pp. 261–298). Hershey, PA: IGI Global.

Rousselle, C. (2017, May 08). President Trump's star on Hollywood walk of fame vandalized again. Retrieved from https://townhall.com/tipsheet/christinerousselle/2017/05/08/president-trumps-star-on-hollywood-walk-of-fame-vandalized-again-n2323920

Ryan, W. (2002). The Unz initiatives and the abolition of bilingual education. *Boston College Law Review, 43*(1/2), 487–519.

Ryan, J. (2016, November 09). 'This was a whitelash': Van Jones' take on the election results. Retrieved from http://www.cnn.com/2016/11/09/politics/van-jones-results-disappointment-cnntv/index.html

Samaha, A., Hayes, M., & Ansari, T. (2017, June 6). Kids are quoting Trump to bully their classmates and teachers don't know what to do about it. Retrieved from https://www.buzzfeed.com/albertsamaha/kids-are-quoting-trump-to-bully-their-classmates?utm_term=.ccD1LY82o#.pvOK7M3bQ

Schegloff, E. A. (2007). *Sequence organization in interaction: A primer in conversation analysis* (Vol. 1), Cambridge, England: Cambridge University Press.

Seligman, M., & Csikszentmihalyi, M. (2014). Positive psychology: An introduction. In M. Csikszentmihalyi, *Flow and the foundations of positive psychology* (pp. 279–298). Berlin, Germany: Springer.

Services, T. N. (2016, July 20). Trump speechwriter apologizes for plagiarism in Melania Trump's speech. Retrieved from http://www.chicagotribune.com/news/nationworld/politics/ct-melania-trump-speechwriter-plagiarism-20160720-story.html

Shin, H. B., & Kominski, R. A. (2010). *Language use in the U.S.:* 2007. American Community Survey Reports, ACS-12. Washington, DC: U.S. Census Bureau.

Silverstein, M. (1996). Monoglot 'standard' in America: Standardization and metaphors of linguistic hegemony. In D. Brenneis & R. Macaulay (Eds.), *The matrix of language: Contemporary linguistic anthropology* (pp. 284–306). Boulder, CO: Westview Press.

Southern Poverty Law Center. (2016). *The Trump effect: The impact of the 2016 election on the nation's schools.* Retrieved from https://www.splcenter.org/sites/default/files/trump_effect_final_comments_2.pdf

Starr, K. (1998). *The Starr report: The findings of independent counsel Kenneth W. Starr on President Clinton and the Lewinsky affair.* New York, NY: Public Affairs.

Stokes, B. (2017). *What it takes to truly be 'One of Us.'* Washington, DC: Pew Research Center.

Taylor, K. Y. (2016). *The anti-inauguration: Building resistance in the Trump era.* Chicago, IL: Haymarket Books.

Theodossopoulos, D. (2013). Laying Claim to Authenticity: Five Anthropological Dilemmas. *Anthropological Quarterly, 86*(2), 337–360.

Three Times a Liar. (2017, April 17). Retrieved from http://www.snopes.com/donald-trump-lie-truth/

Trump, D., & Schwartz, T. (1987). *Trump: The art of the deal.* New York, NY: Random House.

CHAPTER 3

DUAL LANGUAGE TEACHERS AS A POTENTIALLY DEMOCRATIZING FORCE IN ENGLISH LEARNER EDUCATION

Donaldo Macedo
University of Massachusetts Boston

Lilia I. Bartolomé
University of Massachusetts Boston

ABSTRACT

This chapter argues that teachers, particularly in dual language education, must develop a critical consciousness about the sociopolitical and socioeconomic inequities that affect their lives and those of their students. This political clarity, which recognizes language as a fundamentally ethical practice, invites teachers to interrogate macro-level systems and micro-level practices to understand if and how societal inequalities are reproduced in the classroom. Teachers can then intervene as a democratizing force to transform the edu-

Transforming Schooling for Second Language Learners, pages 43–59
Copyright © 2019 by Information Age Publishing
43

cational experiences of diverse students into humane opportunities for learning. Teachers' political clarity and pedagogical expertise thus work together in their ability to effectively teach emergent bilingual students.

> *If they are here in the U.S. illegally, I won't teach them.*
> —Campbell High School teacher in Hawaii (Gaydos, 2017)

As the adage so correctly captures, the more things change, the more they stay the same: one teacher's refusal to teach students who are labeled "illegal" does not represent a new ideological stance since attacks on select groups of immigrants, English learners (ELs), and other linguistically minoritized students have been a constant in U.S. history. In this chapter, we argue that the challenge for all educators, including dual language teachers, is to cut the ideological yoke of colonialism by helping students decolonize the mind and reject all forms of subjugation or the seductive propaganda of White supremacy that equates being White to being human—a yardstick teachers often use in their evaluation and judgement of students' worth and humanity (Macedo, 2006).

Currently, as in the past, targeted attacks serve to foment racist policies euphemized as "populism." For example, President Trump's unvarnished categorization of Mexicans as "rapists" touched the submerged racist ideological nerve that wires a large segment of the White population in the United States as millions of voters remained unconcerned with his blatant bigotry and voted for him to become the 45th President. These same voters also provided the political base for President Trump to appoint Steve Bannon as his main adviser and strategist even though Bannon has close links with Nazi-influenced organizations and praises the racist French novel, *The Camp of the Saints*, a "[s]tunningly Racist French [n]ovel... [that]...tells a grotesque tale about a migrant invasion to destroy Western Civilization" (Blumenthal & Rieger, 2017).

While the mainstream media and most academics are enthralled with forms of globalization that adhere to the dictates of the neoliberal doctrine of free markets and freer movements of goods, there has been little substantive discussion regarding the globalization of racism and the legacy of colonialism which, coincidently, has its roots in the academy under euphemistic terms such as the "clash of civilization" by prominent intellectuals such as Allan Bloom, Samuel Huntington, and even the liberal author Arthur Schlesinger, Jr., with his celebrated book, *The Disuniting of America: Reflections on a Multicultural Society* (1998), which provided the platform for the reemergence of racist anti-immigrant sentiments exploited by far-right politicians such as David Duke, Patrick Buchanan, and others.

These far-right political pundits, academics, and authors work to propagate colonial legacies that still permeate all level of society by subjugating people that the ruling class typecasts as inferior. The colonizers' control either administratively through rules and laws they create (e.g., laws banning bilingual education or the closing down of Mexican-American studies in Tucson, Arizona Public Schools) or through the colonization of the mind—a subtle process through which a portion of the minoritized groups are inculcated with myths and beliefs about their own inferiority and begin to aspire to be like the oppressors by imitating their tastes, ways of speaking, bourgeoisie aspirations, and ways of being in the world (Freire, 2004). That is, the colonizer always has a

> predatory presence, his unrestrained desire to overpower not [just] the physical space but also the historic and cultural spaces of the invaded, his domineering manner, his subordinating power over lands and peoples, his ambition to destroy the cultural identity of the indigenous, regarded as inferior quasi-beasts. (Freire, 2004, pp. 53–54)

The colonizers' legacies are played out, for example, in President Trump's incessant attacks on Mexican-Americans, Mexicans, Muslims, and other minoritized groups—attacks that have licensed racist outbursts such as those in Charlottesville, Virginia where Neo-Nazis and KKK members violently displayed their racial animus with impunity.

The intellectual normalization of racism and neocolonial ideologies is not, however, restricted to U.S. intellectuals, journalists, and politicians. In France, the ultra-right National Front party headed by Marine LePen had mounted an incessant attack on immigrants, particularly Muslims from former French colonies, and was one of the top contenders in this last presidential election, a significant shift to the right. In Germany, there has been a significant increase in the number of neo-Nazi groups that have been responsible for a number of house bombings against Turkish immigrants and where far-right parties are increasingly gaining political ground. In Austria, Russia, and some Scandinavian countries, the level of anti-Semitism is also on the rise as far-right parties are gaining ground. For example, in the Netherlands' last election, the far-right candidate Geert Wilders sent shock waves throughout Europe even though he lost the election. His campaign was based on an anti-immigrant platform, referring to Moroccan immigrants as "Moroccan scum" and calling for banning of the Koran, "which won him the moniker, 'Dutch Trump'" (Bilefsky, 2017, p. A3). After his election loss, Wilders posted on Twitter, "We were the third largest party of the Netherlands. Now, we are the second largest party. Next time we will be number one" (Bilefsky, 2017, p. A3). Similar normalization of racism has been attested in Spain, particularly against North African immigrants and the Roma (more commonly known as "Gypsies").

It is against this sociopolitical and ideological context that teachers of immigrant, ELs, and other linguistic minoritized students, particularly Latinas/os, must acknowledge and challenge nativist ideologies in order to provide effective instruction and student/community advocacy to protect their students from the symbolic and material violence they often experience on a daily basis in their schools and communities. Given the history of Latina/o internal colonization in the United States, in particular Mexican Americans and Puerto Ricans, current racist occurrences against people of color by Whites and repressive efforts such as massive deportation of both citizens and the undocumented, teachers need to understand that, in terms of this current state of siege, there really is nothing new under the sun (Acuña, 2014). Recognizing the need to prepare all teachers to work more humanely and effectively with lower-socioeconomic status (SES) and linguistic minoritized students, we maintain that it is equally crucial to explicitly help prospective dual language education (DLE) teachers develop their political clarity in parallel with their pedagogical expertise so they can begin to link past and current explosive racism and other subordinating mechanisms against immigrants (documented and undocumented) to their ability to effectively teach ELs.

Political clarity refers to "the ongoing process...by which individuals come to understand the possible linkages between macro-level political, economic, and social variables and subordinated groups' academic performance in the micro-level classroom" (Bartolomé, 2004, p. 98). It is important to point out that "political clarity" here does not refer to one particular "party line" or view of sociopolitical and economic realities. Rather, the concept refers to educators' constant struggle to more comprehensively understand if and how societal inequalities are being reproduced at the classroom and school level in order to proactively intervene on behalf of their students. Such actions can take many forms and reflect teachers' particular ideological predispositions. Hence, political clarity, as we conceive it, requires teachers (and all citizenry for that matter) to continually develop a critical comprehension of world events and be able to make historical linkages so as to develop a more rigorous understanding of how they shape reality and can be shaped by it. Political clarity implies having the ability to comprehend and deconstruct the intricate interplay of race, gender, class, among other factors that shape schooling in the United States and often adversely impact minoritized students.

It is important to reemphasize that the need for DLE teachers to harness their ever-developing political awareness in order to more comprehensively understand this current context as reflected, for example, by the racial violence in Charlottesville, North Carolina, lies in its potential to wake up teachers politically so that they can refuse so-called apolitical, decontextualized, lock-step instructional approaches as blind, one-size-fits all solutions to address challenges that emanate from beyond the classroom. Instead, DLE educators can begin to infuse their educational programs and approaches with democratic and ethical principles to both effectively prepare students and invigorate our moribund democracy.

Although our discussion regarding the need for decolonizing pedagogy (Macedo, 2006) applies to linguistic minority education programs in general, for the purposes of this chapter, we focus on DLE or two-way immersion (TWI) education, which de Jong (2010) explains, refer to the "most developed integrated bilingual education model" that includes both native English speakers and native speakers of a minority language (p. 113). Similar to other bilingual programs, DLE/TWI programs have many designs. Two common models are the 90:10 and 50:50 models where the percentages refer to the time dedicated to academic language instruction in English and the minority language. It is important to highlight that despite there being different models of DLE/TWI, for our purposes, we select to focus on DLE/TWI education to make our argument because of three essential features across all types of DLE/TWI which render them potentially ideal learning contexts. De Jong (2010) explains that [DLE] TWI programs

1. are considered enrichment programs that aim at three interrelated goals: high levels of bilingualism and biliteracy, grade-level academic achievement, and cross-cultural competence;
2. TWI programs enroll approximately equal numbers of native speakers of English and of the minority language, and integrate these two groups of students for most or all of the day; and
3. all TWI students receive content area instruction and literacy instruction through both languages [with at least half of the instruction in the minority language]. (p. 192)

In sum, we focus on this academic and language education model because of: (a) its additive multilingualism philosophy and promising success, (b) its dramatic increase nationwide (Center for Applied Linguistics, 2014), and (c) the growing number of research studies that discuss the potential for DLE programs to be implemented in a more egalitarian and decolonizing manner (e.g., Fitts, 2006; Henderson & Palmer, 2015). In fact, current efforts in DLE attempt not only to provide students instruction in their native language and in English, but, as our previous discussion of decolonized education suggests, conscious efforts are made to shield and protect minoritized students from greater societal denigration and mistreatment (Alfaro & Bartolomé, 2017; Sayer, 2008, 2013).

In this chapter, we discuss the potential strengths of DLE, as an example of an academic and language learning model that, *under the vigilant implementation of critical DLE educators*, potentially situates language education within a context that ruptures ELs' generally low-status primary languages and their low socioeconomic standing. That is, we argue that even against the current highly xenophobic context, DLE that decolonizes has the potential to democratize schools and society, particularly if teachers move away from the rigidity of separate, two standard colonial languages and begin to introduce a translanguaging pedagogy that "returns the power of language to speakers and engages their communicative potential, rather than authorizes only the conventions of named languages that have been codified by the nation-state to develop governable subjects" (García, in press). However, we advise teachers to understand that the potential democratization of DLE must meet at least two conditions—continued development of teachers' political clarity and their ethics (teachers' coherence in terms of their critical reflections and subsequent actions). In the sections that follow, we elaborate on these two conditions. Before doing so, we first briefly discuss the colonial legacy of bilingualism in the United States, particularly as it relates to non-White immigrant and EL populations.

FRACTURING OUR COLONIAL LEGACIES

It is only through a more comprehensive understanding of our colonial legacy that we can begin to comprehend the complexity of bilingualism in the United States, which is almost always predicated on the superiority of English and its corresponding Anglo culture, which is reminiscent of colonial policies. This named superiority of English (a) devalued non-English native languages, (b) disparaged these languages' corresponding cultures, and (c) used the colonial language as a tool for cultural invasion and assimilation which typically results in the subtraction of native linguistic and cultural expressions and ways of being in the world.

Given the colonial legacy that informs most bilingual programs in the United States, DLE teachers must understand that, for most ELs and other linguistic minority students, their bilingualism is not simply characterized by the ability to speak two languages. In fact, there is a radical difference between a dominant culture student learning a second language and a minority culture student acquiring the dominant language (Pimentel, Diaz Soto, Pimentel, & Zurrieta, 2008; Valdés, 1998). This can easily be seen in the language acquisition dynamics in DLE programs. While the former involves the addition of a second language to one's linguistic repertoire, the latter usually provides the minority speaker with the experience of subordination in speaking both his or her language, which is devalued by the dominant values, and the dominant language that he or she has learned, often under coercive conditions (Macedo, 2006; McCollum, 1999; Henderson & Palmer, 2015). Thus, in DLE programs in which one of the languages is devalued, as in the case of Spanish, a colonial dynamic can easily permeate the interaction between the two linguistic and cultural groups. For this reason, DLE teachers need to acquire the necessary political clarity so as to understand that they cannot simply teach content in two languages while asymmetrical power relations continue to negatively undergird instruction and interactions (Scanlan & Palmer, 2009).

Both the neocolonial context and the asymmetrical power relations with respect to language use in some DLE programs create, on the one hand, a form of forced bilingualism and, on the other, what Albert Memmi (1965) calls a linguistic drama during which

> two tongues are in conflict; they are those of the colonizer and the colonized . . . Furthermore, the colonized's mother tongue, that which is sustained by [her/]his feelings, emotions, and dreams, that in which [her/]his tenderness and wonder are expressed . . . is precisely the one which is the least valued. . . . In short, colonial bilingualism is neither a purely bilingual situation, in which an indigenous tongue coexists with a purist's language nor a simple polyglot richness benefiting from an extra but relatively neutral alphabet; it is a linguistic drama. (p. 10)

An example *par excellence* concerning how current linguistic dramas and how society treats different forms of bilingualism is reflected in how tolerance toward certain types of bilingualism versus lack of tolerance towards other types is expressed. Most of us have tolerated various degrees of bilingual proficiency on the part of foreign language professors that range from heavy English-accented foreign language proficiency to serious lack of fluency in the foreign language they teach. Nevertheless, these professors, with rare exceptions, have been granted tenure, have been promoted within the institutions where they teach and, in some cases, have become "experts" and "spokespersons" for various cultural and linguistic groups in local immigrant and language minority communities. On the other hand, if bilingual teachers are native speakers of a low status language and speak English as a second language with an accent, the same level of tolerance is not accorded to them.

Although the example that follows is dated, it clearly reflects current negative views of teachers from subordinated linguistic minority groups who speak English with a low prestige accent and whose intelligence and teaching ability are often suspect precisely because they speak with an accent perceived and treated as low status and undesirable. In Westfield, Massachusetts, "about 400 people there signed a petition asking state and local officials to ban the hiring of any elementary teacher who speaks English with an accent" (Lupo, 1992, p. 19) because according to them, "accents are catching" suggesting that non-English accents can be involuntarily picked up by native English-speaking students.

The petition was in response to the hiring of a Puerto Rican teacher assigned to teach in the school system. In contrast, we believe that if the teacher had spoken English with a French accent, the exaggerated prestige of the French language would have likely shielded him from the English-spewing parents' attacks. As is evident, DLE programs that neglect to fully investigate this linguistic drama and treat bilingualism as mere communication in two languages invariably end up reproducing those ideological elements characteristic of the communication between the colonizer and colonized. Thus, teachers involved in DLE programs need to develop sufficient political clarity to move their understanding beyond conventional descriptions of DLE classrooms as containing a mixture of English-speaking and native-speaking children of non-English languages so as to factor in minoritized language practices and use them as pedagogical platforms for learning other subject matters, including the development of academic discourses.

While the presence of native speakers of both English and the other target language may provide spaces for both language groups to communicate with one another, this descriptive definition of DLE programs fails to capture the fact that, if speakers of the non-English language are subordinated in the society, then students belonging to the two linguistic groups do not typically engage in communication from the same symmetrical power relation position. Further, native English speakers seldom experience subordination in speaking the second language they are learning or experience what it means to have your tongue "yanked" (Anzaldúa, 1987) in order to learn a target language effectively as preached by the English language learning folk theory to which most U.S. educators and policy makers subscribe. In other words, this folk theory proposes that the supposed success of English language learning of ELs must depend on the subtraction of one's mother tongue—a requirement not applied to native English speakers learning a second or foreign language. Thus, DLE teachers empowered by their political clarity, not only can challenge this erroneous assumption, but they can also advocate for the equal treatment of both languages and their respective speakers.

NEOCOLONIAL IDEOLOGIES IN MULTICULTURAL
EDUCATION: CULTURAL TOLERANCE IS STILL RACISM

While DLE teachers focus heavily on establishing a pedagogically sound balance regarding instruction in two languages, what they rarely address is the reality that language is part and parcel of the culture that generates it. Consequently, we cannot stress enough the full integration of the cultures that are intimately tied with the two languages of instruction in DLE programs. However, our notion of culture integration goes beyond what conventional multicultural education literature correctly stresses: the need to valorize and appreciate cultural differences as a process for students to come to voice. However, the underlying assumption is typically that the celebration of other cultures will take place solely in English, a language that may provide linguistic minority students with the experience of subordination. In fact, some conventional multiculturalists, without saying so, assume that multicultural education can be effectively implemented in English only. Such an assumption neglects to recognize how English, as the societal dominant language, even in a multicultural DLE classroom, holds superior status often to the detriment of other primary languages and the students who speak them. That is, one cannot celebrate different cultural values through the very dominant language that devalues, in many ways, the cultural experiences of minoritized cultural-linguistic groups. Multiculturalists need to understand that language is one important means through which one comes to consciousness.

With the exception of some critical multiculturalists such as Christine Sleeter, Henry Giroux, Antonia Darder, and Peter McLaren among others, most conventional multicultural educators have simply failed to undertake the necessary critical analysis of the politics of language and its role in multicultural education. By critical multicultural education, we refer to the process through which the act of teaching culture is recognized as a political act that must interrogate power asymmetries that lead to the minoritization of ELs. Regrettably, the dearth of critical work concerning the ideological construction of language and its cultural manifestation is due, primarily, to two fundamental factors: (a) the teaching of cultural tolerance as an end in itself, and (b) the lack of political clarity in the bilingual education movement (including many involved in DLE efforts), which, in turn, prevented even the most committed educators from recognizing the neocolonial language policy that has informed and shaped bilingual program developments in general, and DLE programs, in particular.

As we mention above, there is preponderance in the field of conventional multicultural education to focus on teaching tolerance of the *Other*. This posture is not only paternalistic but it also fails to critique its underlying assumptions so as to understand the power asymmetry that characterizes the constellation of cultures within which we live, particularly in the age of globalization. The emphasis on teaching cultural tolerance often fails to denude the privilege inherent in such a posture. In other words, promising the Other a dose of tolerance so we can get along, not only eclipses real opportunities for the development of mutual respect and cultural solidarity but also hides the privilege and paternalism inscribed in the proposition, "I will tolerate you even though your culture is repugnant." It is the same paternalism that is often encoded as: "We need to empower minorities" or "We need to give them voice." First of all, we need to become keenly aware that voice is not something to be given by those in power. Voice requires struggle and the understanding of both possibilities and limitations. The most educators can do is to create structures that will enable submerged voices to emerge. Voice is not a gift. Voice is a human right. It is a democratic right.

The teaching of tolerance that has ushered multicultural education into the 21st century has brought with it highly complex and challenging realities that are still ill understood but have enormous ramifications for creating a more humanized world. Against a background of increased globalized racism, xenophobia, and continued neocolonial ideologies and practices, we doubt very much that the teaching of tolerance alone will enable us to critically understand how capitalist forces construct, shape, and maintain the cruel reality of racism. We also doubt that the teaching of tolerance can equip educators with the necessary critical tools to understand how language is often used to ideologically construct realities that veil the raw racism that devalues, disconfirms, and poisons other cultural identities.

Even within bilingual education, many teachers lack political clarity or embrace neocolonial ideologies that view (a) English as a superior language to ELs' primary languages, (b) standard English and primary languages as superior to nonstandard varieties, and (c) lighter-skinned EL students as more intelligent and attractive than their darker-skinned peers (Bloom, 1991). Consequently, in the past, many language educators failed to understand the neocolonialist ideology that informs the bilingual education debate to the extent that they structured their arguments within a reductionist view of language that overemphasized English language teaching and learning while disarticulating it from its interconnection to social and historical forces. For example, because most bilingual programs, including DLE, are predicated on the teaching two separate standard languages that correspond to the nation-state (typically former colonial powers) that socially constructed these categories to begin with, according to García (in press),

> The knowledge-power of invented named languages and elite bilingualism continues to marginalize many multilingual communities of brown and black bodies. To disrupt this cycle of failure, the ways in which named languages have been used in society and schools, and their relationship to racism and governability, need to be unmasked. If we were truly interested in the academic success of Latinx students, we would be accepting of what we call here their translanguaging, and not insist in monolingual performances, especially in English, in order to give them access to educational and economic opportunities.

In other words, teachers, in general, and DLE teachers in particular need to move beyond their tolerance of language practices of their EL students and begin to respect students' ways of speaking as valid, creative, and necessarily hybrid as all languages are or have been.

ETHICS AND THE USE OF LANGUAGE AS A DEMOCRATIZING FORCE IN DLE

Most educators agree that language is central to education but often hold views of it as merely a vehicle for communication and a focus of instruction. Beyond teaching students the technical mastery of language, educators rarely examine how using language is a fundamentally ethical practice. How words are deployed to "name" the reality behind the language so as to make dominant ideologies visible, or how a word can be used to obscure or reproduce the same dominant ideologies. For example, using a euphemistic concept such as "the affluent" can perpetuate a myth of a classless society, in contrast to a term like "the ruling class," which provokes questions about power and who the "ruled" are. Asking such questions about the language we use also demands that we address the importance of *how* and *for what reasons* we teach—and to do so in ways that challenge rather than replicate oppressive conditions. In the context of DLE, this means not just scrutinizing the content of what is being taught, but supporting the capacity for ELs and their linguistic communities to exercise agency, in the language of their own choosing, including the open use of language practices which are part and parcel of their languaging (García, in press; Pennycook, in press). Inviting students to be and to become in the language of their own choosing positions DLE teachers and researchers to be intellectuals along the lines of Edward Said's insistence that intellectuals should be "moved by metaphysical passion and disinterested principles of social justice and truth, [who] denounce corruption, defend the weak, and defy imperfect or oppressive authority" (Hussein, 2004, p. 306)—including our own.

Even among liberals and many progressives, employing a language that names the crude racism is often considered impolite and using a language that ruptures unethical perspectives or behaviors within the academy is almost certainly dismissed as deliberately provocative. Hence, we are conditioned through our membership in the academy to avoid using terms such as "oppressed" that may implicate us in oppressive systems and are instead encouraged to use euphemisms such as "disenfranchised" or "economically marginal." The same self-serving contradiction deeply informs the liberal approach to human suffering—an approach that positions a person as *ethical* precisely through distancing themselves from society's crimes. This approach, according to Paulo Freire (2004), is steeped in "false generosity" (p. xxi). That is, "[i]n order to have continued opportunity to express their 'generosity,' the oppressors must perpetuate injustice as well. [Hence] true generosity consists precisely in fighting to destroy the causes which nourish false charity" (Freire, 2000, p. 44–45). The key point is that redressing injustice means to *change* our approach, redirect our actions, not merely to accept, through our acknowledgement, the conditions that underlie any and all forms of oppression.

The analysis of the role of language and the ethics of language instruction is very important, especially when terms such as "ethics" and "morals" are often banalized by academic discourse. These terms, when they do appear, are usually used as a type of window dressing. The ethical content that should undergird morality is routinely emptied out, leaving us with a carcass best described as moralism without morals. We need to reduce the gulf between academic posturing *and* authentic intervention in the world. How can we speak of morality concretely when we remain gated in academic oases while writing about the oppressed, reducing our activism in the oppressed community to "tours of the oppressed?" These "tours of the oppressed" can be later transcribed, analyzed, narrated, and published, guaranteeing the academic tourists' promotion, tenure, and in some cases, celebrity status. Meanwhile children, the elderly, and other folks in the community remain trapped in hunger, despair, hopelessness—a compromised human dignity that can only be described as sub-humanity.

By refusing to deal with the issue of linguistic oppression—when expression in the nondominant language or accented English speech becomes a means to shame, exclude, and humiliate EL student communities—liberal educators often dogmatically pronounce that they "empower" EL students and "give them voice" so long as that voice is in English. This position often leads to a pedagogy of entrapment: while proclaiming to empower students, educators who go into linguistic minoritized communities to provide services in English only risk strengthening their own privileged position by shielding themselves from the reality that created the oppressive conditions they supposedly want to ameliorate in the first place. At the same time, liberal educators need to understand that they should not prevent marginalized community members from appropriating the very cultural and linguistic capital from which they, as middle-class educators, have greatly benefited. In other words, accessing educational content in language varieties that ELs and other linguistic minoritized students' master should not exclude English language acquisition. What educators need to be reminded of is Adrienne Rich's poem, "The Burning of paper Instead of Children" when she wrote the poignant verses: "This is the oppressor's language yet I need it to talk to you" (cited in hooks, 1994, p. 167).

bell hooks (1994) cautions, "it is not the English language that hurts me, but what the oppressors do with it, how they shape it to become a territory that limits and defines, how they make it a weapon that can shame, humiliate, and colonize" (p. 167). Thus, DLE teachers need to have a critical understanding about how dominant ideologies weaponize language to oppress, and teachers in general, and DLE teachers in particular, have the ethical duty to deconstruct and oppose forms of oppression designed to dehumanize EL students, as we discuss below.

POTENTIAL ROLE OF DLE TEACHERS IN DISMANTLING OPPRESSION: CONCLUSION AND IMPLICATIONS

Against a backdrop of language and cultural discrimination, most EL and other linguistic minoritized students often do not feel welcome in U.S. society and schools. Hence, DLE teachers who consider themselves agents of change and want to make a positive difference in their students' lives need to factor into their practice issues of language and cultural discrimination. DLE teachers need to critically understand that a society that can be so blatantly unwelcoming to ELs and other linguistic minoritized students cannot expect these same students to be highly motivated to embrace the dominant culture (and its language) that, for many of them, particularly students of color, often devalues their cultural identities, their languages, and, too often, their dignity. This process is akin to what Amilcar Cabral viewed as quasi-cultural genocide designed to enable the dominant cultural group to consolidate its cultural and language hegemony, a process that "succeed[s] in imposing itself without damage to the culture of the dominated people—that is, [it] harmonizes economic and political domination of these people with their cultural personality" (Cabral, 1973, p. 40). This is why you will hear proponents of English-only education argue that EL students can still speak their native language *in their home*, while learning English in schools will ensure their future success. But speaking a language is not equivalent to being literate in that language, and this is no less a form of coercive assimilation.

We maintain that it is always possible for ELs to learn English and succeed academically, but this success is often tied to the humanity and quality of teachers that students encounter along their English learning journey (Alfaro, 2008; Bartolomé, 2004, 2008; Beauboeuf-Lafontant, 2002; Lucas, Villegas, & Freedson-Gonzalez, 2008). Most ELs and other linguistic minoritized students consider themselves enormously fortunate when they cross paths with humane teachers who protect them from others who devalue them and who dissuade them from pursuing a college track since they may not be considered conventional "college material."

Thus, teachers in general and DLE teachers in particular *matter* and can positively affect their EL students' academic trajectory. To *matter* means taking on responsibilities beyond contractual agreements to teach the content area. To *matter* means that teachers become politically aware that not all students are treated in schools with the dignity and respect they deserve. To *matter* also means that DLE teachers realize that beyond the temporary English language barriers faced by their students, there are always needs, desires, dreams, and aspirations—an assumption that is always present with respect to dominant English monolinguals who choose to learn a second or foreign language. DLE teachers need to lovingly reject the dehumanization of high stakes testing and announce that behind each standardized test score there is always a human being who yearns to *become*, and who needs a safe pedagogical space to reflect on the tensions, fears, doubts, and hopes which are part and parcel of living in a borrowed cultural existence—an existence that is almost culturally schizophrenic. DLE teachers must consciously and strategically defend students from the oppressive conditions they face in schools and society as well as teach the academic content that they are charged to cover. The duty as DLE teachers also requires that they constantly protect the dignity of all students so as to prevent them from falling victim to the discriminatory educational *bell curve* that often parades under the veil of scientific teaching and democracy.

Under the mantra of scientific and "evidence-based" teaching, DLE teachers are often coerced to engage in the social construction of *not seeing* regarding the demonization of immigrants, which is a world-wide phenomenon that manifests differently in different world contexts. In the case of the United States, the phenomenon is very evident in the present moment but not necessarily unique or new. What DLE teachers need to understand is that the current assault on the Latina/o population across the United States is not dissimilar from the deportation of Roma people from France and the French treatment of Muslim immigrants. DLE teachers need to be able to connect the dots and see a parallel between, for example, the closing down of ethnic studies in Arizona and preventing the building of a Muslim mosque in a global metropolis like New York City. These assaults are not merely reflections of extremist politicians and groups in a particular country, state, or city. They comprise a neocolonial and racist ideology that is typically rendered invisible and not confined to the United States, but constitutes, instead, an insidious global phenomenon. What DLE teachers cannot do is to claim that racism is worse in Europe than in the United States given their frequent bombings of mosques and the constant assaults on immigrants while rationalizing that, although racism remains a problem in "those" countries, race relations are much better here than "elsewhere." That is, as Graham (2017) highlights, "less racism is still racism."

We believe that DLE teachers need to unapologetically embrace the pedagogical principles developed by critical scholars such as Paulo Freire, bell hooks, Howard Zinn, Henry Giroux, Antonia Darder, and others. These scholars exemplify what it means to be engaged in a humanizing pedagogy. Beyond their specific areas of specialization, they share Augusto Boal's conviction that "as humans, we are all born poets but institutions interfere to keep us from continuing to be poets" (personal communication, 1998). What makes these scholars unique is their enormous humanity; their unyielding commitment to social justice; and their courage, as Paulo Freire would say, to denounce the world's ugliness and announce a more humane world.

DLE educators can develop programmatic structures so that excluded linguistic minoritized communities can take their own initiative and chart their own course of action, thus eliminating the need for outside liberal and conservative educators' continued colonialism through "English only" and/or standard Spanish-only paradigms that often result in the suffocation of "nonstandard" language practices that ELs bring to the classroom. DLE educators need to be prepared to take social justice efforts seriously and to prepare to work with EL students in communion with by being engaged in their communities. Freire (2014) often suggested that while change is difficult, it is always possible to make this world less discriminatory, more just, less dehumanizing and more humane. And, to change and transform the world always involves a revolutionary love infused with "just ire," compassion, passion, and an unyielding hope that challenges all teachers to zealously work to transform the ugliness of the world with compassion, passion, and an unwavering commitment to a pedagogy that ceases to dehumanize so it can begin to humanize. A hope imbued in our denouncement of the duplicity of educators who accommodate and who willingly embrace the social construction of not seeing so that they can justify teaching on their knees. While denouncing aggressively the domesticity of most educators, we simultaneously need to announce, "standing up," a language of educational vision based on the permanent struggle against social injustices—a struggle that points to the construction of a future shaped and guided by love, humility, and humanity.

REFERENCES

Acuña, R. F. (2014). *Occupied America: A history of Chicanos* (8th edition). Upper Saddle River, NJ: Pearson.

Alfaro, C. (2008). Teacher education: Examining beliefs, orientations, ideologies, and practices. In L. Bartolomé (Ed.), *Ideologies in education: Unmasking the trap of teacher neutrality* (pp. 231–241). New York, NY: Peter Lang.

Alfaro, C., & Bartolomé, L. (2017). Preparing ideologically clear bilingual teachers: Honoring working-class, non-standard language use in the bilingual education classroom. Issues in Teacher Education: Preparing Bilingual Educators. *International Journal of Teacher Education, 26*(2), 11–34.

Anzaldúa, G. (1987). How to tame a wild tongue. *Borderlands/La frontera: The new mestiza* (pp. 33–45). San Francisco, CA: Aunt Lute Books.

Bartolomé, L. (2004). Critical pedagogy and teacher education: Radicalizing prospective teachers. *Teacher Education Quarterly, 31*(1), 97–122.

Bartolomé, L. (2008). Authentic cariño and respect in minority education: The political and ideological dimensions of love. *The International Journal of Critical Pedagogy, 1*(1), 1–16.

Beauboeuf-LaFontant, T. (2002). A womanist experience of caring: Understanding the pedagogy of exemplary black woman teachers. *The Urban Review, 34*(1), 71–86.

Bilefsky, D. (2017, March 19). Relief washes over European officials after Dutch vote. *The Boston Globe*, p. A3.

Bloom, G. M. (1991). *The effect of speech style and skin color on bilingual teaching candidates and bilingual teachers' attitudes towards Mexican American pupils* (Unpublished doctoral dissertation). Stanford University, California.

Blumenthal, P., & Rieger, J. (2017, March 6). This stunningly racist French novel is how Steve Bannon explains the world. Retrieved from http://www.huffingtonpost.com/entry/steve-bannon-camp-of-the-saints-imigration_us_58b75206e4b0284854b3dc03

Cabral, A. (1973). *Return to the source: Selected speeches of Amilcar Cabral.* New York, NY: Monthly Review Press.

Center for Applied Linguistics (2014). Directory of two-way bilingual immersion programs in the U.S. Retrieved from http://www.cal.org/twi/directory/

de Jong, E. J. (2010). From models to principles, implementing quality schooling for ELLs. In G. Li & P. A. Edwards (Eds.), *Best Practices in ELL Instruction* (pp. 189–206). New York, NY: The Guilford Press.

Fitts, S. (2006). Reconstructing the status quo: Linguistic interaction in the dual language school. *Bilingual Research Journal, 29*(2), 337–365.

Freire, P. (2000). *Pedagogy of the oppressed.* New York, NY: Continuum International.

Freire, P. (2004). *Pedagogy of indignation.* Boulder, CO: Paradigm.

Freire, P. (2014). *Pedagogy of commitment.* Boulder, CO: Paradigm.

García, O. (in press). Decolonizing foreign, second, heritage, and first languages: Implications for education. In D. Macedo (Ed.), *Decolonizing foreign language education: The misteaching of English and other colonial languages.*

Gaydos, R. (2017, March 7). Hawaii teacher under fire for saying he would not teach illegal immigrant students. Retrieved from http://www.foxnews.com/us/2017/03/10/hawaii-teacher-under-fire-for-saying-would-not-teach-illegal-immigrant-students.html

Graham, R. (2017, April 5). Less racism is still racism. *The Boston Globe*, p. A11.

Henderson, K. I., & Palmer, D. K. (2015). Teacher and student language practices and ideologies in a third grade dual language program. *International Multilingual Research Journal, 9*(2), 75–92. doi:10.1080/19313152.2015.1016827

hooks, b. (1994). *Teaching to transgress: Education as the practice of freedom.* New York, NY: Routledge.

Hussein, A. (2004). *Edward Said: Criticism and society.* London, England: Verso.

Lucas, T., Villegas, A. M., & Freedson-Gonzalez, M. (2008). Linguistically responsive teacher education: Preparing classroom teachers to teach English language learners. *Journal of Teacher Education, 59*, 361–373.

Lupo, A. (1992, March 4). Accentuating the negative. *The Boston Globe*, p. 19.

Macedo, D. (2006). *Literacies of power: What Americans are not allowed to know.* Boulder, CO: Westview Press.

McCollum, P. (1999). Learning to value English: Cultural capital in a two-way bilingual program. *Bilingual Research Journal, 23*(2/3), 113–134.

Memmi, A. (1965). *The Colonizer and the colonized.* Boston, MA: Beacon Press.

Pennycook, A. (in press). From translanguaging to translingual activism. In D. Macedo (Ed.), *Decolonizing foreign language education: The misteaching of English and other colonial languages.*

Pimentel, C., Diaz Soto, L., Pimentel, O., & Zurrieta, L. (2008). The dual language dualism: ¿Quienes ganan? *TABE Journal, 10*(1), 200–223.

Sayer, P. (2008). Demystifying language mixing: Spanglish in school. *Journal of Latinos and Education, 7*(2), 94–112.

Sayer, P. (2013). Translanguaging, TexMex, and bilingual pedagogy: Emergent bilinguals learning through the vernacular. *TESOL Quarterly, 47*(1), 63–88.

Scanlan, M., & Palmer, D. (2009). Race, power, and (in)equity within two-way immersion settings. *Urban Review, 41*(5), 391–415.

Schlesinger, A. M., Jr. (1998). *The disuniting of America: Reflections on a multicultural society* (2nd ed.). New York, NY: W. W. Norton.

Valdés, G. (1998). Dual-language immersion programs: A cautionary note concerning the education of language-minority students. *Harvard Educational Review, 67*(3), 391–429.

SECTION II

TRANSFORMATIVE POLICIES

TRANSFORMING SCHOOL DISTRICT POLICY FOR EMERGENT BILINGUALS IN NEW IMMIGRANT DESTINATIONS

The Role of Community-Based Organizations

Megan Hopkins
University of California, San Diego

Kristina Brezicha
Georgia State University

ABSTRACT

This chapter explores one school district's response to shifting demographics in the Northeastern United States. Despite a normative and political environment hostile towards the new immigrant population, members of a

Transforming Schooling for Second Language Learners, pages 63–79
Copyright © 2019 by Information Age Publishing
All rights of reproduction in any form reserved.

community-based organization served as boundary spanners who facilitated communication between community members and school district leaders, thereby encouraging more equity-minded policies for their growing emergent bilingual population. The chapter highlights the coalition building necessary to support and sustain transformative school district policies, or those that enable more inclusive school cultures, improved learning supports, and enhanced engagement with emergent bilingual students and families.

Over the last two decades, increasing immigration has shifted the cultural and linguistic makeup of communities across the United States, particularly in emerging gateway states with little history of ethnic or racial diversity (Wortham, Murillo, & Hamann, 2002). In these locales, school districts that have typically enrolled White, monolingual students are experiencing unprecedented growth in their immigrant and emergent bilingual student populations. This chapter explores one school district's response to shifting demographics in the Northeastern United States. Specifically, we show how, despite a normative and political environment hostile towards the new immigrant population, members of a community-based organization served as boundary spanners who facilitated communication between community members and school district leaders, thereby encouraging more equity-minded policies for their growing emergent bilingual population. Our findings have implications for the coalition building necessary to support and sustain transformative school district policies, or those that enable more inclusive school cultures, improved learning supports, and enhanced engagement with emergent bilingual students and families.

SCHOOL DISTRICTS AS ZONES OF NORMATIVE AND POLITICAL MEDIATION

School districts, as institutions situated within broader social and cultural contexts, are often limited by external normative and political forces that define the boundaries within which district policies are constructed (Oakes, Welner, Yonezawa, & Allen, 2005). For example, school districts in communities that are antagonistic toward new immigrant populations may struggle to implement policies that reallocate resources to support immigrant students' educational needs, as such policies could challenge xenophobic norms or confront contentious political climates. In order for more equity-minded policies to succeed in such contexts, district leaders must confront these external forces and work to shift norms related to race, class, language, and/or immigrant status, thereby expanding the boundaries within which district policy can develop (Oakes et al., 2005). As negotiators of these broader forces, school districts are often zones of normative and political mediation (Renee, Welner, & Oakes, 2010).

Within these zones of mediation, boundary spanners can facilitate change by aligning stakeholder interests around a common vision or goal. Boundary spanners are individuals who broker the exchange of practices and perspectives from one community of practice (i.e., a group of individuals interacting around a common goal) to another (Wenger, 1998). For example, district and school leaders work as boundary spanners when they interpret and convey information from external reformers to facilitate their implementation among district and school staff (Camburn, Rowan, & Taylor, 2003; Honig, 2006). While much of the educational literature has focused on boundary spanners who reside within school districts, in this chapter we look to a community-based organization to explore how its members worked as boundary spanners to coordinate and transform school district and community perspectives around a new immigrant population. In doing so, we show how community-based boundary spanners began to shift the boundaries of the zone of mediation and open up possibilities for the development of more equity-minded policies for immigrant and emergent bilingual students.

DEMOGRAPHIC CHANGE IN CHESTERFIELD

Chesterfield (a pseudonym) is a former coal-mining community of about 25,000 residents located outside a large Northeastern city. While proud of its origins as a home to diverse groups of western European immigrants, declining industry resulted in steady decreases in Chesterfield's predominantly White population over the last several decades. In an attempt to revive its contracting economy, Chesterfield leaders opened several industrial complexes in the late 1990s and early 2000s, creating thousands of blue-collar jobs that attracted many first-generation immigrants, most from the Dominican Republic. As a result, the percentage of Latino/a residents dramatically increased in Chesterfield, from just under 5% in 2000 to almost 40% in 2010. Not unlike other new immigrant destinations in the United States (Massey, 2008), this rapid population shift raised fears among long-standing Chesterfield residents that the community was, as one participant stated, being "invaded" with undocumented immigrants.

Heightened crime in the community fueled tensions, as many White residents blamed the new immigrant population. In 2006, Chesterfield's mayor used increasing crime rates to justify the introduction of a restrictive immigration act that penalized employers and landlords if they knowingly hired or rented to undocumented immigrants. In a speech, the mayor stated that the ordinance "intended to make [Chesterfield] one of the most difficult places in the U.S. for illegal immigrants" to live, and that, "only legal immigrants are welcome."[1] A Dominican community member noted that the ordinance created a normative context in which all Latinos/as were presumed undocumented: "Everybody that was looking as a stranger, as Hispanic, has an accent... [was treated as] illegal." This hostile political context narrowed possibilities for Chesterfield Public Schools (CPS) as they made decisions related to their new immigrant students, as these students were viewed as part of the negative changes in the community.

A CONCERNED COMMUNITY

The demographics of CPS, a K–12 district with nine elementary-middle schools and one comprehensive high school, mirrored those of the broader community. While the student population grew by about 25% to 10,000 students between 2000 and 2010, students receiving free or reduced-price lunch grew by 300%, and the Latino/a student population grew by 900%. A substantial proportion of these students were emergent bilinguals; by 2010, students designated as English learners (ELs) comprised about 10% of the district's population. As has been the case in other U.S. school districts (Frankenberg & Orfield, 2012), CPS schools within the city's urban center experienced the greatest population growth, while schools in outlying areas did not experience the same changes.

As we will describe in more detail below, the CPS school board, whose members held much of the decision-making power in the district, made minimal policy changes to address the needs of its changing student population. Concerned with the lack of support provided for new immigrant students and parents, three Dominican immigrants who had been living in the community for a number of years, Hector, Jose, and Marcos, founded *Parents Engaged* in 2008, an organization that offered translation services, reading programs, and English-as-a-second-language (ESL) classes to adults. Volunteers for Parents Engaged included bilingual Latino/a community members who were relatively new to Chesterfield, as well as long-standing White community members, many of whom were former public and private school teachers.

Jose, Hector, and Marcos marshaled institutional support for Parents Engaged by seeking assistance from Rebecca, a White Italian-American and Chesterfield native who served on the district's school board from 2005 to 2009. Based on increasing demands for Parents Engaged services, Rebecca, Hector, and Rebecca's husband, John, also a longstanding White community member, organized a larger initiative in 2011, the *Chesterfield Unity Project*. The Unity Project's stated goal was to integrate the White and Latino/a communities by providing sports and educational programs for children and youth, and by hosting events for all community members. In 2012, the project opened a community center that offered adult ESL classes, after-school tutoring, a bilingual preschool program, and several sports-re-lated activities. In the remainder of this chapter, we explore how Unity Project leaders worked as boundary spanners to coordinate perspectives and practices between the community and school district, and to transform district policy for immigrant and emergent bilingual students in Chesterfield.

EXPLORING THE WORK OF COMMUNITY BOUNDARY SPANNERS

We used case study methodology (Yin, 1994) to explore how these community boundary spanners worked to transform school district policy in Chesterfield. Such methods are appropriate when examining the social and cultural context essential for understanding the case (Yin, 2012). We analyzed several sources of data, including: (a) minutes from school board meetings held between 2002 and 2014; (b) publicly available district policy documents; (c) local newspaper articles; and (d) semi-structured interviews collected between 2012 and 2014 with four school board members, three district and school leaders and teachers, five Unity Project leaders, and nine community members and parents. While our sample included 21 interviewees, we conducted 27 interviews, as both Rebecca and John were interviewed four times over the 2-year period.

We first analyzed school board meeting minutes and district policy documents to develop a timeline of district policy changes. Through this analysis, we identified the types of resources allocated to the new immigrant population in the district, and how these changed over time. Absent from these documents, however, were descriptions of how the community context influenced school board decisions, or how community members perceived and responded to school board actions. As such, we drew on articles from the local newspaper as well as our interview data to explore these areas.

All interviews were semi-structured using protocols developed around the interviewee's role in the school district and/or community. For example, we asked school board members about changes in the community and district over time, the board's response to those changes, and their opinions of those actions, while we asked community leaders to describe Chesterfield's demographic change, how they perceived those changes and corresponding community responses, and what actions they had taken as a result. Interviews ranged from 30 minutes to 3 hours and were recorded and transcribed verbatim.

We analyzed interview transcripts collaboratively to develop broad thematic categories (Maxwell, 1998; Strauss & Corbin, 1998) related to our interests in district policy change and boundary spanning, including: community attitudes, barriers to community involvement, school district response, and brokering. Using these categories, we developed an initial list of codes, applied them to one-quarter of the data, and met to discuss and revise the coding scheme. We then applied hypothesis coding (Saldaña, 2009) to confirm and/or disconfirm the theories we were developing related to boundary spanners' work (Miles, Huberman, & Saldaña, 2013). Upon completion of coding, we met again to develop assertions based on the analysis and to instantiate them with appropriate evidence.

As we did not set out to study how boundary spanners influenced school district policy in Chesterfield, we did not explicitly ask participants to discuss this topic and may not have fully captured all of the details and nuances of their work, or of the community context. We became interested in reanalyzing our data through the lens of boundary spanning because of the work that we observed community members taking on related to the education of emergent bilinguals and immigrant students. Our subsequent data analysis provided sufficient evidence to present Chesterfield as a case of community organizing in a new immigrant destination, and to raise important questions deserving of further exploration.

NAVIGATING THE ZONE OF MEDIATION

Chesterfield school board members were initially ambivalent and at times outright hostile towards the idea of developing policy focused on meeting the needs of immigrant students and emergent bilinguals. This response reflected the broader normative and political context that constructed many new immigrants as criminals. Over time, however, Unity Project leaders worked to shift perspectives of the new population, and to model responsive practices, in ways that began to change the normative and political environment and increase possibilities for more equity-minded district policy.

School District Ambivalence and Hostility

As the population of immigrant and emergent bilingual students began to increase in the early 2000s, CPS implemented cursory measures to address the new population's needs, primarily focused on hiring a handful of bilingual translators and ESL teachers. Despite growing need, funding for these positions relied solely on federal educational sources such as Title III,[2] as school board members were reluctant to spend taxpayer dollars on programs for new immigrants or emergent bilinguals. This reluctance to spend local funds limited the district's ability to hire additional staff or offer professional development to teachers for much of the next decade.

Reliance on the federal funding stream also meant that resources for translators and ESL teachers were unstable. When asked at a 2005 board meeting what would happen to the district's translators when Title III funds ran out later that year, the superintendent responded, "The Chesterfield Public Schools cannot offer the services and [the translators] understand that." Rather than shift local funds to cover the translation services, school board members voted to cut translator positions until the next federal funding cycle. With respect to ESL teachers, their positions were among the first eliminated during budget difficulties in 2012. A majority of the school board approved these cuts despite one member's concerns: "Why would you cut your staff by five ESL teachers while your population is going up by three, four, five percent every year?" Despite acknowledging the need for professional staff to work with emergent bilinguals, district leaders remained ambivalent about sustaining resources to support them. Indeed, CPS' response to its rapid demographic change seemed slow to many in the community, including a school board member: "We had a population changing so rapidly that it took us a while to catch up. They still haven't caught up."

In addition to this cursory and at times ambivalent response, district leaders implemented several policies that created an unwelcoming environment for the new immigrant population. These policies reflected broader community norms that constructed newcomers as "illegal" and more likely to engage in criminal acts. In 2006, for instance, the school board approved the creation of a newcomer center for high school students, yet enrollment policies essentially precluded any immigrant students from enrolling, as a board member explained, "At one time we did have a newcomer's center next to the high school. But... it didn't last long. Unfortunately, we had a registration policy that—they wanted parents to have these three forms of identification." This policy made many new immigrant parents feel unwelcome, as few had three forms of identification deemed acceptable by the district. As a result, the newcomer center did not achieve sufficient enrollment to remain open. Instead, the board decided to offer a newcomer class to a limited number of students at the high school, providing 1 year of sheltered instruction before integrating newcomers into mainstream classes.

The school district also implemented extensive security measures shortly after the student population began to change. In 2003, CPS hired a director of security and "temporary security officers" to oversee hallways and lavatory areas in the trailers being installed near the high school. In 2010, the school board voted to hire full-time security guards for every school, to install metal detectors, and to require students to carry clear backpacks. One board member attributed these changes to "the nature of the population," who "were concealing things in their pockets and their backpacks." Nevertheless, none of our interviewees could cite an incident or infraction that warranted such safety concerns. These measures did, however, align with the normative construction of the immigration population as "illegals" and hence criminals in the broader community.

Beyond security policies, the director of security also advocated for a tougher dress code, as a school board member described, "The security director advised us, 'We have to get rid of these cargo pants and blue jeans.' He convinced us that that's where all these kids are hiding things that they shouldn't have in school." These security and dress code initiatives, passed as the new immigrant population increased, constructed the new students as dangerous, which mirrored perceptions of immigrants in the community. As one Latina community member shared, "I think the perception they [long-standing community members] have, it's like everybody was criminal." The broader normative and political context shaped the kinds of policies that were implemented in the district, limiting the extent to which more equity-minded reforms were implemented.

Working to Shift Perspectives and Practices

While CPS policies often reflected a hostile community context, boundary spanners worked to shift perspectives of the new immigrant population and to model responsive practices that challenged the normative and political dimensions in both the community and district.

Shifting Perspectives

An atmosphere of mistrust permeated Chesterfield for much of the 2000's, with long-standing White residents depicting the new population as a "disaster" for the community. As John, a White Unity Project leader, noted, "People were saying, 'Ah, [Chesterfield's] not the same anymore. It's horrible, it's all changed. These new people that came in, these Latinos, they're a disaster. They're just not like us.'" While many White community members tended to view the new Latino/a population as the other, and "just not like us," a small subset connected their family histories with the newcomers' experiences. Rather than othering the newcomers, long-standing White Chesterfield residents, such as Rebecca and John and other Unity Project leaders, constructed a narrative of commonality that acknowledged the community's immigrant roots. For instance, Rebecca, one of the White Unity Project leaders and a former school board member, consistently described how the new Latino/a immigrants reminded her of her family:

> They reminded me so much of my own grandparents. The kind of issues that they were facing were probably a lot of the issues that my grandparents faced.

> My own mother started school speaking only Italian. I mean we are so similar—Italian families and Latino families.

Similarly, John argued, "These people are exactly like the way we grew up. Let's not repeat what happened to our parents."

Unity Project leaders tended to invoke this narrative in public forums in their efforts to shift perspectives of the Latino/a newcomers. Rebecca often recounted the story of her mother at school board meetings, as her mother was a first-generation Italian immigrant who could not attend school in Chesterfield until her family could afford to buy her shoes. She argued that the new immigrants shared similar experiences, and that district leaders should take care of them: "Every child deserves the kind of an upbringing where people look out for each other... [and] look at everybody like a human being." More recently, at a pro-immigrant, Unity Project organized community walk that drew about 500 people, John read the following comments:

> As we begin today's event, please remember we are walking on the same dirt, the same path as was traveled by our fathers, grandfathers and great-grandfathers who came here from Italy, Poland, Ireland, Germany, and other European countries. And today we are proud to share the same direction with our new brothers and sisters from the Dominican Republic, Puerto Rico, Mexico.... Same path, same walk. We are Chesterfield.

In this speech, John publicly constructed the immigrant population as "our new brothers and sisters" who shared a similar history and path, a perspective that contrasted with the broader narrative of othering that depicted newcomers as illegals and "not like us."

Over time, district leaders began to shift their perspectives of the new immigrant population, from one of illegality to commonality. The focus on commonality and a shared history is evident in one school principal's description of the Latino/a population:

> When my grandparents came to this country, they were ostracized. So, it's the same thing. We have to be open-minded and respectful of each other's culture. I think I have a connection more with the Hispanics because of my Italian heritage. There are a lot of similarities... there's a lot of family stuff, there's a lot of food, a lot of ways we do things.

Similar to Unity Project leaders, this principal drew on his Italian heritage to connect with the Latino/a newcomers. Nonetheless, although he expressed generally positive sentiments about "Hispanics," his understandings seemed to hover at surface-level constructions, as he emphasized similarities related to "family stuff" and "food."

While Unity Project leaders worked to change the White community's perspectives of the new immigrant population, these leaders did not work alone, nor would they have been aware of the issues facing newcomers without collaboration from local Latino/a community leaders. In 2007, Hector, a leader in the Latino/a community who had children in CPS, heard from several families that few language services were offered to students or parents. A former resident of New York City, Hector compared CPS' services for emergent bilinguals to those offered in the city:

> I was receiving a lot of complaints from parents, especially with the language barrier. Because ... in New York, in all departments, there is a bilingual person to help you. However, here, when I went to the schools, that was a surprise. There were only two bilingual people [in the district].

After observing the need for more translators, Hector and two other parents presented the problem to Rebecca, then a school board member, who worked with them on forming Parents Engaged and providing translation and other services (more on this initiative below).

Rebecca's involvement with Latino community leaders opened her eyes to the inequities permeating the school district, which eventually led her to step down from the school board in 2009 to focus on supporting Parents Engaged and developing the Unity Project. Rebecca recounted how her interactions with newcomer students gave her a better understanding of the lack of instructional services for emergent bilinguals:

> Often, I heard from [Spanish-speaking] students that it was very frightening to be in a classroom and not know any of the words that were being spoken. I didn't think of that until I had two little girls tell me that.

While Rebecca had not previously considered the challenges that emergent bilingual students face, her engagement with the Latino/a community brought her into interaction with students who made her aware of their needs and the district's lack of responsiveness to them. In an interview in 2014, Rebecca demonstrated broader awareness of the institutional changes needed:

> The way our schools are doing it, it's not working for these kids. ... Just because they're in the classroom, and they don't speak English doesn't mean they don't deserve a quality education. Instead of [the focus] being on your administration, your principal, your superintendent, your principals, your teachers, it has to turn over, and the student needs to be on top of that priority list and work its way down.

As Rebecca realized that the district's approach was "not working," she decided she could affect more change outside the system, so that she could "take the gloves off" and "be [an] advocate."

By advocating for a shift in perspective of the new immigrant population, Rebecca and other community leaders began "break[ing] down...barriers," as the CPS superintendent described, "I think Rebecca's group had a lot to do with minimizing and breaking down some of those barriers that existed." As barriers shifted, school board members began to acknowledge the need for change and to emphasize community involvement:

> Programs like the Unity Project are absolutely critical. And I'm doing my very best to push a relationship between programs of that type and the school district....You've got to get the parents involved, and you've got to provide adequate services.

This board member's comment indicated a shift from ambivalence and hostility toward a desire to partner with the Unity Project and to provide appropriate services for immigrant students and emergent bilinguals.

Modeling Practices

In addition to shifting community perspectives of the new immigrant population, Unity Project leaders modeled equity-oriented practices that challenged the district to allocate more resources to serve immigrant and emergent bilingual students. These efforts stemmed from the organizing efforts of Parents Engaged, which launched an initiative in 2008 to help bilingual community members gain the clearances needed to enter schools as translators. Hector, a Parents Engaged leader, described their work: "At the beginning, it was a bridge to helping in the school district with anyone who had a problem with the language barrier.... It meant that... every time that we were called, someone was there to help." Parents Engaged volunteers became an important resource for the school district, so much so that 2 years later the school board decided to hire a full-time translator for every school.

After stepping down from the school board in 2009, Rebecca became more involved with Parents Engaged, which culminated in the formation of the Unity Project and opening of the community center in 2012. In 2013, Rebecca led the development of an afterschool program focused on supporting emergent bilingual students in grades K–8. The program was designed to provide academic and linguistic support through homework help and project-based enrichment activities. Acknowledging their limited understanding of the educational supports that emergent bilinguals need, Rebecca and other Unity Project leaders sought support from university faculty to develop the program curriculum. Still, responding to reports from Latino/a students about a dearth of teachers who knew or encouraged them, Unity Project leaders decided they wanted to create a different type of learning environment. As Hector described it:

> That's why we're here. It's to teach them and to go little by little until they feel—that you and I are different from the school. Because the teachers don't take the opportunity to be closer with the student, face to face, to encourage and let them know what they need and why they need it.

Rebecca echoed these sentiments: "We want programs that are enriching for the kids, that make them feel good about themselves. . . . I want them to feel, 'I can do this. I'm smart.'" Through the afterschool program, Unity Project leaders worked to implement practices that differed from students' school experiences, in that they supported a sense of belonging and helped students feel confident in their abilities.

Unity Project leaders often invited district administrators to visit the afterschool program, including the assistant superintendent and director of elementary and middle level education. Hector noted the importance of these visits for showing administrators the types of supports that could be provided to students:

> They [district administrators] are seeing that so many people are involved in the students' educational progress. . . . This is what we wanted, to work together and get that type of confidence that you can see. If they did what we're doing, they would have a bigger impact [on students] than us.

In modeling supportive programs and practices for emergent bilinguals, Unity Project leaders expanded the district leaders' understanding of the possible. Indeed, in 2014 the school board voted to reallocate district funds to provide after-school programming in all K–8 schools serving emergent bilinguals.

Simultaneously, the district hired a full-time community liaison to improve relations with the Latino/a community, which, as one school member noted, was "the most important position we hired this year." This liaison spent half his time in the schools, and the other half at the Unity Project working with students and parents. Though just one position, its creation demonstrated district leaders' understanding of the importance of developing positive relationships with the community, and indicated a willingness to allocate additional resources beyond those supported by Title III.

Although the school district was becoming more responsive, Unity Project leaders were still concerned with more systemic change, with John noting that it was not enough to simply change perspectives:

There's institutional problems too. This is not just about people's individual attitudes. They might not recognize that they're part of the problem. "I'm the least prejudiced guy you've ever met," they'll say. Then I'll say, "Then why aren't there any teachers with the last name Gonzalez?" They [the people of Chesterfield] are only going to start to change when the district adopts more proactive policies in terms of bringing English learners into the system in a more realistic way.

As John suggested, changing "people's individual attitudes" would not be enough to facilitate change, and the school district needed to support more inclusive policies to "bring English learners into the system." At the time of our study's conclusion, there was some evidence that district leaders were beginning to respond to this charge. As one board member noted, "We need to get new teachers, new Hispanic staff and particularly with the eye toward establishing some level of respect within the Hispanic community." The school board was quick to react, with district administrators hiring the first two bilingual teachers in the district: "We have two bilingual teachers and the superintendent pointed out that he wishes he could clone them. He said they are just really, really wonderful." In addition, the district was in the process of recruiting up to 20 bilingual instructional aides. These actions suggest that district leaders were beginning to understand the importance of establishing more comprehensive hiring practices that included members of the Latino/a community. Thus, as district leaders' awareness grew, they began to support more responsive and equitable policies and practices for immigrant and emergent bilingual students.

IMPLICATIONS FOR POLICY, PRACTICE, AND RESEARCH

This chapter presents one example of how boundary spanners shifted the normative and political contexts of a community to allow for the implementation of more equity-oriented policies and reforms for immigrant students and emergent bilinguals. Findings present numerous implications for transforming policy, pedagogy, and practice.

Transforming Policy and Policymaking Processes

Our account highlights the influential role that community leaders can play in motivating positive policy change for immigrant and emergent bilingual students in new immigrant destinations. By brokering the exchange of perspectives and practices between the community and school district, Unity Project leaders served as boundary spanners who shifted community members' and district leaders' perspectives regarding the new population and their needs. In doing so, they shifted the normative and political context in ways that expanded the school district's policy options. School district policy for immigrant students and emergent bilinguals in Chesterfield was originally developed amidst broader views that Latino/a immigrants were criminals; thus, district policy tended to focus on addressing security concerns stemming from "the nature of the population," rather than meeting students' educational needs. Over time, however, community-based boundary spanners began to reconstruct perspectives of the Latino/a immigrant population as a continuation of Chesterfield's shared immigration history, allowing for changes in school district policy and practice.

These findings have several implications for school district policymakers. First, district leaders in new immigrant destinations must be cognizant of the broader community context and the role that the school district plays in shaping that context. This is particularly important in communities where tensions between long-standing residents and newcomers may prevent the allocation of institutional support for immigrant students. Second, with this awareness comes a need for district leaders to develop proactive responses to demographic change. Cursory responses are neither sufficient nor sustainable, as they do not address systemic issues and are easily eliminated. Instead, district leaders must address the broader normative and political contexts that constrain available policy options. They do not, however, have to do this work alone, as our findings show that community-based organizations can be important allies in this work. That is, rather than relying solely on internal personnel to develop community-district connections, district leaders may benefit from building coalitions with community leaders who are part of or are actively engaged with the newcomer population.

Transforming Pedagogy

As equity-minded change continues in Chesterfield, it will be important to build on and strengthen community-district relationships in order to transform pedagogy in schools and classrooms. Although initial changes in district practice were promising, more attention to teaching and learning efforts is needed, including curriculum development and teacher education. Community leaders can and should be instrumental in this work, such that newcomers' funds of knowledge are valued and directly inform these efforts. Indeed, nascent efforts to support teacher professional development in Chesterfield aim to include parents and community members in curriculum development efforts. Though still in the planning phases, the proposed model represents a significant shift in the district's approach to professional development and community engagement that has the potential to transform pedagogy for immigrant students and emergent bilinguals.

Transforming Practices

In collaborating with community organizations and hearing from community leaders, school district leaders can learn strategies for transforming district practice. In Chesterfield, Parents Engaged and Unity Project leaders were instrumental in shifting the narrative around newcomers and modeling responsive practices, which opened up possibilities for the district to adopt practices that had the potential to transform schools for newcomer immigrants, such as hiring translators for every school, recruiting bilingual teachers and a community liaison, and offering after-school support to emergent bilinguals. Community leaders' efforts thus helped to shift the zone of mediation in the school district, which facilitated the adoption of more equity-minded policy and practices.

Notably, the boundary spanners in our study represented both the White and Latino/a communities in Chesterfield. While engagement of Latino/a community members was invaluable in understanding newcomers' perspectives and needs, the involvement of White community members likely helped to facilitate some of the changes we observed, especially given that the school board was entirely White. Thus, change efforts in new immigrant destinations need to involve diverse coalitions that can negotiate between and build alliances among distinct community groups. Moreover, it will be important to support more diverse representation on Chesterfield's school board in the coming years to further transform practice in the district.

Future Research

Although the boundary spanners in our study pushed district policymakers to shift their perspectives of and practices for Chesterfield's new immigrant population, they did so in a race-neutral way. That is, community leaders in Chesterfield did not explicitly use race or racial inequality in their arguments for more equitable policies, and instead focused on immigration status and emphasizing similarities between the Latino/a and White communities. Though this focus was useful in shifting district perspectives, it did not address the underlying racism that undergirds many inequities in the Chesterfield community and society writ large. It is thus unclear whether and how the normative and political shifts we observed will persist over time. As transformation continues to unfold in the community and school district, future research should consider the implications of failing to address underlying issues of racism, and explore how racism can and should be addressed in change efforts focused on immigrant students and emergent bilinguals. Attending to these issues is essential in supporting long-term and sustainable change efforts focused on emergent bilinguals in new immigrant destinations.

NOTES

1. We do not include specific references for certain quotes or demographic data in order to preserve the school district's confidentiality.
2. A statute in the federal *Every Student Succeeds Act* that provides funds for "supplemental services that improve the English language proficiency and academic achievement of ELs, including through the provision of language instruction educational programs (LIEPs) and activities that increase the knowledge and skills of teachers who serve ELs" (U.S. Department of Education, 2016, p. 4).

REFERENCES

Camburn, E., Rowan, B., & Taylor, J. (2003). Distributed leadership in schools: The case of elementary schools adopting comprehensive school reform models. *Educational Evaluation and Policy Analysis, 25*(4), 347–343.

Frankenberg, E., & Orfield, G. (2012). Why racial change in the suburbs matters. In E. Frankenberg & G. Orfield (Eds.), *The Resegregation of Suburban Schools: A Hidden Crisis in American Education* (pp. 1–25). Cambridge, MA: Harvard University Press.

Honig, M. (2006). Street-level bureaucracy revisited: Frontline district central-office administrators as boundary spanners in education policy implementation. *Educational Evaluation and Policy Analysis, 28*(4), 357–383.

Massey, D. (2008). Assimilation in a new geography. In D. Massey (Ed.), *New faces in new places: The changing geography of American immigration* (pp. 343–353). New York, NY: Russell Sage Press.

Maxwell, J. A. (1998). Designing a qualitative study. In L. Bickman & D. S. Rog (Eds.), *Handbook of applied social research methods* (pp. 69–100). Thousand Oaks, CA: SAGE.

Miles, M., Huberman, A. M., & Saldana, J. (2013). *Qualitative data analysis: A methods sourcebook* (3rd ed.). Thousand Oaks, CA: SAGE.

Oakes, J., Welner, K., Yonezawa, S., & Allen, R. L. (2005). Norms and politics of equity-minded change: Researching the "zone of mediation." In M. Fullan (Ed.), *Fundamental change* (pp. 282–305). Dordrecht, Netherlands: Springer.

Renee, M., Welner, K., & Oakes, J. (2010). Social movement organizing and equity-focused educational change: Shifting the zone of mediation. In A. Hargreaves, A. Lieberman, M. Fullan, & D. Hopkins (Eds.), *Second international handbook of educational change* (pp. 153–168). Dordrecht, Netherlands: Springer.

Saldana, J. (2009). *The coding manual for qualitative researchers* (2nd ed.). Los Angeles, CA: SAGE.

Strauss, A., & Corbin, J. (1998). *Basics of qualitative research: Techniques and procedures for developing grounded theory.* Thousand Oaks, CA: SAGE.

U.S. Department of Education. (2016). Non-Regulatory guidance: English learners and Title III of the Elementary and Secondary Education Act (ESEA), as amended by the Every Student Succeeds Act (ESSA). Retrieved from https://www2.ed.gov/policy/elsec/leg/essa/essatitleiiiguidenglishlearners92016.pdf

Wenger, E. (1998). *Communities of practice: Learning, meaning, and identity.* Cambridge, England: Cambridge University Press.

Wortham, S., Murillo, E. G., & Hamann, E. T. (Eds.). (2002). *Education in the new Latino diaspora: Policy and the politics of identity.* Westport, CT: Ablex.

Yin, R. (1994). *Case study research: Design and methods.* Thousand Oaks, CA: SAGE.

Yin, R. (2012). *Applications of case study research* (3rd ed.). Thousand Oaks, CA: SAGE.

CHAPTER 5

REIMAGINING THE EDUCATIONAL ENVIRONMENT IN CALIFORNIA FOR EMERGENT BILINGUALS

The Implications of the Passage of Proposition 58

Ursula S. Aldana
University of San Francisco

Danny C. Martinez
University of California, Davis

ABSTRACT

This chapter profiles multiple interest groups working to influence statewide and local policies that shape the schooling of emergent bilinguals. It draws on the example of California to showcase the sociopolitical context in which Proposition 58 (California Educaiton for a Global Economy Initiative [2016] aimed at overturning most of Proposition 227 (English for the Children

Transforming Schooling for Second Language Learners, pages 81–100
Copyright © 2019 by Information Age Publishing
All rights of reproduction in any form reserved.

[1998]) sought to transform education for emergent bilinguals. In this context, educators and policymakers drew on growing evidence of the benefits of bilingual education and frustration at the constraints imposed by Proposition 227, to shift the language policy landscape from a *language as problem* framing to one of *language as right* and *resource* for emergent bilinguals.

This chapter examines the recent struggle for bilingual education in California, from the passage of Proposition 227 (English for the Children) in 1997, to the more recent passage of Proposition 58 (SB 1174 [Chapter 753, Statutes of 2014]). Both initiatives were approved by California voters who overwhelmingly supported each proposal, the former which severely limited primary language instruction in schools, and the latter which sought to rescind much of the former law, expanding bilingual and dual language instruction in schools. We draw on Ruiz's (1984) orientations in language policy framework to examine Proposition 227 and the growing resistance amongst educators interested in employing a language as right/resource approach with emergent bilinguals. We highlight the role of educators and policymakers as part of a movement aimed at shifting the language policy landscape in California from a *language as problem* framing, to a framework of *language as right* and *language as resource* orientation for emergent bilinguals. This shift, we argue, grew from frustration over the difficulty caused by Proposition 227 for educators to promote or institute any kind of bilingual program despite a growing body of research that maintained and touted the benefits of bilingual education, throughout the 2000s (Gándara & Contreras, 2009; Gutiérrez, Asato, Santos, & Gotanda, 2002).

We explore how policymakers, researchers, and interest groups contributed to the pro-bilingual education movement that eventually led to the passage of Proposition 58 (2016). We share our own work with the Secondary On-Line Learning project (known as Project SOL), a research study of the UCLA Civil Rights Project/*Proyecto Derechos Civiles* led by Dr. Patricia Gándara, to highlight bilingual teachers' resistance of English-only ideologies and policies by providing primary language instruction and support to emergent bilinguals in secondary math and science courses. Data from the 4-year project show the transformative nature of bilingual education in academic and social contexts, especially for newcomer youth. For students in Project SOL, access to bilingual education in high school meant they benefited from college preparation content area courses in their native language while accessing bilingual teachers who impacted their sense of belonging in marginalized contexts (Aldana & Martinez, 2018). We reflect on the shortcomings of Proposition 58 and discuss how educators will need to continuously operate with a language as right and resource orientation to ensure emergent bilinguals have access to bilingual education. We discuss the statewide policy that promotes the use of languages other than English and how those in California might use this policy to transform education for emergent bilinguals.

THEORETICAL FRAMEWORK: LANGUAGE AS PROBLEM, RIGHT, RESOURCE

In this section we consider the language as problem, right, and resource (Ruiz, 1984) orientations that characterize language policy and planning in California. Understanding how the language-as-right impacts the language-as-resource orientation is critical to framing Proposition 58 (2016) as a shift in language policy rights towards a language-as-resource approach.

Language-as-Problem

The language-as-problem orientation to language planning focuses on the identification and resolution of language problems, and is framed in the context of national development (Ruiz, 1984). From this perspective, poverty, disability, low educational achievement, and low levels of social mobility can be marked by language: particularly in speaking a nondominant language that is treated as a problem to be resolved by transitioning speakers to the dominant language. This persistent and negative view of bilingual students often leads to negative perceptions of minority groups, especially Latinos, and can alter their educational experience for the worse.

Language-as-Right

Ruiz (1984) notes that, "since language touches many aspects of social life, any comprehensive statement about language rights cannot confine itself to merely linguistic considerations" (p. 11). The right to use and learn one's home language has been recognized as a human right. To this end, the United Nations Declaration on the Rights of Persons Belonging to National or Ethnic Religious and Minorities indicates that states should provide opportunities for linguistically minoritized individuals to learn their mother tongue, including instruction in that language (García, 2009). UNESCO signed a Universal Declaration of Linguistic Rights in 1996, which argues that education should foster linguistic and cultural diversity, as well as harmonious relations among different language communities worldwide (García, 2009).

In the United States however, language rights have been tested in the courtroom several times and court decisions help illustrate the language-as-right perspective. (For a full review of the history of U.S. language policy, please see Ovando, 2003.) The Supreme Court case *Lau v. Nichols* (1974) ruled that schools were in violation of non-English-speaking students' civil rights. *Castañeda v. Pickard* (1981) operationalized the spirit of the Lau decision by establishing three criteria for determining whether school districts are appropriately serving language-minority students. Ovando (2003) notes that while these court decisions have driven many bilingual education initiatives, there has been considerable variation in the types of programs conceptualized and materialized. Furthermore, legal manipulation has been utilized to avoid compliance.

Language-as-Resource

Bilingual education programs, for example, generally adopt a language ideology that regards their students who speak the target *language* (i.e., Spanish or other non-English language) *as a resource* (Ruiz, 1984). In dual immersion programs, students who speak the target language are seen and used as linguistic resources for their English dominant peers (Angelova, Gunawardena, & Volk, 2006). Dual immersion programs adopt an additive language approach to teaching and build upon the home languages of the target language-speaking students (Freeman, 1996; Gomez, Freeman, & Freeman, 2005; Lindholm-Leary, 2001). In the same manner, late exit developmental, bilingual education programs by design serve to use the home language of the student as a linguistic tool in the classroom (García, 2009). These types of bilingual education programs have resulted in successful academic outcomes for language minority students because of their commitment to the use of children's first language or home language for 5 to 6 years. Empirical research demonstrates the strengths of a bilingual academic experience (both dual immersion and bilingual education) versus English-only structured immersion programs (Ramírez, Yuen, Ramey, & Pasta, 1991; Thomas & Collier, 2002; Willig, 1985).

Ruiz' orientations to language planning and policy have been influential to the various fields who consider bilingualism and seek to raise the prestige of languages other than English. Ricento (2005) reminds us, however, that while we can argue that language is a resource, we have yet to convince the public of this given the passage of voter-approved laws such as Proposition 227 (1998) in California, along with other restrictive language policies in Arizona and Massachusetts. He argues, "The field of language planning has yet to demonstrate adequately how such an approach can move beyond academic theorizing and affect societal attitudes towards non-English languages in U.S. society (or anywhere else, for that matter)" (Ricento, 2005, p. 349).

As we explore Proposition 227 (1998), we consider the affordances and constraints of a language-as- resource and language-as-right approach in the future, given the passage of Proposition 58 (2016).

CONTEXT OF EDUCATION POST-PROPOSITION 227: PERSONAL VIGNETTES

Through our own experience as teachers of emergent bilinguals, we saw the injustice of educating emergent bilinguals within an English-only approach, particularly as we saw how a language-as-problem approach mediated policies and practices of many administrators and teacher colleagues. Those working with bilingual communities in schools (e.g., classrooms, school districts, research organizations, and university teacher education programs) seemed to agree with a language-as-resource ideology, but our district, state, and national assessments constantly reminded us that English was the primary and only valuable language of instruction.

We approach this chapter with dual lenses, as both former teachers of emergent bilinguals and as university researchers working with future educators of emergent bilinguals and interested in promoting the benefits of linguistic diversity in schools. Ursula was a sixth grade and high school teacher to emergent bilingual students in the Compton Unified School District, while Danny was a middle and high school teacher of emergent bilinguals in the Los Angeles Unified School District. We taught in districts with high percentages of emergent bilinguals (over 40% and close to 30%, respectively) and student bodies afflicted by triple segregation: by language, race, and socioeconomic status (Gándara & Aldana, 2014). Commencing our teaching careers during the early implementation of Proposition 227 (1998), we witnessed Spanish print materials and books being tossed into trash bins or storage pods.[1] These acts were visual reminders that many of our educator colleagues were acting in compliance with English-only policies rather than resisting them. Years later, in graduate school, we shared our stories, noting how we belonged to a generation of bilingual education activists born out of the frustration of the passage of 227. We were part of a growing number of Latinxs, particularly those in positions of power within policy and education contexts, making it a goal to resist anti-bilingual learning environments in our schools. As authors, we witnessed many of these groups collaborate to effectively set the stage for the repeal of Proposition 227 and its English-only rhetoric. It would take 18 years, but a deliberate and pro-bilingual education campaign helped influence the California electorate to support bilingual education and the passage of Proposition 58 in the November 2016 elections.

THE HISTORY OF BILINGUAL EDUCATION POLICY
IN THE UNITED STATES

California has played a significant role in both moving us toward providing effective instruction for bilingual students (*Lau v. Nichols*, 1974, and subsequent), and by creating one of the most restrictive learning environments for students for whom English is not their primary language (elimination of bilingual education via Proposition 227, 1998). Next we consider the history behind this movement toward bi- and multilingualism as a priority.

In the 1990s, legal protections for bilingual education met their strongest challenge. California, the state with the highest number of emergent bilinguals, was the first to experience Ron Unz's campaign to eliminate bilingual education. Unz was the Silicon Valley entrepreneur who funded state-level propositions that asked voters to decide the fate of bilingual programs that he declared unsuccessful and fiscally draining. California's "English for the Children Initiative" was passed by voters, ending bilingual instruction and replacing it with "structured emergent" instruction in English-only classrooms that was to last only 1 year. While a waiver process allowed parents to exercise their right to opt their children out of structured emergent programs, the process was burdensome and confusing with access and support for parents varying across the state depending on the local support for bilingualism. Gándara and Gómez (2009) report that after the passage of Proposition 227 (1998), bilingual instruction in the state of California dropped from approximately 30% to less than 6%.

Despite the political context, educators throughout the United States and California continued teaching in increasingly culturally and linguistically diverse classrooms. During this time, emergent bilinguals were attending schools in new destinations where they and their families changed the demographic landscapes of communities (Gándara & Contreras, 2009). An additional layer to this context came with the reauthorization of the Elementary and Secondary Education Act (ESEA) in 2001, known as No Child Left Behind (NCLB), which made all public schools accountable for the academic growth of their emergent bilinguals for federal accountability purposes (NCLB, 2001). With NCLB, attention was placed on several subgroups of students, including emergent bilinguals (referred to as English Language Learners in NCLB), for whom schools had to demonstrate growth to meet federal accountability benchmarks. However, scholars have critiqued the lack of attention to assessments, teacher preparation, and teacher capacity-building for emergent bilinguals despite this added attention (Hopkins, Thompson, Linquanti, Hakuta, & August, 2013). In effect, NCLB focused on the educational achievement and growth of emergent bilinguals in English and impeded many school communities from utilizing the waivers as a language right or leveraging languages other than English in the instruction of emergent bilinguals (Martinez, Morales, & Aldana, 2017).

After the passage of Proposition 227 in 1998, California dismantled more than half of its bilingual education programs, and today less than 5% of schools offer multilingual programs (Ulloa, 2016). As English immersion programs became the norm, the need for bilingual teachers decreased resulting in a decrease in the number of certified bilingual teachers (Mongeau, 2016). But by the early 2000s, California experienced a steady increase in the number of dual immersion programs and other forms of bilingual education programs (Linton & Franklin, 2010). Over time, school districts and schools looking to develop and expand their bilingual education programs struggled to find teachers, and in some cases looked outside California to fill bilingual teacher positions. By 2010, the sociopolitical context of California had changed since the passage of Proposition 227. To explore the resistance to such restrictive language policies, we highlight the educators in Project SOL, a project of the UCLA Civil Rights Project/ *Proyecto Derechos Civiles.*

PROJECT SOL: CHOCOLATE CON CHEMISTRY

Despite the restrictive language policy environment created by Proposition 227 (1998), various teachers, counselors, and administrators pushed back against this environment through their participation in Project SOL. During the 2008–2012 academic years, Project SOL teachers taught a range of science courses, including chemistry, geometry, physics, and biology, in addition to math courses in algebra, geometry, and algebra 2. While these courses are taught in high schools across the United States, the unique contribution of Project SOL courses was that instruction occurred in Spanish using Mexican curriculum developed in a binational partnership between the UCLA Civil Rights Project/ *Proyecto Derechos Civiles* and Mexico's *Colegio de Bachilleres*. Specifically, emergent bilingual Project SOL students were enrolled in math and science courses taught in Spanish at the high school level. Additionally, courses offered by Project SOL satisfied California State University (CSU) and University of California (UC) admissions requirements, known in California as the A-G requirements.[2] Few secondary emergent bilingual youth were provided this opportunity. Given Proposition 227's requirements, these courses were legally possible given the use of waivers by parents requesting primary language instruction. Additionally, the schools these youth attended had administrative and teacher support for bilingual instruction.

Our research team made its way to several Southern California high schools to observe Project SOL teachers and counselors working with students. Two schools were in "border towns," with one in San Diego and the other in Imperial County, while the other two schools were located in Los Angeles County, one near downtown Los Angeles, and the other in the "valley" region. Danny recalls his usual drives into the valley of Los Angeles to a predominately Latinx community.

> During one of Danny's visits to Ms. V's class, he witnessed many youth waiting in a line to fill empty beakers with water toward the back of the classroom. Youth immediately placed their beakers onto burners set on their lab tables. Youth waited patiently, chatting with one another until bubbles began to dance in the water, and they took notes about the changes they observed. Next, youth ripped opened white packets filled with hot chocolate mix! Before pouring the content into the water, they noted the characteristics of the powdery substance, very familiar to them, yet somewhat unfamiliar through their young chemist eyes. As they poured the powdery mix into boiling water students noted how the chocolate powder dissolved to form the rich, sweet, and tasty treat. On this day, Ms. V was teaching a lesson on chemical reactions to a group of emerging bilinguals in her chemistry course. After each student quickly participated in the "warm up" hot chocolate lab, they returned to their seats sipping on their cozy drinks, prepared to dig deeper into instruction about chemical reactions, in Spanish.

The students in Ms. V's class, and students enrolled in the Project SOL classes across the four sites, were enrolled in ESL/ELD[3] courses to facilitate their learning of English. Traditionally, a course like chemistry might not be offered to emergent bilinguals since their ESL/ELD courses often required more than one course from their schedules, and a CSU/UC required course might be seen as too difficult or rigorous for youth learning English. When such a course *is* offered, emergent bilingual youth might sit in a class with very little support in their primary language. However, through Project SOL, school staff worked to ensure emerging bilingual students could access courses required for college entrance by the state university systems. This vignette from the Project SOL classroom illuminates the possibilities, now that Proposition 58 (2016) has rescinded most of Proposition 227.

PROPOSITION 58: CALIFORNIANS TOGETHER

Immediately after the passage of Proposition 227, a number of researchers and bilingual education activists organized to advocate for equal access to a quality education for emergent bilingual students. In 1998, Californians Together (CT) formed as a larger coalition of organizations aimed at improving the educational landscape for emergent bilinguals. Since 2001,

CT had galvanized 26 parent, teacher, education advocates and civil rights organizations to work to promote quality programs of instruction for emergent bilinguals. By 2008, CT had laid the foundation for a seal of biliteracy that would honor graduating seniors who could demonstrate proficiency in two languages. The Seal of Biliteracy serves as a practical policy aimed at supporting the value of bilingualism at the school level and countering English-only ideologies within the state policy at the time. California would be the first state to adopt the State Seal of Biliteracy in 2012.

By 2014, CT announced the California Campaign for Biliteracy, which according to executive director Shelly Speigel-Coleman would inspire educators to work towards more opportunities for students to become biliterate: "The California Campaign for Biliteracy seeks to engage educators, policymakers, parents and students who share the vision for multilingualism, and also understand the enormous benefits to individuals, society, and the economy" (Californians Together, 2016). CT made the announcement for the California Campaign for Biliteracy at the annual California Association for Bilingual Education (CABE) conference. At this event, they also awarded San Francisco Unified School District and Glendale Unified School District with the first Multiple Pathways to Biliteracy District Recognition Award. CABE became not only the annual meeting for those interested in expanding bilingual education in California but served to praise and bring positive attention to bilingual educators. Given the negative experiences of many bilingual teachers post-Proposition 227 (1998), the role CABE played in supporting and honoring the labor bilingual educators do for English learners cannot be overstated. Californians Together was uniquely positioned to leverage its member organizations (see Appendix A), such as CABE, to promote bilingual education to a broader audience.

STATE SENATOR RICARDO LARA

Ricardo Lara was elected to the California State Legislature in 2012 to represent an area of southeast Los Angeles and Long Beach, home to a working-class Latinx majority. As a junior state senator, much of his platform focused on improving the lives of immigrant and Latinx families, which included the development and promotion of California Senate Bill 1174. The Project SOL team met Ricardo Lara early in his new appointment, when he helped us honor Project SOL teachers. Even then, his commitment to bilingual education was clear. In 2012, nine Project SOL teachers received the "Courage to Act" Bilingual Teacher Awards from CABE (UCLA Ed & IS, 2012), and Lara helped recognize them as a member of the state legislature. For Lara, the introduction of SB1174 was influenced by his experience as a child of immigrants and as a teacher's assistant. In a 2016 editorial in support of SB1174,

Lara began with a personal anecdote about his family and said, "My parents came to California so their children could have a better life. Like most other Spanish-speaking parents, they believed their kids' path to success had two main requirements: learning English and doing well in school." Although his words reaffirmed the importance of learning English for many immigrant families and their children, he attributed his family's success to being able to choose the right language instructional program for each child:

> In my family, English immersion classes worked well for my sister and me. However, some of my other siblings did better in a transitional English class. The fact that my parents had the ability to choose the best approach—and our schools had the flexibility to teach us what worked best—helped us succeed.

> Our experience is reflected in a wide body of research that shows students learn languages in a variety of ways. In addition to my first-hand experience learning English as a child, I also worked my way through college as a teacher's assistant in an English immersion classroom. I saw how it worked for some students and how it didn't meet the needs of others. (Lara, 2016, paras. 5, 6)

Lara's experience as a teacher's assistant working with English learners also led to his nuanced understanding of language as an instructional tool. Lara's admission that English immersion did not work for everyone countered anti-bilingual education rhetoric with expertise from educators working with emergent bilinguals. Notably, Lara leveraged his experience as a child of immigrants and educator to develop a better policy for emergent bilinguals. As a teacher working with emergent bilinguals, he witnessed the effects of an overreliance on English-only instruction and how it often rendered bilingual educators less effective when communicating with students.

In February 2014, Lara sponsored the bill, known then as California Education for a Global Economy Initiative, which was passed by both houses and would be put before the voters as a ballot measure for the 2016 election. Senate Bill 1174 (Proposition 58, 2016) outlined specific changes made to Section 300 of the California Education Code, which promoted the use of other languages in the instruction of English Language Learners (State of California, 2014). The proposal aimed to repeal most of the 1998 Proposition 227 (1998), which effectively reduced the use of non-English languages in instruction. According to the California voter information guide, Proposition 58 (2016) would do the following:

- Preservice requirement that public schools ensure students obtain English language proficiency.
- Require school districts to solicit parent/community input in developing language acquisition programs.

- Require instruction to ensure English acquisition as rapidly and effectively as possible.
- Authorize school districts to establish dual-language immersion programs for both native and non-native English speakers.
- Allows parents/legal guardians of students to select an available language acquisition program that best suits their child.

—State of California, 2016

In effect, the ballot measure would require local school districts and county offices of education to develop a process for collecting annual community stakeholder/parent feedback on the language instructional programs. The measure eliminated the need for parental waivers if they opted to enroll their children in a bilingual program. At its best, SB1174 asked voters to overturn Proposition 227 (1998) and was designed to redress the curtailing of bilingual education effectively done by the "English for the Children" policy. Proposition 58 (2016) would eventually be changed to the California California Educaiton for a Global Economy Initiative (Senate Bill 1174) and was approved in November 2016 with over 73% of the vote (Ballotpedia, 2016). Later still it was re-named as the California Education for a Global Economy Initiative. Notwithstanding Proposition 58's move to use language as a resource for emergent bilinguals, the policy maintains English as the goal for emergent bilinguals. In another example of interest convergence, Proposition 58 asked school districts to support bilingualism for emergent bilinguals but also called on support for dual immersion programs for native English speakers.

EDUCATIONAL ORGANIZATIONS

For 18 years, schools in California generally failed to provide multilingual pathways for students. However, despite the restrictive language policy and the underuse of primary languages as a resource in educational contexts, a movement of educators and researchers has always worked to provide emergent bilinguals with the best instruction, including primary language instruction. By 2010, a growing number of educators working with emergent bilinguals continued to educate and share stories of successful bilingual education programs in the face of English-only rhetoric, backed by the research to prove it (Gándara & Hopkins, 2010). Research pointed to the overwhelming cognitive, social, and academic benefits of being bilingual (e.g., García & Kleifgen, 2010; Morales & Aldana, 2010, Valenzuela, 2010; Zentella, 1997) and parents' positive views of bilingual education were increasingly informed by this research (Linton & Franklin, 2010). Dual immersion programs were increasingly in demand and yet schools faced pressure to meet yearly progress for English learner growth on English assessments, and an implementation of a dual immersion program might decrease test scores given a reliance on English-only assessments (Menken, 2010).

A number of schools and school districts shared their endorsement of Proposition 58 (2016) once it was on the ballot. For example, the San Diego County Office of Education publicly endorsed the measure, as did 18 school districts and universities (see Appendix B).[4] School districts such as Chula Vista and San Francisco rapidly expanded their bilingual education options, while some school districts were slow to respond to this demand. The Los Angeles Unified School District (LAUSD) waned in their expansion of dual immersion and multilingual educational pathways for students initially but has recently shifted this approach. Hilda Maldonado, executive director of multilingual and multicultural education at LAUSD, publicly supported Proposition 58 and is working with school board members to expand these offerings (Medina, 2016).

IMPLICATIONS OF THE PASSAGE OF PROPOSITION 58

The passage of Proposition 58 (2016) in California suggests an ideological and cultural shift that promotes bilingualism and multilingualism in schools. The policy on its own does little to expand bilingual or dual immersion programs, but it does give schools permission to use languages other than English for instruction. At its best, Proposition 58 could anchor a major shift in the history of schooling for emergent bilinguals in California. To this end, we consider various implications of the policy on ideology, instruction, and research. If Proposition 58 is going to transform the educational experience for emergent bilinguals in California schools and communities, educators will need to adopt and engage in transformative pedagogies and practices. In particular, we identify challenges and opportunities that the passage of Proposition 58 affords school districts, higher education (e.g., schools of education), and stakeholders in local contexts. We next provide future directions for research in this area.

Bilingual Teacher Pipeline

The passage of Proposition 58 (2016) has implications for schools of education and teacher education programs. School districts across California need more credentialed bilingual teachers than they currently have in their hiring pools, and there is an increasing demand for bilingual education programs throughout the state (Mongeau, 2016). The passage of Proposition 58 shifted the policy context to support language rights for emergent bilinguals, but a critical need for well-prepared and skilled bilingual

TABLE 5.1 District Language Planning		
Conserving: Building on Student Assets	**Growing: Monolinguals to Be Bilingual**	**Maintaining: Developing Language Competencies Over Time**
• Heritage Language Programs • Dual Language Programs • Bilingual Programs • Parent Literacy Programs • Bilingual Teacher Certification	• Dual Language Programs • Foreign Language Programs	• Middle school Dual Language Programs and High School International Baccalaureate (IB) Programs • Professional Development/Other Language Resources for Bilingual Teachers

educators that can employ a language-as-resource approach remains. In Table 5.1, we envision how school districts might build a bilingual teacher pipeline through long-term investments in various bilingual education programs and short-term policies that support adult bilinguals. We focus on how school districts might conserve and leverage emergent bilinguals' language skills but also how they might serve monolinguals and adults.

Districts will need robust plans to grow these programs given the loss of institutional memory around bilingual education in many schools because so much time and expertise has been lost in these intervening years of Proposition 227 (1998) in an overall long history of bilingual education (Hopkins, Malsbary, & Morales, 2016). As demand increases, schools of education should consider how various preparation programs might better equip school counselors, administrators, literacy and curriculum specialists, and librarians to serve multilingual learning environments. School leaders face multiple challenges when they establish language programs, especially for emergent bilinguals in underserved communities (Menken & Solorza, 2014, 2015), but can ensure their faculty employ a language-as-resource (Ruiz, 1984) and community cultural wealth (Yosso, 2005) approach towards their students. Schools of education can play a significant role in the development of school leaders that better understand how emergent bilinguals learn and are able to enact a pedagogical shift that leverages the linguistic skills of emergent bilingual students. Over time, the passage of Proposition 58 (2016) will lead to an increase in multilingual learning environments and accordingly, schools of education will need to adapt their coursework.

Transformative Practices

We caution that the passage of Proposition 58 (2016) should not mean a sudden move to open bilingual education programs without conducting the necessary intake of information to ensure their success. School districts should self-study their current language programs that serve emergent bilinguals and determine what models of bilingual education or other programs have worked well. We recognize that schools with successful bilingual education programs (at the primary and secondary level) might not look the same, and district officials will have the important task of identifying the various reasons why model programs are working. School districts can identify the conditions, resources, and expertise of their schools' communities that have facilitated the expansion and success of multilingual programs and share this information with stakeholders. In turn, parents, teachers, and school leaders interested in the expansion or development of a bilingual/foreign language program can then better organize and share their vision for new programs while calling attention to the areas the school district can better support.

Before the expansion of bilingual and dual immersion programs, district leaders should identify struggling programs and determine how the school district falls short of supporting them. As the number of schools that provide a STEM, STEAM, the arts, social justice, or ethnic studies curriculum increases, school district supervisors will need to consider how they provide professional development and school support within multilingual learning environments. If they have not already, districts should engage in strategic planning to outline how they might better support and expand bilingual education programs. Although it might be tempting to proliferate dual immersion programs in communities where there is interest, we caution this could result in an increase in dual immersion programs for middle class communities and make them inaccessible to emergent bilinguals in low-income communities (Morales & Rao, 2015). In fact, districts need to examine student outcomes in these particular bilingual programs in an effort to ensure that the needs of emergent bilinguals are in fact being met, rather than prioritizing the needs of English dominant (and overwhelmingly White) students (Valdés, 1997). A slow and deliberate self-study of how school districts have been able to establish and sustain bilingual education programs is critical if we want school districts to expand multilingual pathways in a thoughtful and successful manner.

Future Research

Professors of education might consider how the expansion of language programs impact education research. Research on bilingual education and dual immersion programs already point to a number of academic, social, and cognitive benefits of learning in two languages (Morales & Aldana, 2010) as well as the economic benefits (Callahan & Gándara, 2014).

Research should move beyond outcome-based measures to better understand how to implement and support emergent bilinguals especially those from low-income homes. Critical literacy, translanguaging[5] practices, and culturally relevant pedagogy can help scholars and practitioners improve bilingual education in the context of multilingual communities. We urge researchers in other disciplines of education to consider how their research might be shaped by multilingual learning environments.

NOTES

1. In our work with preservice teachers and education leaders, we often screen *Immersion* the film to demonstrate how Proposition 227 shaped the experiences of emergent bilinguals and their teachers. (http://www.immersionfilm.com)
2. A-G courses are those that fulfill requirements for admission to University of California and California State University system.
3. Depending on a school district, courses were either titled ESL (English as a Second Language) or ELD (English Language Development).
4. It is important to underscore the commitment schools take on when they want to expand their language programs and understandably, there are a number of educators not interested in doing this work. Before Proposition 58 even passed, 18 school districts and a county office of education endorsed this measure because of their commitment to providing students with a quality multilingual education.
5. Translanguaging practices recognize the unbounded nature of language use for bilinguals and multilinguals. García and colleagues call attention to how bilingual and multilingual speakers seamlessly draw on any languages available to them.

APPENDIX A
Californians Together (2016) Member Organizations

2-Way California Association for Bilingual Education (2-Way CABE)
Advancing Justice
Asian Pacific Islanders California Action Network (APIsCan)
Association of Mexican American Educators (AMAE)
Association of Two Way Dual Immersion Education (ATDLE)
California Association for Asian Pacific Bilingual Education (CAFABE)
California Association for Bilingual Education (CABE)
California Association of Bilingual Educators-Political Action Committee (CABE- PAC)
California Council on Teacher Education (CCTE)
California Federation of Teachers (CFT)
California Latino School Boards Association (CLSBA)
California Rural Legal Assistance Foundation (CRLAF)
California Teachers of English to Speakers of Other Languages (CATESOL)
Center for Equity for English Learners (CEEL)
Centro Latino for Literacy
Coalition for Quality Early Education (CQEE)
Early Edge California
Excellence and Justice in Education (EJE)
Families in Schools (FIS)
Institute for Social Innovation (ISI)
National Association for Multicultural Education (NAME)
National Council of La Raza (NCLR)
Parent Institute for Quality Education (PIQE)
Parents for Unity
Transforming Education for English Learners Consulting (TEEL)
United Teachers Los Angeles (UTLA)

APPENDIX B
SUPPORTERS OF PROPOSITION 58

	School Districts and Universities in Public Support of Proposition 58
1	San Diego State University
2	Alhambra Unified School District
3	Alum Rock Unified School District
4	Anaheim City School District
5	Berkeley Unified School District
6	El Rancho Unified School District
7	Firebaugh-Las Deltas Unified School District
8	Garvey Unified School District
9	Hueneme School District
10	Los Angeles Unified School District
11	Lynwood Unified School District
12	Montebello Unified School District
13	Norton Space and Aeronautics Academy Board of Education
14	Ocean View School District
15	Pajaro Valley Unified School District
16	San Bernardino City School District
17	San Francisco Unified School District
18	Woodland Joint Unified School District

REFERENCES

Aldana, U. S., & Martinez, D. C. (2018). The development of a community of practice for educators working with newcomer, Spanish-speaking students. *Theory into Practice, 57*(2), 137–146.

Angelova, M., Gunawardena, D., & Volk, D. (2006). Peer teaching and learning: Co constructing language in a dual language first grade. *Language and Education, 20,* 173–190.

Ballotpedia. (1998). *California Proposition 227, English Language in Public Schools Statute.* Retrieved from https://ballotpedia.org/California_Proposition_227,_the_%22English_in_Public_Schools%22_Initiative_(1998)

Ballotpedia. (2016). California Proposition 58, Non-English Languages Allowed in Public Education. Retrieved from https://ballotpedia.org/California_Proposition_58,_Non-English_Languages_Allowed_in_Public_Education_(2016)#cite_ref-quotedisclaimer_3-3

California Education Code, Chapter 3, Article 1. Section 305

Californians Together. (2016, November 9). Victory for Proposition 58 guarantees that parents and educators can choose the best language education program for students in California. Retrieved from [Press release]. https://www.californianstogether.org/victory-for-proposition-58-guarantees-that-parents-and-educators-can-choose-the-best-language-education-program-for-students-in-california/#more-1581

Callahan, R. H., & Gándara, P. C. (2014). *The bilingual advantage: Language, literacy, and the labor market.* Bristol, England: Multilingual Matters.

Castañeda v. Pickard, 648 F. 2d 989 (1981).

Freeman, R. D. (1996). Dual-Language planning at oyster bilingual school: "It's much more than language." *TESOL Quarterly, 30,* 557–582.

Gándara, P. C., & Aldana, U. S. (2014). Who's segregated now?: Latinos, language, and the future of integrated schools. *Educational Administration Quarterly, 50*(5), 735–748.

Gándara, P. C., & Contreras, F. (2009). *The Latino education crisis: The consequences of failed social policies.* Cambridge, MA: Harvard University Press.

Gándara, P. C., & Gómez, M. C. (2009). Language policy in education. In G. Sykes, B. Schneider, & D. N. Plank (Eds.), *Handbook of education policy research* (pp. 581–595). New York, NY: Routledge.

Gándara, P. C., & Hopkins, M. (2010). *Forbidden language: English learners and restrictive language policies.* New York, NY: Teachers College Press.

García, O. (2009). *Bilingual education in the 21st century: A global perspective.* Malden, MA: Wiley-Blackwell.

García, O., & Kleifgen, J. A. (2010). *Educating emergent bilinguals: Policies, programs, and practices for English language learners.* New York, NY: Teachers College Press.

Gomez, L., Freeman, D., & Freeman, Y. (2005). Dual language education: A promising 50–50 model. *Bilingual Research Journal, 29*(1), 145–164.

Gutiérrez, K. D., Asato, J., Santos, M., & Gotanda, N. (2002). Backlash pedagogy: Language and culture and the politics of reform. *The Review of Education, Pedagogy & Cultural Studies, 24*(4), 335–351.

Hopkins, M., Malsbary, C. B., & Morales, P. Z. (2016). Responsive federal policy for bi/multilingual students. *The Education Law and Policy Review, 3,* 31–57.

Hopkins, M., Thompson, K. D., Linquanti, R., Hakuta, K., & August, D. (2013). Fully accounting for English learner performance: A key issue in ESEA reauthorization. *Educational Researcher, 42*(2), 101–108.

Lara, R. (2016, October 20). Guest commentary: Proposition 58 will help students learn language. *OC Register.* Retrieved from http://www.ocregister.com/articles/students-732798-english-parents.html

Lau v. Nichols, 414. U.S. 563 (1974).

Lindholm-Leary, K. J. (2001). *Dual language education.* Clevedon, England: Multilingual Matters.

Linton, A., & Franklin, R.C. (2010). Bilingualism for the Children: Dual-Language Programs Under Restrictive Language Policies. In P. Gándara & M. Hopkins (Eds.), *Forbidden Language: English Learners and Restrictive Language Policies.* New York, NY: Teachers College Press.

Martinez, D. C., Morales, P. Z., & Aldana, U. S. (2017). Leveraging students' communicative repertoires as a tool for equitable learning. *Review of Research in Education, 41*(1), 477–499.

Medina, J. (2016, October 17). Californians, having curbed bilingual education, may now expand it. *New York Times.* Retrieved from https://www.nytimes.com/2016/10/18/us/californians-having-curbed-bilingual-education-may-now-expand-it.html?_r=0

Menken, K. (2010). No child left behind and English language learners: The challenges and consequences of high-stakes testing. *Theory Into Practice, 49,* 121–128.

Menken, K., & Solorza, C. (2014). Where have all the bilingual programs gone?!: Why prepared school leaders are essential for bilingual education. *Journal of Multilingual Education Research, 4*(1), article 3.

Menken, K., & Solorza, C. (2015). Principals as linchpins in bilingual education: The need for prepared school leaders. *International Journal of Bilingual Education and Bilingualism, 18*(6), 676–697.

Mongeau, L. (2016). California voters overturn English-only instruction law. *The Hechinger Report.* Retrieved from http://hechingerreport.org/california-voters-poised-gut-english-instruction-law/

Morales, P. Z., & Aldana, U. S. (2010). Learning in two languages: Programs with political promise. In P. Gándara & M. B. Hopkins (Eds.), *Forbidden language: English learners and restrictive language policies* (pp. 159–174). New York, NY: Teachers College Press.

Morales, P. Z., & Rao, A. (2015, September 28). How ideology and cultural capital shape the distribution of Illinois' bilingual education programs. Online commentary. *Teachers College Record.* https://www.tcrecord.org/content.asp?contentid=18139

No Child Left Behind Act of 2001, P. L. 107-110, 20 U.S.C. § 6319 (2001).

Ovando, C. J. (2003). Bilingual education in the United States: Historical development and current issues. *Bilingual Research Journal, 27*(1), 1–24.

Ramírez, J., Yuen, S., Ramey, D., & Pasta, D. (1991). *Final Report: Longitudinal study of structured English immersion strategy, early-exit and late-exit bilingual education programs for language-minority children. (Vol. 1; Prepared for U.S. Department of Education).* San Mateo, CA: Aguirre International. (No. 300-87-0156)

Ricento, T. (2005). Problems with the 'language-as-resource' discourse in the promotion of heritage language in the U.S.A. *Journal of Sociolinguistics, 9*(3), 348–368.

Ruiz, R. (1984). Orientations in language planning. *NABE journal, 8*(2), 15–34.

State of California. (2016). *California general election November 8, 2016, official voter information guide.* Sacramento: California Secretary of State Elections Division, 2016.

State of California. SB 1174. (2014). "California Education for a Global Economy Initiative." Retrieved from http://elections.cdn.sos.ca.gov/ballot-measures/pdf/sb-1174-chapter-753.pdf

Thomas, W. P., & Collier, V. P. (2002). A national study of school effectiveness for language minority students' long-term academic achievement. Washington, DC: Center for Research on Education, Diversity and Excellence.

UCLA Ed & IS. (2012, April 17). Bilingual high school teachers of Project SOL receive "Courage to Act" awards: The Civil Rights Project/Proyecto Derechos Civiles initiative supports teachers of English language learners. Retrieved from https://ampersand.gseis.ucla.edu/bilingual-high-school-teachers-of-project -sol-receive-courage-to-act-awards/

Ulloa, J. (2016). Bilingual education has been absent from California public schools for almost 20 years. But that may soon change. *L.A. Times*. Retrieved from http://www.latimes.com/politics/la-pol-ca-proposition-58-bilingual-educa-tion-20161012-snap-story.html

U.S. Supreme Court. (1974). Lau v. Nichols (No. 72-6520). Retrieved from http:// caselaw.find-law.com/us-supreme-court/414/563.html

Valdés, G. (1997). Dual-language immersion programs: A cautionary note concern-ing the education of language-minority students. *Harvard Educational Review, 67*(3), 391–430.

Valenzuela, A. (2010). *Subtractive schooling: U.S. Mexican youth and the politics of caring* (2nd ed.). Albany: State University of New York Press.

Willig, A. C. (1985). A meta-analysis of selected studies on the effectiveness of bilin-gual education. *Review of Educational Research, 55*(3), 269–317.

Yosso, T. J. (2005). Whose culture has capital? A critical race theory discussion of community cultural wealth. *Race Ethnicity and Education, 8*(1), 69–91.

Zentella, A. C. (1997). *Growing up bilingual: Puerto Rican children in New York*. Mal-den, MA: Wiley-Blackwell.

CHAPTER 6

HOW SCHOOL-LEVEL PRACTICES TRANSFORM FEDERAL AND STATE POLICIES

One Dual-Immersion School's Response to the Common Core State Standards

Jamy Stillman
University of Colorado, Boulder

ABSTRACT

This chapter investigates teachers' response to the Common Core State Standards in English Language Arts in the context of a high-performing, dual-immersion school in California. Drawing on ethnographic case study data, it analyzes how school-level practices that were strength- and asset based powerfully transformed schooling experiences for emergent bilingual students by supporting teachers' ethical responses to reductive education policies that stand to disadvantage these students' access to responsive instruction. When provided with professional autonomy, strong leadership, and meaningful

Transforming Schooling for Second Language Learners, pages 101–120
Copyright © 2019 by Information Age Publishing
101

learning opportunities, teachers can engage with educational policies to advance equity-oriented goals.

THE CENTRALITY OF POLICY IN TEACHING EMERGENT BILINGUAL STUDENTS

Educational policies have, over the last 2 decades, played an increasingly powerful role in the lives of public school teachers and students. This is especially true for Latinx emergent bilingual (EB)[1] youth and their teachers, who have had to contend with federal and, in some cases, state legislation aimed at limiting immigrants' rights, including the right to public education. Restrictive language policies, or policies that intend explicitly to control language use in schools, have played a similarly powerful role in shaping the educational experiences of EBs. Within just the last 20 years, laws in several states with large EB populations, including California, Arizona, and Massachusetts, passed restrictive language policies that prohibited the use of languages other than English in public school classrooms other than for the purpose of foreign language instruction[2] (Gándara & Hopkins, 2011). These policies severely reduced the number of bilingual education offerings, while simultaneously barring teachers and students in English-instruction classrooms from drawing on EBs' linguistic resources—arguably their most critical tool for learning and development.

In addition to targeted policies such as these, wider reaching policies, including high-stakes accountability policies and standards-based reforms have also been shown to negatively affect EBs' access to high-quality, appropriate instruction (Menken, 2010). Purportedly aimed at raising achievement among all students, such policies often press teachers to "teach to the test" and, in so doing, to take up teacher-centered, skill-driven instructional practices known to undermine EBs' opportunities to learn, particularly in literacy (e.g., Pacheco, 2010; Stillman, 2011). Gutiérrez, Asato, Santos, and Gotanda (2002) have argued that such policies can lead teachers to employ "backlash pedagogies," or pedagogies that, while framed as neutral or culture-free, put Latinx EBs at risk by treating their cultural and linguistic resources as barriers to their English acquisition, performance on English standardized tests, and academic success.

Despite the challenges imposed on EBs by some educational policies, growing evidence illustrates that teachers can positively impact policy enactment. Various accounts, for example, illustrate how equity-minded teachers who have been explicitly prepared to teach culturally and linguistically diverse students are especially well equipped and inclined to challenge and/or adapt policy mandates in the service of teaching in student-responsive ways. Whether called "principled resistance" (Achinstein & Ogawa, 2006), "critical professional practice" (Stillman, 2011), and/or "creative insubordination" (Gutiérrez, 2013), each involves teachers privileging local student needs as they navigate policies they view as contradicting their own knowledge and expertise and as potentially posing harm to students. Policymakers and traditional policy scholars often frame such actions as wrongheaded or deviant, particularly because they can lessen the degree to which a policy is implemented as policymakers intended. However, research increasingly suggests that critical policy engagement represents essential efforts to advocate for students who are underserved by public schools (Pease-Alvarez & Samway, 2012), can lead teachers to experience meaningful professional learning (Stillman, 2011), and is at the heart of public school teachers' roles as keepers of a democratic society (Santoro, 2016).

This chapter grows out of and builds on this literature by considering school-level practices that can support teachers' ethical responses to policies that stand to disadvantage EBs' access to responsive instruction. It does so by drawing on data from a 2-year ethnographic case study of one high-performing, dual-immersion (Spanish/English) K–8 school in California and ten of its teachers' responses to the Common Core State Standards (CCSS) in English Language Arts (ELA)/literacy. The account demonstrates the potentially powerful ways school-level practices can transform schooling for EBs by reducing the negative effects of reductive federal, state, and district policies.

THE COMMON CORE STATE STANDARDS: POTENTIAL PROMISES AND LIKELY RISKS

Developed by a Gates Foundation-funded consortium that included the Council of Chief State School Officers and the National Governor's Association and released in 2010, the CCSS represent the latest iteration of standards-based reform. Unlike their state-derived predecessors, the CCSS are the United States' first national standards and as of 2017 were in use in 42 states. The CCSS' broad adoption is partially attributable to *Race to the Top* (2009), the Obama administration policy which promised CCSS-adopting states additional federal school funding.

Advocates claim the CCSS have the capacity to meet wide ranging goals, such as increasing coherence across states and school systems (e.g., Reville, 2014) and enhancing the nation's global competitiveness (e.g., National Governors Association, Council of Chief State School Officers, & Achieve, 2008). Perhaps most notably, CCSS supporters tout the standards' power to raise academic expectations—to "raise the bar" for all students, which CCSS authors allege prior standards have failed to do (Common Core State Standards Initiative, 2010).

Responses to the Common Core ELA/Literacy Standards are mixed. Some educators trouble the potential for national standards to *standardize* the curriculum by taking debates about what constitutes knowledge out of the hands of local communities (Sleeter & Flores Carmona, 2017); others raise questions about the CCSS' tendencies to promote instructional approaches that dismiss strong evidence from literacy scholarship about, for example, how to determine a text's difficulty or how to support a range of readers to make meaning of various texts (e.g., Hiebert & Mesmer, 2013). Meanwhile, some praise the CCSS for their commitment to high expectations for all and for offering direction for authentic, rigorous literacy instruction as compared to some states' prior standards (Pearson, 2013).

Variation likewise characterizes responses that speak directly to the CCSS' potential impact on EBs. Some argue that the CCSS' emphasis on "raising the bar" for all may prompt teachers to hold higher expectations for Latinx EB students, who, because of pervasive deficit ideologies, have long been subjected to low expectations. In particular, education and language scholars have pointed to the CCSS' potential to open up EBs' access to more advanced instruction and materials, including more complex texts (e.g., Wong, Fillmore, & Fillmore, 2012). Others suggest the CCSS may have a "silver lining" when it comes to language and literacy instruction for EBs, by offering a conceptualization of language use and language development that aligns with how bilinguals authentically use language (Rymes, Flores, & Pomerantz, 2016).

Despite these potential benefits, criticisms of the CCSS and their use with EBs abound. Multiple scholars problematize the CCSS' monolingual/monocultural focus, pointing especially to the standards' potential to engender biased treatment of EBs. Wiley (2015), for example, challenges the CCSS' proclivity to cater exclusively to students from the dominant group, which he argues creates a "false image of deficiency for language minority students" (p. 11). Menken, (2015), meanwhile, underscores the risks imposed by CCSS-aligned assessments which, like other monolingual standardized tests, cannot fully measure EBs' knowledge and skills, and are likely "detrimental" to EBs because of the reductive instructional approaches they encourage.

The CCSS' monolingual focus is compounded by the standards' cursory attention to EBs, who are referenced explicitly only once (within the document's Appendix B), where it's suggested that teachers offer them "special accommodations." Notably, these accommodations are not named or described, suggesting they are perhaps optional, and/or that teachers are already knowledgeable about how to facilitate EBs' learning, despite evidence indicating most U.S. teachers are underprepared to teach EBs (Lucas, Villegas, & Freedson-Gonzalez, 2008). Indeed, because the CCSS present new demands, professional development that provides teachers with explicit support to implement these standards with EBs in needed (Valdés, Kibler, &

Walqui, 2014). Scholars have also criticized the CCSS' advancement of instructional approaches that conflict with key conditions for effective instruction for EBs. These criticisms have focused on: (a) the recommendation that students remain "within the four corners of the page" (e.g., rather than draw on prior knowledge and experiential understandings) when making meaning of new texts and providing evidence for text-based arguments; and (b) press on teachers to accelerate instruction by increasing text difficulty for all, and to withhold scaffolding, such as pre-reading activities, so that students can engage in "productive struggle" (Au & Waxman, 2015; August & Shanahan, 2015).

In light of these concerns and the challenges they potentially impose on EBs and their teachers, it is important to understand how teachers are interpreting and enacting the CCSS in schools serving EBs. The remainder of this chapter explores this question.

GETTING TO KNOW PLAYA: CONTEXT AND HISTORY

This chapter reports on an ethnographic case study that explored ten teachers' interpretations and enactments of the CCSS during the standards' first 2 years of implementation at a high-performing 50/50 dual-immersion school, referred to here as "Playa."[3] Playa sits on a neighborhood street adjacent to the U.S./Mexico border and near a fairly large metropolitan area. A charter school that emerged as a mechanism for offering a bilingual program in the wake of Proposition 227's 1998 passage, in 2017 Playa spanned grades PreK–12 and served more than 1400 students. Though the demographics have varied somewhat over the years,[4] in 2017 approximately 94% of Playa's students were Latinx, 38% were labeled as English Learners[5] and 64% were eligible to receive free or reduced priced lunch.

Playa considers itself a literacy-focused school committed to equity and social justice. These commitments manifest in the enthusiastic schoolwide support for bilingualism and biliteracy, and the staff's stated passion for critical pedagogy, inspired by the teachings of Paolo Freire. After the staff read *Pedagogy of the Oppressed* (1970) in summer 2012, two particular ideas took hold. First, teachers embraced Freire's criticism of "banking" education—or education that expects teachers to deposit knowledge, while students passively accept it. In response, teachers sought to tip the balance of intellectual heavy-lifting toward students, and to position students as knowledge generators (not just knowledge consumers). Second, teachers subscribed to Freire's ideas regarding dialogical teaching and believed that engaging students in dialogue could scaffold students' learning and disrupt hierarchical student–teacher relationships.

Playa's perhaps most notable characteristic is that for almost 10 years, it has been considered a high-performing school when compared to schools with similar demographic profiles. This is no small matter, particularly given Playa's initial designation as a "low-performing" school facing state takeover. This fraught history was evident in Playa's everyday practices and school identity, especially in how much pride staff, students, and community members took in the school; how hard school staff were willing to work on behalf of students; and in staff's hyperawareness of Playa's performance status.

During my first visit to Playa in Fall 2012, my colleagues and I were struck almost immediately by the school's positivity and clarity of purpose. It felt like a place where good things were happening for children, Latinx EB students especially, and we were excited to learn about the staff's work. While talking with three fourth grade teachers that day, they unexpectedly began discussing the CCSS in uncommon ways. Despite the mostly negative discourse at the time about the CCSS and their potential use with EBs, these teachers spoke with enthusiasm about their adoption. One teacher, Justin, offered that with CCSS, they could "finally do what we're supposed to be doing," meaning that their established instructional practices would be sanctioned by standards. Curious, my colleagues and I asked if we could follow them as they learned about and enacted the CCSS. They agreed, and seven more teachers eventually agreed to participate as well (see Appendix A).

USING CULTURAL-HISTORICAL ACTIVITY THEORY TO EXPLORE TEACHERS' ENACTMENTS OF THE CCSS

Unlike many traditional policy studies that focus on the fidelity of teachers' policy implementation (which assumes that a given policy is worthy of faithful implementation), this study conceives of teachers' work with policy as a situated learning phenomenon. Accordingly, my colleagues and I used learning theory—specifically, cultural-historical activity theory or CHAT—to guide our inquiry. From a CHAT perspective, all human activity is understood as situated, dialectical, and mediated. Thus, when using this lens to examine teachers' CCSS interpretations and enactments, we were compelled to consider how teachers' work and learning were mediated by the social, cultural, and historical contexts within which they occurred, while also attending to the ways in which teachers and other community members mediated those very contexts (Cole & Engeström, 1997; Engeström, 1987). Put another way, the study aimed to understand, as Britzman (2003) wrote in her seminal study of learning to teach, "what teachers make happen because of what happens to them and what it is that structures their practices" (p. 70).

The inquiry was guided by the following questions: (a) "What meaning do teachers make of the CCSS, particularly in language arts/literacy?" "What does that meaning-making entail?"; (b) "How do teachers use the CCSS in their language arts/literacy teaching practice?" "How does their meaning-making shape their instruction and vice versa?"; and (c) "What role does context play in teachers' responses to the CCSS?" "Which mediating factors matter most, and with what implications for students' opportunities to learn?" To pursue these questions, my colleagues and I designed a 2-year ethnographic case study. Data were collected across 11 school visits, each organized around weeklong "cycles of learning" lasting 4 to 5 days (Greene, 1994). During each visit, the research team conducted extensive school and classroom observations. In the first year, "the team" also conducted semi-structured individual and focus group interviews with teachers and individual interviews with school administrators. In the second year, video clips of teachers' literacy and language instruction were used as a springboard for conversations with individual teachers about their practice and the decisions they made "behind the scenes." These video-mediated interviews were designed to get at aspects of teachers' CCSS enactments that were perplexing in some way. Data analysis was ongoing and relied on both inductive and deductive coding, the latter of which involved drawing on CHAT.

Our analysis revealed that, in some ways, CCSS-driven instruction at Playa fell short of teachers' stated ideals regarding equity-oriented, responsive literacy instruction. Addressed in the chapter's "Discussion and Conclusion," these compromised aspects of Playa's instruction often reflected the cautions (some described above) administered by literacy and language scholars. In other ways, however, teachers successfully transformed some of the CCSS' potentially harmful dimensions, including their monolingual emphasis. As described below, our analysis revealed that several school-level practices were particularly essential to teachers' capacities to use the CCSS in ways that made the standards better suited to, and less disadvantageous for, EBs.

SCHOOL-LEVEL POLICIES AND PRACTICES THAT SUPPORTED TEACHERS' NAVIGATION OF THE CCSS

The school-level practices that supported teachers' ethical navigation of the CCSS most consequentially can be described in terms of how Playa's administrative team *organized* teachers' work and learning, in general, and in relation to the CCSS, specifically. The subsequent section describes some of Playa's most prevalent school-level practices in relation to two overarching administrative goals: (a) to develop and enable teacher autonomy and professionalism, and (b) to develop and deepen teachers' asset-based orientations and related teaching practices. As illustrated below, teachers' work was largely organized around these goals, particularly as they engaged with the CCSS.

Organizing for Autonomy and Professionalism

Playa's principal, Dr. Ruiz , organized Playa teachers' work and learning with the explicit aim of cultivating their professional autonomy and agency. This proved to be critical in how teachers understood their work with the CCSS and how they viewed themselves as policy actors, more generally.

Taking Policy and "Making It Playa's"

When my colleagues and I asked teachers to talk about the CCSS and policy mandates in general, it was clear they thought differently about policies than many teachers. While teachers commonly experience policy as something that happens *to* them, Playa teachers talked almost universally about policy, including the CCSS, in agentive terms meaning they viewed themselves as agents in the implementation process. These perspectives were closely tied to Dr. Ruiz's own beliefs that teachers must "engage with policies, *not* resist them" because "that's the way it is...so you need to work within that structure."

The reasoning that teachers ought to engage with rather than resist, even potentially harmful policies because they're part of the existing "structure," may strike some as odd; particularly coming from a "critical" school like Playa, and in light of accounts that illustrate the essential role of resistance in some equity-minded teachers' principled efforts to serve their students well (e.g., Achinstein & Ogawa, 2006). This struck us as odd, too, until we understood that Dr. Ruiz's brand of policy engagement was guided by his belief that "success" required ensuring EBs could compete in the existing educational system—a perspective that privileged engagement over resistance. Dr. Ruiz also understood policy engagement to mean "getting out in front of policies," or determining as a school how a policy would be enacted before any "outsider" could. As he contended, when it came to policy, "We're in the driver's seat. We're moving things. We're gonna continue to move regardless of the obstacles." Importantly, Dr. Ruiz's claim that Playa would "move regardless of the obstacles," reflected a broader, school-wide cultural norm that seemed to emerge out of Playa's journey from "low" to "high-performing." With Dr. Ruiz at the helm, Playa's ascendancy helped build in staff a sense of self-confidence and capability that led them to view any challenge as surmountable and helped them resist feeling subject to any "structure" or policy. One teacher aptly explained that, at Playa, "things aren't done to us, we handle things."

As a practice, being in "the driver's seat" and "handling things" mostly appeared to mean trying to adapt policy mandates in alignment with Playa-specific goals, values, and practices. According to Ms. Cook, Playa's middle school assistant principal, "the best teachers are the ones who know how to adapt," who take policy, subject matter, and pedagogy and "make it their own." Teachers embraced this outlook, which middle school teacher Miriam expanded upon as follows: "[Playa's] philosophy is, you're presented with something new, you take it, and you make it your own, you make it Playa's." Teachers also spoke often about "going beyond" policies—not just complying, but doing *more* than what was actually asked for.

This general stance toward policy powerfully mediated teachers' responses to the CCSS. For example, teachers tended to view the CCSS as unremarkable and as just one more dimension of "the structure" to which they would adapt. This perspective manifested when teachers worked diligently and collaboratively to determine how they would use the CCSS within their dual-immersion program and with the goal of supporting student learning across grade levels, languages, and subject matter. Teachers were especially well positioned to take ownership of the CCSS when they developed units of study from scratch that—per administrative mandate—included *all* of the literacy standards and incorporated Playa's core tenets of bilingual education and critical pedagogy. As described below, teachers received support to engage in this policy-related labor during regularly scheduled collaborative grade-level meetings.

Recognizing and Supporting Teachers' Policy Navigation

School-level policy additionally supported Playa teachers to use the CCSS in ways that were more responsive to EBs than was stipulated by the standards, through the requirement that all teachers participate in regularly scheduled, structured collaborative meetings. Every 2 weeks, teachers gathered for 2½ hours with their grade-level colleagues to plan instruction, develop assessments, examine student work, and figure out how to incorporate new initiatives. During our 2 years visiting Playa, we sat in on many such meetings. In each, almost all of teachers' time and efforts were geared toward interpreting and implementing the CCSS.

Providing teachers with structured and protected time for professional work is largely what enabled teachers to use the CCSS to promote bilingualism and biliteracy and supported teachers' capacities to incorporate dialogical approaches into their instruction. It's also what signaled to teachers that administrators viewed them as professionals who could be trusted to use the CCSS without relying on prepackaged and/or scripted standards-based curricula. Teachers took this autonomy seriously, as evidenced by the rigorous and meaningful thematic units they developed (described later in the chapter), many of which incorporated social justice themes. During the meetings my colleagues and I attended, for example, we observed: first-grade teachers puzzle over how they might "teach beyond" the first-grade standards so that students would have opportunities to reach their full potential; fourth-grade teachers develop complex graphic organizers for scaffolding students' learning about character analysis; and middle school teachers draw on strategies from the GLAD program—a set of instructional approaches designed for EBs for which all teachers had received training—as they developed CCSS-based instruction aimed at teaching students how to make text-based arguments within a unit entitled, "Racial, Cultural, and Socioeconomic Differences Can Lead to Misunderstandings, Prejudice, and Violence." Collaborative meetings provided teachers with essential time and resources for "engaging" (rather than "resisting") the CCSS, in order to support learning in two languages and to realize high expectations for EBs.

Organizing for the Development and Support of Asset-Oriented Teaching for EBs

Another key aspect of Playa teachers' capacities to use the CCSS in EB-responsive ways involved drawing upon their well-developed, asset-oriented views about and treatment of Latinx EBs. Playa leadership, and especially Dr. Ruiz, was instrumental in organizing teachers' work in ways that cultivated these perspectives and practices, in particular through established schoolwide policies concerning bilingualism and biliteracy and labeling. As illustrated below, these policies—developed mostly by Dr. Ruiz—were often quite top-down in nature, and therefore seemed to contradict Playa's more critical and democratic values and practices, particularly those that aimed to cultivate professional autonomy. This inconsistency sometimes rubbed teachers the wrong way, and observations indicate it also often undermined teachers' efforts to be as responsive to students as they would have liked and were equipped to be. That said, these school-level policies simultaneously provided teachers with clear direction and structures for enacting their asset-based orientations. Thus, they were consequential in supporting teachers to transform the CCSS to better serve EBs.

Cultivating Students' Bilingualism and Biliteracy

Playa teachers' strong asset-oriented, anti-deficit views of students were expressed most explicitly through Playa's commitment to bilingualism and biliteracy and played a central role in enabling teachers to transform the CCSS to better support EBs. This commitment was also at the heart of Playa's identity, largely due to Dr. Ruiz, a devoted bilingual education advocate. So strong was Playa's commitment, the CCSS' monolingual focus never came up during our school visits. Rather, guided by school leaders,

Playa teachers understood the CCSS to be a tool for guiding Spanish and English instruction. This was apparent in several key ways.

First, administrators expected the CCSS to play an equally prominent role in English and Spanish language arts' classrooms. As he introduced the CCSS to teachers, Dr. Ruiz explained that all language arts teachers, in collaboration with their grade-level partners, would be expected to develop four standards-based literacy units per year—two focusing on narrative texts, and two focusing on informational ones. Over the course of the school year, teachers were instructed to use *all* of the CCSS ELA standards to develop these units for use in Spanish and English. We understood this policy as Dr. Ruiz's effort to ensure instruction would be equally rigorous across languages, and that students would be able to perform at a similarly "high bar" in Spanish and English. In response, teachers worked diligently and enthusiastically to create curriculum, mostly, it seemed, because the mandate aligned so well with their own asset orientations, personal commitments to EBs and bilingual education, and desire, as professionals, to craft the curriculum on their own terms, instead of using prepackaged programs. Even though the curriculum development demanded appeared to exhaust teachers, and as middle school teacher Sonya explained, was not for teachers who view teaching as a "cakewalk," teachers rarely complained and mostly took the extra responsibility in stride.

To be sure, the standards featured in equal measure across Spanish and English language classrooms. This was especially true for two of the CCSS' "anchor" literacy standards (featured across all grade levels) that CCSS authors and teacher guidebooks have emphasized more than other standards: (a) pressing students to read increasingly "complex texts" (as stipulated by the CCSS' "text complexity staircase," which recommends text levels and specific texts that students, beginning in second grade, ought to read); and (b) requiring students to engage in a reading strategy called "close reading" (what others have called "cold reading"), to navigate complex texts (Common Core State Standards Initiative, 2010).

In first grade, for example, students in Spanish-language classrooms completed multiple close readings of complex informational texts about child labor and about the impacts of deforestation on *los lacandones* (an indigenous Mexican community); meanwhile, in English-language classrooms, the same first graders were expected to do close readings of literary texts, in one case, of a poem entitled, "I am" that conveyed complex messages about identity through figurative language. Expectations in fourth grade and middle school were similarly rigorous. Fourth graders, for example, did close readings of complex texts about topics like immigration and Mexican politics, while middle schoolers with varying reading levels were expected to do close readings of complex texts about the Islamic Empire, school segregation, and racial violence. Across classrooms, texts surpassed CCSS' text complexity staircase recommendations.

While notable on its own, it wasn't just that teachers engaged in the technical act of ensuring standards "showed up" in their instruction. Rather— per administrative mandate—teachers worked together to figure out how standards could be used across classes, content areas, and languages to deepen and broaden students' learning, including their language learning. This was exemplified in the example above of first-grade teachers assigning texts that aimed to cultivate understandings across languages about their grade level's overarching unit theme: Human Rights. This was also exemplified when these same teachers spent hours hunched over the CCSS, unit and lesson plans, and student work to figure out how they might facilitate learning in relation to several standards addressing verb usage.[6] In typical fashion, teachers decided to embed verb-related skills and concepts in content-rich texts while emphasizing various aspects of the same standards. Thus, students identified verbs and their role within the aforementioned "I am" poem; teachers then introduced students to the idea of verb tense in the context of a complex Spanish text about deforestation. In other words, grade-level teammates worked to support students' mastery of the same standards, contextualized in similar content (since grade-level teams collectively determined unit themes), but through different yet complementary learning experiences that relied on a range of instructional materials. The goal was for students to understand how meaning and conventions travel across settings, concepts, and languages in similar and divergent ways, but always informing one another. This is not to suggest that the CCSS themselves advance (holistic notions of) bilingualism or biliteracy; rather, with the right school-level supports and expertise (discussed below), teachers were able to use the CCSS to advance their own and Playa's goals and values. This was no small feat given the risks that monolingual standards impose on EBs and on dual language education, more broadly.

Relatedly, administrators pressed and supported teachers to use the CCSS to advance bilingualism/biliteracy by requiring that teachers administer all school-level, standards-based assessments in Spanish and English. This involved teachers drawing on state exemplars of CCSS benchmark assessments (developed by Smarter Balanced) to develop assessments for each ELA and SLA literacy unit. Although this required significant labor of teachers, teachers mostly valued the process because it lent status and legitimacy to teaching bilingually and provided more accurate information about their students' progress than monolingual assessments could (Hopewell & Escamilla, 2014). It also positioned teachers and other Playa staff to use the official language of policy and accountability to advocate for Playa's bilingual program, while making it less risky for teachers, who would, despite Playa's charter status, be more vulnerable to scrutiny if they acted individually and without school-level protection as they assigned equal status to Spanish and English, rather than privileging English, as the CCSS suggest they should have.

Resisting Labels

Playa administrators additionally cultivated asset-oriented views and treatment of EBs through their mandate that teachers resist assigning labels to students. Labeling students according to perceived ability and language proficiency is a common practice in most schools. While this practice confers certain benefits—namely by informing teachers about students' particular needs and aiding in efforts to address them, it can also have harmful effects. This is particularly true for students from historically marginalized communities, as evidenced by long-standing problems with over- and under-representation of students of color and EBs in special education, tracking practices that curtail culturally and linguistically diverse students' access to high-status courses, and rampant deficit ideologies among educators about students from nondominant cultural and linguistic communities (Artiles, Kozleski, Trent, Osher, & Ortiz, 2010; Callahan, 2005).

Aware of these trends, administrators called for the elimination of "language, special needs, or economic status" labels and demanded that teachers devise more holistic ways to discuss students. Like Playa's CCSS-related curriculum unit policy, teachers enthusiastically complied. First-grade teacher Ramón, for example, suggested that assessments unfairly label students: "You can't give them a test and say, ok, you're literate, you're not literate . . . you have . . . to really know your students to understand how they are developing." Teachers also shared concerns about the term *English learner*, problematizing its power to limit opportunities, despite their sense that the label itself does not accurately capture how language learning occurs. Justin, a bilingual, native English-speaking teacher, shared: "I don't like that idea of English language learner. . . . I'm still an English language learner. It's my native language but I'm still learning English. . . . I've been making [errors] for 34 years." Multiple teachers additionally talked about how the school's no-labeling mandate discouraged them from considering ability levels when planning instruction, or from treating individual students as more or less capable.

Playa's no-labeling policy powerfully mediated teachers' uptake of the CCSS. Because teachers were expected to treat all students as highly capable, they, in turn, expected all students to master all standards usually through uniformly challenging learning experiences. This was true even in the early grades, where teachers treated perseverance as a crucial accomplishment. First-grade teacher, Sofia, recounted how students initially struggled with CCSS-driven expectations, but had eventually learned to handle them:

> At the beginning of the year I had some that cried because (crying voice) I
> don't understand anything, teacher!...It is becoming more normal I guess
> for them to get exposed to this type of text....They don't say, "Oh wow that's
> a lot of reading." No. They don't complain at all now...now they just take it
> as normal. "OK, we'll read it....Yeah. Oh OK."

The no-labeling, high-expectations-for-all ethos was just as prevalent in
the upper grades, where teachers expected students of all reading levels
and language proficiencies to complete "close readings" of the same "complex" texts. As middle school ELA teacher, Sonya, put it, expecting all students to read the same text was a key expression of her belief in students'
capacities:

> I do use the same text [for all students]....It wasn't logical for me to say, "Okay,
> well, we're gonna study the American Revolution, and you're gonna study this
> text, and you're gonna study this different text."...Why are we gonna water
> down or dumb down lessons for our kids when they should all [learn]?

Together, these comments counter deficit ideologies about Latinx EBs, as
well as patterns of withholding rigorous instruction from students considered "unready" for academic challenge.

DISCUSSION AND CONCLUSION

This account highlights the role that school-level policies and practices can
play in supporting teachers to transform educational policies that impose
potential harm on EBs. In this case, several school-level policies and practices supported Playa's teachers to use the CCSS to advance Playa's EB-focused
values and goals, particularly by enabling teachers to use the CCSS as a tool
for enacting asset-oriented views of students and for expanding students'
access to rigorous instruction. These were not inconsequential accomplish-
ments, particularly since pressures associated with high-stakes accountability policies, including standards-based reform, have led to decreases in bilingual education offerings (Menken & Solorza, 2014), and to the privileging
of English, even in bilingual programs (Palmer & Rangel, 2011).

Nevertheless, the impact of Playa's school-level policies and practices
wasn't exclusively positive. Because teachers offered all students the same
rigorous instruction, we frequently observed students struggle through
challenging academic tasks with little support. Relatedly, teachers commonly embraced dimensions of the CCSS that scholars have suggested may
undermine EBs' learning. Teachers, for example, often pressed students to
adhere to the CCSS' charge to "remain within the four corners of the page"
while reading, demanding that students holster prior understandings while

making meaning of new text. This practice contradicts research that establishes the importance, for EBs especially, of bridging new understandings with existing ones (e.g., Walqui, 2006). Teachers' encouragement that students read texts of ever-increasing complexity, even when students were working in their less-dominant language, likewise counters cautions about imposing onto bilingual learners expectations that overlook biliteracy development's nonlinear trajectories (Hopewell & Escamilla, 2014).

Whether positive or negative, the contributions of school level policies and practices to teachers' CCSS enactments were connected to Playa's specific context, its norms and practices. In other words, what teachers "made happen" with the CCSS was linked strongly to "what happen[ed] to them" (Britzman, 2003, p. 70), both in terms of the school-level policies and practices described in this chapter, and also how such policies and practices were instantiated in context-specific ways. Thus, implementing similar policies at different schools wouldn't necessarily generate the same outcomes as those described here. For example, when the CCSS came on the scene, Playa educators were already well equipped to use them responsively. As a high-performing school with an established bilingual program, Playa staff possessed the confidence, infrastructure, and autonomy necessary for tailoring the CCSS to their EBs. This, combined with Dr. Ruiz's hiring practices—which included recruiting from a highly regarded university-based bilingual preservice program with whom he had a longstanding partnership—meant that Dr. Ruiz could count on teachers to hold the specialized knowledge and ideological stances regarding Latinx EBs needed for using the CCSS adaptively.

It would also be remiss to attribute teachers' lack of awareness of compromised CCSS-based instruction to individual shortcoming. Teachers, rather, seemed susceptible to troubling CCSS enactments because of how seamlessly some of Playa's sanctioned practices and ideologies mapped onto the CCSS and their surrounding discourse. For example, teachers often equated their commitments to dialogical teaching and the related commitment to have students do the intellectual "heavy lifting," with the CCSS' press to increase academic rigor without also increasing support. This was (ironically) compounded by teachers' asset orientations and resistance to labeling, which many teachers read as the same as CCSS calls to "raise the bar."

Playa's context also seemed to compromise teachers' proclivities to apply a critical eye to the CCSS. For one, teachers seemed to interpret Playa's high-performing status as an indication that what they were doing was "working" and did not require reflection or modification. Just as significantly, the policy context itself undermined teachers' propensities to critically consider their CCSS enactments. Teachers experienced so much pressure to sustain Playa's high-performing status by "keeping up" with policy demands that they typically interpreted their CCSS responsibilities as covering all standards. Although they tackled this task in earnest, doing so superseded teachers' propensities to critically analyze the CCSS or CCSS-driven practice.

IMPLICATIONS

Taken together, findings point to several important implications for policy, transformative practice and pedagogy, and future research. First, findings underscore the need for flexible federal and state policies that are designed to inspire responsive, contextually sensitive teaching, instead of promoting blind replication of predetermined instructional practices and/or policy fidelity. Although teachers were able to use the CCSS to advance Playa's own goals and values to some degree, had teachers been able to use the CCSS without the pressure of looming high-stakes CCSS-aligned assessments, perhaps they would have been less inclined to privilege high-status dimensions of the standards (e.g., close reading of complex texts), and more inclined to lend a critical eye to the standards and their standards-driven practices.

Findings additionally underscore a need for transformative school-level policies and practices that help minimize harm imposed by external policies. If Playa's case teaches us anything, it's that, when provided with professional autonomy, strong leadership, and meaningful learning opportunities, teachers can use even suboptimal policies to advance equity-oriented goals. Notably, Playa's case also suggests that school-level policies and practices are more likely to take hold when they align with a school's own norms, values, and capacities.

Yet, findings also intimate that the presence of transformative school-level policies and practices cannot fully protect teachers—even those who are specially prepared to serve EBs, have asset orientations, and work in "high-performing" schools with equity commitments—from the colonizing power of reductive policies. As illustrated elsewhere (Stillman & Anderson, 2017), in order to stave off the encroachment of potentially harmful policies, teachers of EBs, especially, need school-level practices that aim to cultivate teachers' *critical* policy responses. This could involve practices that support teachers to move beyond policy engagement, even adaptation—which at Playa mostly led teachers to privilege CCSS coverage and compliance—and toward policies and practices that center teachers' critical reflection and interpretation. Put another way, in today's policy and political context, administrators might establish school-level policies and practices that do more than generate for teachers harmonious, "horizontal interaction" (Engeström, 1991), as Playa's collaborative planning time and professional development sessions tended to do. Instead, schools could reorganize or *remediate* teachers' working and learning conditions in ways that help surface "stories of problematic situations," upon which teachers could thoughtfully reflect about taken-for-granted understandings, what we might think of as planting the seeds for teachers' future policy-related, expansive learning. This, in turn, may increase possibilities for positively transforming EBs' learning experiences.

Teacher education has a potentially important role to play, as well. In particular, teacher preparation programs might move beyond helping candidates learn to comply with standards, by instead employing transformative pedagogies that support candidates to engage critically with policy mandates. This would hopefully position graduates to take full advantage of school-based opportunities to adapt educational policies, and/or to exercise agency for initiating critical policy engagement, even when school-level policies or practices don't support it.

Finally, findings point to a need for policy scholarship that generates understandings about how policy impacts teachers and students, rather than privileging questions about implementation fidelity, especially in relation to potentially harmful policies. Certainly, the study reported on here begins to deepen our understandings of the challenges EBs and teachers of EBs face in these policy-heavy times, and to offer insights regarding the kinds of conditions that can help transform such challenges into positive learning experiences for EBs. That said, a single story of a single school can do little on its own to disrupt harmful policies, to impress upon policymakers and the public the need for better policy, or to sufficiently illustrate the transformational work of EBs' most talented and committed teachers.

APPENDIX A

TABLE 6.1 Teacher Assignments and Characteristics			
Teacher Names	Language of Instruction	Bilingual	Race/Ethnicity
Ana	English	✓	Latinx
Sofia	Spanish	✓	Latinx
Ramón	Spanish	✓	Latinx
Rocio	English	✓	Latinx
Paco	Spanish	✓	Latinx
Justin	English	✓	White
Julie	English		White
Sonya	English	✓	Latinx
Miriam	Spanish	✓	Latinx
Lynette	English		White

NOTES

1. Throughout the chapter, I use the term Latinx in lieu of Latino/a because it currently represents the most established gender neutral and nonbinary option. In addition, I use the term Emergent Bilingual to describe students who are developing two languages as a way to signal the importance of viewing such students through a lens of potential, rather than a lens of deficiency, and to frame the overall goal for students' learning as bilingualism/ biliteracy instead of positioning English monolingualism/monoliteracy as schooling's primary goal.
2. In 2016, almost 20 years after the passage of Proposition 227, 70% of California voters passed Proposition 58, again allowing "non-English languages" to be used in the state's public school classrooms.
3. All names of people and sites are pseudonyms.
4. As recently as 2013, close to 55 % of Playa's students were considered English Learners. The more recent statistics reflect Playa's changing population, which have resulted from more students entering school as simultaneous bilinguals and an increasing demand in the community (admittance is determined by lottery), in light of the school's consistent high-performing status and a growing desire in California for bilingual education.
5. Although not captured in typical demographic data, it's important to note that many of Playa's students are *simultaneous* bilinguals, or students who have grown up speaking both Spanish and English and now have relatively equal proficiency in both. These students are often not considered English Learners.
6. Such standards included: CCSS.ELA-LITERACY.L.1.1.E: "Use verbs to convey a sense of past, present, and future." and CCSS.ELA-LITERACY.L.3.1a: "Explain the function of nouns, pronouns, verbs, adjectives, and adverbs in general and their functions in particular sentences."

REFERENCES

Achinstein, B., & Ogawa, R. (2006). (In)fidelity: What the resistance of new teachers reveals about professional principles and prescriptive educational policies. *Harvard Educational Review, 76*(1), 30–63.

Artiles, A. J., Kozleski, E. B., Trent, S. C., Osher, D., & Ortiz, A. (2010). Justifying and explaining disproportionality, 1968–2008: A critique of underlying views of culture. *Exceptional Children, 76*(3), 279–299.

Au, W., & Waxman, B. (2015). The four corners not enough: Critical literacy, education reform and the shifting instructional strands of the Common Core State Standards. In K. Winograd (Ed.), *Critical literacies and young learners: Connecting classroom practice to the Common Core* (pp. 14–32). New York, NY: Routledge.

August, D., & Shanahan, T. (2015). What are the language demands for English language arts in the Common Core State Standards? In G. Valdés, K. Menken, & M. Castro (Eds.), *Common Core bilingual and English language learners: A resource for educators* (pp. 155–156). Philadelphia, PA: Calston.

Britzman, D. P. (2003). *Practice makes practice* (rev. ed.). Albany: State University of New York Press.

Callahan, R. (2005). Tracking and high school English learners: Limiting opportunities to learn. *American Educational Research Journal, 42,* 305–328.

Cole, M., & Engeström, Y. (1997). A cultural-historical approach to distributed cognition. In G. Salomon (Ed.), *Distributed cognitions: Psychological and educational considerations* (pp. 1–46). New York, NY: Cambridge University Press.

Common Core State Standards Initiative. (2010). *Common Core State Standards for English language arts & literacy in history/social studies, science, and technical subjects.* Retrieved from http://www.corestandards.org/wp-content/uploads/ELA_Standards1.pdf

Engeström, Y. (1987). *Learning by expanding: An activity theoretical approach to developmental research.* Helsinki, Finland: Orienta Konsultit.

Engeström, Y. (1991). Toward overcoming the encapsulation of school learning. *Learning and Instruction, 1,* 243–259.

Freire, P. (1970). *Pedagogy of the oppressed.* New York, NY: Continuum.

Gándara, P., & Hopkins, M. (Eds.). (2011). *Forbidden language: English learners and restrictive language policy.* New York, NY: Teachers College Press.

Greene, J. C. (1994). Qualitative program evaluation: Practice and promise. In N. K. Denzin & Y. S. Lincoln (Eds.), *Handbook of qualitative research* (pp. 530–544). Thousand Oaks, CA: SAGE.

Gutiérrez, R. (2013). Why (urban) mathematics teachers need political knowledge. *Journal of Urban Mathematics Education, 6*(2), 7–19.

Gutiérrez, K., Asato, J., Santos, M., & Gotanda, N. (2002). Backlash pedagogy: Language and culture and the politics of reform. *Review of Education, Pedagogy, and Cultural Studies, 24*(4), 335–351.

Hiebert, E. H., & Mesmer, H. E. (2013). Upping the ante of text complexity in the CCSS: Examining its potential impact on young readers. *Educational Researcher, 42*(1), 44–51.

Hopewell, S., & Escamilla, K. (2014). Struggling reader or emerging bilingual student? Reevaluating the criteria for labeling emerging bilingual students as low achieving. *Journal of Literacy Research, 46*(1), 68–89.

Lucas, T., Villegas, A. M., & Freedson-Gonzalez, M. (2008). Linguistically responsive teacher education: Preparing classroom teachers to teach English language learners. *Journal of Teacher Education, 59*(4), 361–373.

Menken, K. (2010). No child left behind and English language learners: The challenges and consequences of high-stakes testing. *Theory into Practice, 49*(2), 121–128.

Menken, K. (2015). What have been the benefits and drawbacks of testing and accountability for English language learners/emergent bilinguals under No Child Left Behind, and what are the implications under the Common Core State Standards? In G. Valdés, K. Menken, & M. Castro (Eds.), *Common Core bilingual and English language learners: A resource for educators* (p. 246). Philadelphia, PA: Calston.

Menken, K., & Solorza, C. (2014). No child left bilingual: Accountability and the elimination of bilingual education programs in New York City schools. *Educational Policy, 28*(1), 96–125.

National Governors Association, Council of Chief State School Officers, & Achieve. (2008). *Benchmarking for success: Ensuring U.S. students receive a world-class education.* Retrieved from http://www.achieve.org/files/BenchmarkingforSuccess.pdf

Pacheco, M. (2010). English learners' reading achievement: Dialectical relationships between policy and practices in meaning-making opportunities. *Reading Research Quarterly, 45*(3), 292–317.

Palmer, D., & Rangel, V. S. (2011). High stakes accountability and policy implementation: Teacher decision making in bilingual classrooms in Texas. *Educational Policy, 25*(4), 614–647.

Pearson, P. D. (2013). Research foundations of the Common Core State Standards in English language arts. In S. Neuman and L. Gambrell (Eds.), *Quality reading instruction in the age of Common Core State Standards* (pp. 237–262). Newark, DE: IRA.

Pease-Alvarez, L., & Samway, K. D. (2012). *Teachers of English learners negotiating authoritarian policies.* The Netherlands: Springer.

Reville, P. (2014, April 21). How to create a new K–12 engine. *Education Week, 33*(29), 24, 28

Rymes, B., Flores, N., & Pomerantz, A. (2016). The Common Core Standards and English learners: Finding the silver lining. *Language, 92*(4), 257–273.

Santoro, D. (2016). "We're not going to do that because it's not right": Using pedagogical responsibility to reframe the doublespeak of fidelity. *Educational Theory, 66*(1/2), 263–277.

Sleeter, C. E., & Flores Carmona, J. (2017). *Un-Standardizing the curriculum: Multicultural teaching in the standards-based classroom* (2nd ed.). New York, NY: Teachers College Press.

Stillman, J. (2011). Teacher learning in an era of high-stakes accountability: Productive tension and critical professional practice. *Teachers College Record, 113*(1), 133–180.

Stillman, J., & Anderson, L. (2017). *Teaching for equity in complex times: Negotiating standards in a high-performing bilingual school.* New York, NY: Teachers College Press.

Valdés, G., Kibler, A., & Walqui, A. (2014, March). *Changes in the expertise of ESL professionals: Knowledge and action in an era of new standards.* Alexandria, VA: TESOL International Association.

Walqui, A. (2006). Scaffolding instruction for English language learners: A conceptual framework. *International Journal of Bilingual Education and Bilingualism, 9*(2), 159–180.

Wiley, T. G. (2015). In what ways are the Common Core State Standards de facto language education policy? In G. Valdés, K. Menken, & M. Castro (Eds.), *Common Core bilingual and English language learners: A resource for educators* (pp. 10–11). Philadelphia, PA: Calston.

Wong Fillmore, L., & Fillmore, C. J. (2012, January). *What does text complexity mean for English learners and language minority students?* Understanding Language, Stanford University.

SECTION III

TRANSFORMATIVE PEDAGOGIES

CHAPTER 7

SOCIO-SPATIAL REPERTOIRES AS TOOLS FOR RESISTANCE AND EXPANSIVE LITERACIES

Arturo Córtez
University of California, Berkeley

Kris D. Gutiérrez
University of California, Berkeley

ABSTRACT

This chapter profiles a site of resistance, navigated by emergent bilingual youth, that sparked new literacies, language practices, and stances. It examines this site to understand the socio-spatial repertoires essential to meaningful learning and powerful forms of literacy, including learning in local resistance practices. Additionally, the chapter analyzes how preservice teachers can design pedagogical spaces that leverage these socio-spatial repertoires in order to foster transformative learning within schools. This teacher preparation requires intentionally designing learning spaces where teachers can work with youth to engage in consequential learning by building and employing powerful literacies.

Transforming Schooling for Second Language Learners, pages 123–142
Copyright © 2019 by Information Age Publishing
All rights of reproduction in any form reserved.

123

Translinguals[1] traverse and move in and across a diverse and complex set of spaces that index a rich range of linguistic and sociocultural practices and identities. As in many parts of the United States, in California, the focus of this chapter, these spaces are circumscribed by language, racialized, and classed ideologies that mediate everyday life for youth from nondominant communities. Bilingual youth are continually engaging in, developing, expanding, and revising a repertoire of cultural practices and linguistic tools that help them navigate the developmental, sociopolitical, and sociocultural demands of what it means to be human and an adolescent. These tools and practices serve as resources to mediate everyday life, as well as to negotiate the additional set of developmental demands imposed by a range of racialized, economic, sociopolitical, and linguistic forms of inequity and, thus, have significant implications for the transformation of schooling. We argue that youths' engagement in a cultural habitus marked by difference results in the development of what we term *socio-spatial repertoires*. Such practices challenge and resist the injustices of everyday life—inequities connected to the larger global project of neoliberalism, which advances the linguistic dominance of English (Alim, 2016) and reproduces historically unjust spatial arrangements.

In this chapter, we first illustrate how emergent bilingual youth navigate cities in which particular sites of resistance serve as the crucible for new literacies, language practices, and stances. Toward this end, we focus on San Francisco as it provides a rich site for understanding how emergent bilingual youth develop socio-spatial repertoires that leverage particular linguistic practices—those that are essential to meaningful learning and powerful forms of literacy, including learning in local resistance practices. We argue that the everyday practices of emergent bilingual youth are often transformative undertakings that are essential to consequential learning across space, timescales, and sites of power.

Second, we examine some of the challenges and possibilities for preservice teachers who attempted to design pedagogical spaces that leveraged the tools and sensibilities of bilingual youth, particularly their socio-spatial repertoires. By supporting teacher learning in this way, we contend that schools can become sites of transformative learning in which the linguistic, cultural, and spatial practices of youth are seen as resources for learning, as well as for supporting their participation in larger civic and political spheres. We argue, however, that supporting students' development of more expansive socio-spatial repertoires and tool kits requires intentionality, both in the design of systems and for teacher learning such that teachers work side by side with youth to engage in consequential learning and build and employ powerful literacies (Hamilton, 1997). Before we address this key point, we turn to a fuller discussion of the relationship among bilingual youth, the reimagining of the city, and linguistic and spatial dominance.

TRANSLINGUALS, EVERYDAY RESISTANCE,
AND THE DEMANDS OF NEOLIBERALISM

Neoliberalism (Harvey, 2005) mediates the developmental, sociocultural, and sociopolitical demands of everyday life and advances cultural and demographic shifts under the banners of urban renewal, revitalization, and neighborhood beautification. Neoliberalism here is understood as "an ensemble of economic and social policies, forms of governance, and discourses and ideologies that promote individual self-interest, unrestricted flows of capital, deep reductions in the cost of labor, and sharp retrenchment in the public sphere" (Lipman, 2011, p. 6). In this chapter, we highlight bilingual youths' everyday negotiations with neoliberal reforms and discourses in sites across spaces: the neighborhood, the parks, and schools. Specifically, we present a telling case in which bilingual youths' ongoing resistance efforts (Pacheco, 2012) in public spaces led to the development of new linguistic and cultural practices that served as resources for consequential learning.

We focus on neoliberalism to make visible the source of everyday contradictions that bilingual youth experience and to highlight their engagement in resistance practices, as well as the possible futures to which they aspire. In San Francisco, the city places a particular set of demands on speakers of marked languages, who have tentative citizenship status, and who are frequently denied access to the political process. Specifically, we identify how community resistance and the organizing efforts of bilingual youth prevented neoliberal reforms from advancing unabated. One mechanism for engaging in resistance is to challenge the very notions of space, asking, "Who belongs?"; "Where?"; "How?"; and "How do spaces come to be places of valued cultural life?" As Lefebvre (1991) and Soja (1989; 1996) have argued, people are always producing space through their moment-to-moment interactions in their efforts to organize and live culturally. From this perspective, space does not have a given material form or ideal representation, but is contested and reproduced in everyday social interactions. As such, cities are ideological battlegrounds where nondominant communities' cultural practices are pitted against the interests of corporations, elites, and the middle class (Gulson, 2011; Lipman, 2011). In this respect, cities and their institutions are the sites of enduring and ongoing political, economic, educational, and cultural struggles.

In this section, we take up this issue and highlight how neoliberalism circumscribes the everyday lives of nondominant youth. Paradoxically, while cities are sites of intense communicative diversity (Blommaert & Rampton, 2011), dominant linguistic practices are privileged through the expansion of ideological reforms and discourses. For emergent bilinguals in California's public schools, neoliberal educational policies, and the concomitant practices privileged therein, orient the purposes of schooling towards the demands of the economy. As a result, the bilingualism of nondominant populations is seen as a valued resource neither in its own right nor in schools or other valued social spaces. Such perspectives are not grounded in empirical, historical, or observer-participant understandings of how people deploy language, particularly as a means for asserting and achieving one's own dignity. However, rather than succumbing to a totalizing narrative about nondominant people who inhabit the city, we instead foreground how community resistance efforts by long-time residents (e.g., artists, business owners) became part of a larger movement to reimagine the city for new futures (Gutiérrez, 2008). Specifically, we examine the resistance efforts of a diverse group of translingual youth who revised, expanded, and deployed linguistic and space-producing practices that resisted the advancement of neoliberal reform.

In our view, San Francisco is a robust case illustrating how broader cultural and political dynamics shape cities for elites, corporations, whites, and the middle class (Gulson, 2011; Lipman, 2011). During the past 20 years, the San Francisco Bay Area has witnessed economic growth tied to the creation of new private-sector, technology-related industries as corporations such as Twitter, Google, Airbnb, Facebook, Uber, and Lyft have opened up or expanded offices within San Francisco and the broader metropolitan area—as a result of the tax incentive legislation devised by San Francisco policymakers to keep or attract such businesses, irrespective of the impact on the public welfare. Thus, the demand for housing, as a result of newly arrived technology workers in an already overly-subscribed market, has led to increased real estate prices and rents to levels that the middle class cannot afford (Hutson, 2015). Nondominant neighborhoods have been disproportionately affected, including the Mission District, a predominantly Latinx[2] neighborhood at the center of this controversy, which experienced over a 10% decline in the Latinx population between 2000–2010 (Hutson, 2015). However, long-time residents, business owners, and artists living in the Mission have not conceded space and their organizing efforts are challenging the demographic and cultural shifts in the neighborhood.

Thus, our focus on these "resistance practices" provides an opportunity to examine how these practices become resources for bilingual youth to overcome dilemmas advanced by neoliberal and deficit-oriented social and educational policies. Further, as learning scientists interested in the role of culture in the learning and sociocultural development of nondominant populations, we are motivated to attend to youths' everyday practices and the learning therein to capture the *everyday resistance* (Pacheco, 2012) in which youth and their families and communities currently engage within cities. We are interested in how youth continually negotiate space linguistically to contest notions of language proficiency bounded by context, content, and discipline, subverting the linguistic dominance of English and accompanying dehumanizing practices. Before examining this relationship between sociocultural explorations of learning and the ongoing process of spatial production, we provide a theoretical framing of the notion of socio-spatial repertoires.

SURFACING SOCIO-SPATIAL REPERTOIRES: THE CASE OF SAN FRANCISCO

In this section, we address how, in the context of neoliberalism, bilingual youth engage in efforts to transform the city toward equitable ends, while maintaining that neoliberalism (Harvey, 2005) mediates spatial production, in which socially produced structures "result[ing] from the transformation of given conditions inherent to being alive" are created (Soja, 1989, p. 80). Spatial production, then, is central to human activity, as it is part of the moment to moment social interactions embedded within historically situated sociocultural contexts. These space-producing processes are generative of socio-spatial repertoires—repertoires constitutive of the individual and collective cultural tools and practices that people develop, revise, expand, and deploy to make sense of and produce space.

We argue that translingual youth transform and draw from their socio-spatial repertoire—their linguistic, cultural, spatial, and political tool kit—to produce space that mediates everyday constraints. In this respect, these new cultural practices and tools create opportunities for individual and collective learning that is consequential for gaining full participation in the economic, political, and cultural life in the city. Such practices echo Lefebvre's (1996) notion of *the right to the city*, a "cry and demand" (p. 158) to create socially based spatialities that challenge the production of city life oriented toward the interests of private, middle-class, whites, and corporations. For bilingual youth, the right to the city is a concept that highlights their resistance efforts, their cultural and linguistic practices, and literacies that spatially produce the city. To illustrate, we turn our discussion to a specific case that illuminates the development and expansion of the socio-spatial repertoires of a group of bilingual youths as they negotiated a very public dilemma.

Since 2009, new parks and recreation reforms in San Francisco have led to refurbished parks, outfitted with new equipment, and new rules and policies regarding their use, including pay-to-play reservation systems. In particular, Mission Playground, a park that has long been used by the residents of the community for pickup soccer during the evenings, has been the site of disagreements between long-time, Latinx, primarily Spanish-speaking community members and English-speaking residents new to the neighborhood. In 2014, a video on Youtube (Barton, 2014) emerged showing a heated interaction between white, English-speaking, male employees from two tech companies and male youth, many of whom were Latinx, bilingual, and long-time residents of the Mission District.

We draw our analysis from this publicly available video. For our analyses, we constructed activity logs detailing the talk and interaction in 1-minute segments, coding those segments with top-down and bottom-up processes. We then used discourse analysis to examine the moment to moment discursive moves of the participants heard and seen in the video. We supplemented our analyses with public city and Parks and Recreation Department documents.

In the video, several men approach a group of youths who had been playing soccer and inform them that they had reserved the field using the reservation system. However, the youth, unaware of the new policy, refused to leave the soccer field and deployed a variety of linguistic tools and practices that constituted their socio-spatial repertoires to contest the new policy and their potential displacement. We present this event as a case of the kind of everyday negotiations with which nondominant populations must contend as a result of the convergence of neoliberal policies, demographic and cultural changes within the city, and the emerging technology-related industry.

Translanguaging and Socio-Spatial Repertoires

In what follows, we explore how the youth collaboratively drew on their socio-spatial repertoires. In particular, we examine their understanding of space as a sociocultural production and the power of deploying their rich set of linguistic tools to challenge and resist a neoliberal policy over the use of public land, including the players who tried to invoke new rules in the neighborhood. We argue that the youths' multimodal practices indexed their understanding both of the bureaucracy and official language of neoliberalism's spatial expansion, as well as of the meanings and history of use of the valued sociocultural practices of their neighborhood space. The youth, in our view, were building and deploying translingual practices and tools that supported the (re)imagination about how the park should be used and by whom, and, more broadly, about how youth and communities can engage neoliberal policies that are driving cultural and demographic shifts in the city. Of consequence, youth drew on their socio-spatial knowledge and cultural and linguistic practices as resources to resolve present-day contradictions—practices that can serve to reorganize activity systems toward new ends.

We turn our focus to the specific linguistic practices that were leveraged with the goal of producing a more equitable space—a space where youths' histories of movement, participation, and rights are enacted. In particular, we illustrate how youths' movement within and across diverse social and cultural spaces both exposed them to the relentless microaggressions that are part of everyday life for youth from nondominant communities in the city, as well as provided opportunity to enact "resistance practices." We illustrate the youths' deftness in using their linguistic repertoires, indeed their translingual repertoires, to adroitly navigate social interactions in which they asserted their rightful claims to space.

We find the concept of translanguaging (Canagarajah, 2013; García, 2009) particularly useful in the example that follows, as translingual practices are forms of resistance and negotiations of power (Martínez, 2013). Further, translanguaging practices capture the heterogeneity and hybridity of youths' spatial and linguistic practices. To situate our analysis, we insert a theoretical note about bilingual youth and translanguaging practices to further our discussion. Following García (2014), bilingual youth "use their entire linguistic repertoire to signify and construct meaning" (p. 74). In the context of Latinx youth, García has argued that translanguaging allows bilinguals to "learn and lead their lives with dignity and justice" (p. 74). As a theoretical orientation, translanguaging resists static notions of a language as a complete or overarching system, and indeed resists dichotomizing bilingual youth as speaking two different languages. Rather, it centers the activities within which interlocutors are embedded and looks at how language is deployed, hybridized, and generated anew. In this sense, translingualism rejects the notion that a nation-state is the legitimating body governing an official language, and seeks to trouble the linguistic, geographic, and political boundaries that maintain dominance over how, when, and where to speak a language. Thus, by leveraging the concept of translingualism, we foreground how Latinx youth develop expansive socio-spatial repertoires by deploying an expansive set of translingual and embodied practices to negotiate the production of space.

We find these latter points particularly relevant, as we are interested in how translinguals, as well as youth from nondominant communities more generally, develop sociocritical literacies to fully participate in the economic, cultural, political, and spatial dimensions of city life (Gutiérrez, 2008). Following Soja's (1996) processes of transformation in the Thirdspace, we find that translingual practices (a) surfaced the valued cultural and linguistic practices and tools inscribed in the history of the park, (b) made visible contradictions embedded within the neoliberal imagining of the city and the use of public space, and (c) created new meanings about how people contest the production of space.

With this theoretical grounding in mind, we return to the case about contested space to illustrate how youth produce a socially- and place-based spatiality by leveraging the historical, cultural, and linguistic practices and tools that have been valued, deployed, and unmarked prior to the institutionalization of the reservation system, in short, practices that have had a history of use and meaning in the neighborhood park. In the following interaction, we examine how the specific translingual practices transformed the soccer field from a site for play to a site of protest and contestation where private and individual interests were encroaching on what had been a public and collective space.

The transcript excerpt below documents the beginning of the interaction between a group of neighborhood youth, comprised largely of Latinx youth who were playing on the field, and a male employee of a technology-related corporation,[3] a tech worker (TW1), as he entered the soccer field. The neighborhood group was an intergenerational group that also included a slightly older youth (20 years old) from the neighborhood who appears to be a coordinator or at least a regular participant with the youth (we refer to him as OY, older youth). Another adult who filmed the interaction was a coordinator of the youth soccer group.

1. TW1: that co↑ol that co↑ol we got the field from seven to eig↑ht?
2. Y1: No °no° hablo inglés (I don't don't speak English)
3. TW1: Ye(h)ah you <u>do</u> speak English
4. ((*bounces ball*)) [I heard you earlier]
5. Y1: [no I don't] ((*walks away from TW1*))
6. TW1: Yeah we got it seven to eight, we go↑od? ((*following Y1 with ball in*
7. *hand*))
8. Y1: Reall↑y?
9. OY: Yo there is no seven to eight anything ((*gestures outwardly with*
10. *both hands and arms*))
11. If you want to play pick up ((*clapping back of right hand in palm*
12. *of left hand*)), you play pick up like the rest of us ((*extends both*
13. *arms and hands to gesture toward group of youths*))

In this initial engagement, an important tension emerged in which Youth 1 (Y1) immediately assessed that TW1's entry onto the court and his assertion that "we got the field from 7–8," posed a challenge for the youth who were there to engage in their regular pickup soccer game. Within this interaction, Y1 quickly responded by saying "no no hablo inglés" (no no I don't speak English), allowing him to ignore or not engage TW1's claim, only to be challenged by TW1 with, "Yeah you do speak English; I heard you earlier" (lines 3–4). In an ironic move, Y1 replied in English, "no I don't" as he walked out of the interactional space; here in this public space in the youths' neighborhood, linguistic and spatial practices converged (line 5). Youth 1 leveraged his sociocultural knowledge about when and how to use his linguistic repertoires and, thus, deliberately claimed that he did not speak English, while simultaneously demonstrating that in fact, he did speak English as he walked away toward his peers. We are intrigued by the youth's refusal to engage in English and not respond to the TW1's assertion. Here the young man could have been directing his comment both at TW1, as well as the larger community of people on the field who he now faced, as if to say, "You don't get to tell me in what language I can speak" or "You don't get to dictate the language in which we engage." We note, in particular TW1's authoritative response in line 3 ("Yeah you do. . . ."), in which he attempted to redefine the terms of engagement on his own terms in English (Martínez, 2013).

This initial engagement exemplifies how the processes of spatial production were negotiated linguistically. Utilizing his expansive linguistic tool kit, the youth (Y1) used Spanish to reject English as the language of engagement in this public space (lines 2 and 5), both claiming not to speak English and articulating that claim in Spanish. As García (2009) notes, translinguals may deploy multiple linguistic registers in order to challenge and negotiate everyday dilemmas. In the present case, English, as a linguistic tool, was ingeniously leveraged and repurposed to challenge the dominance of English as the language of engagement. The park, as a public space, was spatially remediated into one where multiple languages once again could be leveraged, hybridized. At this park, the youth, anchored in their cultural engagement and history with the park, resisted engaging with the norms defined by an English-speaking, technology worker. Instead, the youth's deployment of Spanish and English repositioned him, as well as his peers, as the linguistic rule setters in this space.

Following Y1's interaction with the TW1, the OY laid out the cultural practices and rules that had been socially developed and locally agreed upon in the park: players on the soccer field adhered to a system of seven-on-seven "pickup," where teams organized to play (lines 11–13). This practice, in existence for several years at this park, allowed for collaborative and equitable sharing of the space where multiple teams and different people could play over the course of an evening (Hoffman, 2012). In this interaction, OY built on Y1's refusal to allow the TW to set the terms of engagement by suggesting that the park already has a well-established set of practices, "Yo there is no 7 to 8 anything" (line 9). The young men pushed to establish that the park's already culturally and socially inscribed rules superseded the rules of Recreation and Parks Department's reservation system. In lines 14–23, TW1 maintained that the field could be booked through this reservation system, but the youth rejected this proposition.

Importantly, many youth, including Y1, also leveraged Spanish toward several ends. First, Spanish may have worked to exclude the tech employees from conversations, while also facilitating the larger practice of maintaining linguistic and spatial command of the soccer field. In the following excerpt, another youth (Y2) entered the conversation between TW1, Y1, and OY.

24.   Y2:   (out of frame): Es que es muy serio mejor no having the paper . . . for
25.   the rent (It's just that it's too serious not having the paper . . . for the
                rent)
26.   Y: (out of frame) no se muevan (everyone, don't move)

Youth 2 began by acknowledging that a new set of spatial practices have been imposed and that, at least temporarily, the youths' right to the space was in peril. With "es que es muy serio mejor no having the paper" (It's just that it's too serious not having the paper, line 24–25), for Y2 there was a recognition that the paper was consequential, both potentially for the youth as well as the tech workers, even if the field's regular participants disagreed with the policy. However, another youth, outside of the video frame, gave an imperative to the group to mobilize their bodies to stand their ground (no se muevan/everyone, don't move), and, in doing so, marked the park as a space where Spanish was spoken and brown bodies mattered (Cruz, 2001). Here translingualism is a multimodal accomplishment that contributes to the collective resistance to concede space. Thus, while the youth collaborated in maintaining their dominance in the space, they simultaneously expanded their socio-spatial repertoires as they negotiated the dilemma by incorporating a basic understanding of the imposed new rules (and their importance) that were being imposed by outsiders. The function of the youths' use of language here is tactical (Erickson, 2004), using English as a means of challenging the outsiders' legitimacy to the space, while Spanish is used to build solidarity and a united front, as well as a means of marking the space as theirs, as belonging to the community. As we will illustrate, the youth not only occupied the field with their bodies, they worked to produce a space where their translingual practices challenged hegemonic linguistic, political, and spatial practices that circumscribed which kinds of language and social practices were valued and legitimate.

The challenge builds in the next sequence, as the youth worked to spatially maintain the park and its history in the community, as well as their place in it. In an ironic twist, Y2 challenged the legitimacy of TW1's claims and "alleged" documentation and demanded to see their papers, "lemme see the paper the rent you know"—that is, to see proof that the tech workers had legitimate access to the park. Showing proof of one's legitimacy, of course, is a familiar trope in the lives of youth from nondominant communities, of immigrant youth, and youth whose languages are marked. Youth 2, arms stretched in ways that underscore his challenge, walked to TW1 and demanded, "lemme see" (line 27); his imperative was immediately ratified and supported by Y3 ("let me see it," line 28).

27.   Y2:   ((*walks to TW1 with arms open*)) Lemme see

28.   Y3:   let me see it

29.   TW1: ((*bounces ball*)) Tyler has that (doing what people do in that space)

30.   Y2:   Lemme see ((*TW1 bounces ball*)) lemme see lemme see the paper

31.   (.) for the rent y<u>ou</u> know?

32.   TW1: I don't have it, Tyler has it my [friend]= ((*holding ball in left hand,*

33.   *pointing finger out of frame*))

34.   Y2:   [please] please divided in the pe↑ople

35.   (.) (overlapping speech by various people)

36.   Y3:   If he comes, then you guys can get the field.

37.   TW1: ((*walking out of frame, away from group of youth*)) Is Tyler coming?

38.   Y2:   Lemme see, no no no no

39.   ((*Y2 follows TW1 toward TW2*))

40.   Y2:   ((*arms extended and open*)) Because I don't know you know what

41.   I me:↑an?

42.   ((*bowing slightly*)) Can (.) you le<u>mm</u>e see yo<u>ur</u> pa↑per for the rent

43.   TW1: ((*tossing ball back from one hand to the other*)) [so]=

44.   Y2:   ((*gesturing with semi-closed fist toward TW1*)) [you can do it one

45.   hour or] twelve or whatever

46.   TW1: Our friend booked it. Our friend our friend he's not here yet [when

47.   he comes]

Throughout this interaction, the young men (Y2 and Y3) pressed the tech worker (TW1) for "proof," for evidence, jointly contesting TW1's claim to the park. At the same time, TW1, a perceived outsider, repeated that his friend, who had not yet arrived, had the papers, bouncing or handling the soccer ball throughout the interaction, perhaps to underscore his legitimacy to be on the field. At one point, Y3 seemed to concede the legitimacy of the paper, should it surface ("If he comes, then you guys can get the field," line 36), to which Y2 interjected, "Lemme se, no no no no" (line 38). As he followed two tech employees, TW1 and TW2, arms stretched open, Y2 cast doubt on the existence of the paper and asked again to see the "paper for the rent" (lines 40–42).

In the continued interaction, we see an illustrative example of how bilingual youth develop tactics that surface how neoliberal reform is connected to broader historical, racial, and classed contradictions. OY challenged the notion that having a reservation, regardless of the documentation, gives the outsider men permission to have access to the field and, thus, the neighborhood. Of significance, questioning the tech worker's lack of understanding or appreciation of the historical practices in this space is tantamount to declaring that the worker's neoliberal logic does not work in the neighborhood space. Instead, the older youth (OY) invoked a place-based form of authentication ("Yo, you don't understand...it's not about the booking," lines 48–49). He further challenged the legitimacy of the practice of booking, as it contradicted the long-standing practice of use (It doesn't matter this field has never been booked, line 51). We note that the intergenerational and diverse nature of the youth group provided the opportunity for collaborative and distributed expertise, with the various members of the youth group taking up different roles to expand their linguistic and sociospatial repertoires.

48. OY: [Yo] you don't understand you don't understand it's not about
49.   [booking the Field]
50. TW1: [I didn't] book it, I didn't book it
51. OY: It doesn't matter (.) this field has never been booked
52. TW2: ((*approaches Y1*)) (inaudible speech)
53. OY: How long you been in the neighborhood, bro? How long you been
54.   in the neighborhood?
55. TW2: Over a year
56. OY: Over a year?
57.   <youth laughing>
58. TW3: Who gives a shit? Who cares about the neighborhood?
59. OY: We play every... Bro, how long have you been playing here for?
60.   My whole life. I've been born and raised here for 20 years and my
61.   whole life we've been playing.
62. TW3: You can share. One time you let other people play.
63. OY: We will share with you. Why don't you get a team and we play
64.   pickup 7 on 7 like it always is.
65.   <inaudible>
66. OY: There is no permit. It does not matter if there is a piece of paper.
67. Y2: Let me see the paper.

Older Youth advanced the question of legitimate right to the space, asking a second tech employee who had joined the group how long he had been in the neighborhood, punctuated with the inclusive word "bro." The use of "bro" here is not irrelevant, functioning perhaps sarcastically, or as a marker of a temporary and contingent union—someone with whom the group would play. The term also signals a kind of contingent inclusivity. TW2's response, "Over a year" was met with laughter and a sarcastic "Over a year?" (line 56). However, TW3 ruptured the potential compact that had been developing by outright proclaiming "Who gives a shit? Who cares about the neighborhood?" (line 58), in essence proclaiming "Who cares about YOUR neighborhood and right to this space." Almost incredulously, OY exclaimed, "My whole life. I've been born and raised for 20 years and my whole life we've been playing." This history of practice seems insufficient for TW3 who responded that the youth can share. However, the man and the youth seemed to have different understandings of what it means to share. For the male visitor, it meant giving up the space for an hour to let his group play ("One time you let other people play," line 63), while OY proffered an alternative that is consistent with the park's history of practices in which the youth share the field and team up 7 against 7 "like it always is" (lines 63–64); because, after all, he stated, there is no permit and, for that matter, it didn't matter if there was a piece of paper (lines 66–67). This interactional segment ends with Y2 requesting again to see "the paper" (line 67), the artifact that had heightened significance for the park interlopers.

We have presented this empirical example of interaction in a neighborhood soccer field that had a meaningful history for the youth—one that comes to life through a range of everyday linguistic and social practices. We do so to surface the diverse cultural tools and practices that the youth jointly employed as they leveraged their socio-spatial repertoires to negotiate the spatial, linguistic, and sociopolitical demands that are part of everyday life. We argue that these same practices and tools can be leveraged beyond the social situations of the park, and into the classroom, as well as to challenge the larger neoliberal (re)imagining of the city as one that privileges corporations, elites, people from dominant groups, and the middle class. Further, this event is illustrative of the expansive linguistic tool kits and practice that constitute youths' repertoires of practice (Gutiérrez & Rogoff, 2003). These are powerful practices that allow youth to spatially preserve the park as theirs while simultaneously challenging the hegemony of English as the dominant linguistic register. While they do engage the interlopers in English, they also leverage it on their own terms. As such, English and Spanish became tools that translingual youth leveraged to confront and overcome everyday dilemmas, including microaggressions resulting from neoliberal reforms. Overall, this event is a normative everyday practice for youth from nondominant communities and, as such, presents an opportunity for us to reframe how we understand the linguistic practices and socio-spatial repertoires that youth deploy as they navigate everyday dilemmas that emerge in public spaces in San Francisco. We build on the transformative potential of such youths' practices in the following section.

LEVERAGING SOCIO-SPATIAL REPERTOIRES
OF BILINGUAL YOUTH

In the previous section, we analyzed youth engagement in the following ways: (a) they used their own language practices to maintain the park as belonging to the neighborhood; (b) they challenged outsiders' authority to displace them; and (c) they challenged larger neoliberal policy frames and discourses related to linguistic and spatial hegemony (e.g., reservations, fees, documentation, etc.). In this section, we build on our notion of socio-spatial repertoires to argue that teachers must codesign pedagogical spaces with youth and communities that give right to the classroom—the local space in the city—where the linguistic demands involve hybridity and the right to learn (Espinoza & Vossoughi, 2014). In this section, then, we illustrate how we can begin to engage with teachers in designing educational projects that are imbued with tools and sensibilities that advance consequential learning for both teachers and their students.

During the summer of 2017, the first author taught a course for preservice teachers at a private university in the San Francisco Bay Area. Throughout the semester, the teachers applied theories on the sociocultural exploration of learning to their own practice and reflected on their own role in the development, expansion, and deployment of youths' and communities' cultural and linguistic resources. With this goal in mind, teachers were encouraged to engage with youth across a variety of sites within the city to support an examination of how learning and sociocultural development occur within and across everyday life.

As the analysis below will show, teachers began to develop new spatial and linguistic frames to create richer learning environments by viewing everyday spaces and practices as resources for learning; making translingual practices normative, thus challenging notions about how young people do and should learn in formal learning environments; and by challenging the hegemony of English in formal learning environments. Here, we draw on a social design-based experiment (Gutiérrez & Vossoughi, 2010) intended to support the development of transformative pedagogies and the expansion of translingual youths' socio-spatial repertoires. In particular, our findings detail how teachers learned to recognize and leverage the cultural, spatial, and linguistic practices of bilingual youth as essential to deeper and transformative learning. Before exploring this point in detail, we first discuss the design of the course and its participants.

The 25 preservice teachers in the class planned to teach in a variety of contexts, including public and private K–12 classroom environments. Because of this chapter's focus on socio-spatial repertoires and the role of translingualism, we focus on the reflections of a subset of six bilingual teachers who will teach in K–8 bilingual classrooms in San Francisco public schools. The reflections of these six teachers offer key insights into how teachers understood the relationship between space, language, and culture. We learned that as teachers developed expansive notions of emergent bilingual youths' everyday linguistic and cultural practices, they transformed their pedagogical practices to build upon youths' socio-spatial repertoires.

To illustrate how these processes began to emerge, we examined how teachers reflected on the role of linguistic dominance in their interactions with youth while they struggled to privilege the cultural and linguistic practices of bilingual youth. Also, the teachers became aware of how their own practices reproduced traditional, deficit frameworks around language use and development. For example, in the following excerpt, Ruby struggled with such demands after interacting with a bilingual student in a summer program designed to advance English literacy:

> Knowing that she had received instruction almost exclusively in Spanish, I went over to do some scaffolding and help her get her ideas translated into English. Upon reflecting, I am so conflicted with this notion. As a bilingual educator, I was so challenged by the notion of having to almost force a child into second language acquisition—and over the course of 5 weeks...I had become a tool within "the system"—something that I thought I had been fighting hard to change. (Ruby, Field Note 3, p. 6, 6/6/17)

Within the social space of the program, Ruby voiced her concern about reproducing "the system" by "almost forc[ing] a child into second language acquisition." In this respect, Ruby struggled with enacting pedagogical practices that treat language practices as discrete and bounded. Specifically, the social space of the summer program in which Ruby was teaching had been organized to promote English language acquisition, a goal conflicting with her role as a bilingual teacher. However, Ruby reported that she began to see school as a space that could be reorganized beyond the current institutional demands. Ruby's thinking underscored the importance of teachers learning to see the constraints within and across spaces in order to create new learning environments for bilingual youth that challenge the hegemony of English. Further, the teachers' collective reflections illuminated their critiques of the inequitable linguistic aims of the institutions, as they developed new ways of seeing the relationship among space, learning, and language. Of potential consequence for emergent bilingual youths' socio-spatial repertoires, the teachers were "fighting hard to change" the deficit understandings of language acquisition, as Ruby reported, and making these practices known to youth such that schools could become sites that enabled the development of new resistance practices.

The data show that while teachers struggled with the demands of educational institutions, they also began to see everyday resistance in emergent bilinguals' linguistic practices. Consider the following excerpt in which

Jackie reflected on her role in sanctioning everyday linguistic resistance in her classroom:

> I am reminded that culture is an active thing and is constantly changing. My culture is not going to be identical to the culture of these boys, especially in regards to language. However, all of this is with the assumption that our students only speak Spanish at home. This isn't the case now. Several students are speaking both languages and there is a lot of Spanglish occurring in everyday conversation. It is the culture of a lot of our students. I am left thinking, how can I incorporate this into my classroom? Do I accept this very clear hybridity of cultures or do I emphasize the separation of the two languages? (Jackie, Field Note 2, p. 4–5, 6/3/17)

Here, Jackie highlighted how "the assumption that our students only speak Spanish at home" contrasted with students' everyday engagement in Spanglish, a form of resistance (Martínez, 2013) to the institutionally privileged "separation of the two languages." She sought to leverage "this very clear hybridity of cultures," but was uncertain about how to "incorporate this into my classroom." We see how "the encapsulation of schooling" (Engeström, 1991) bounds language spatially such that teachers are expected to compartmentalize youths' everyday linguistic practices by dichotomizing English and Spanish, the school and home languages. By the end of the course, all of the teachers began to explore the role of youths' "everyday conversation," their linguistic expertise, as a valued linguistic practice in its own right. Thus, as the teachers examined where and when such everyday language use occurs across space and time (e.g., home, school, playground, park, etc.), they began to see how youths' desires, hopes, and needs, exercised through youths' linguistic and cultural practices, are consequential in transforming sociocultural contexts and places. We argue that an awareness of the role of space in language practices can provide teachers with an opportunity to build upon the resistance efforts of youths' deployment, development, and expansion of their socio-spatial repertoires to resist everyday linguistic and cultural dominance.

IMPLICATIONS AND CONCLUSION

In this chapter, we have made several arguments. First, we argued that youths' language and literacy practices must always be understood against the backdrop of historical, local, and moment to moment practices shaped by formal and informal policies and practices, and the ideologies indexed therein. In particular, we focus on how neoliberalism is shaping the spatial and linguistic boundaries of many youth from nondominant communities and privilege the agentic practices youth take up in response. Our analyses illustrate how youth leverage rich translingual and embodied practices across everyday life—practices that are central to sensemaking and to consequential learning and identity-making processes. Here, drawing on Pacheco (2012), we document that powerful literacies emerge and take shape in meaningful "resistance practices" in which learning and sensemaking are salient. Pacheco documents the rich set of practices that youth and adults from nondominant communities develop as they contend with dilemmas or double binds that youth and their communities' experience. Similarly, Gutiérrez (2014) cogently argues that expansive and consequential learning is dependent on the synthesis of people's cultural repertoires with scientific or school-based knowledge. However, developing robust understandings of learning, including the role of language—the tool of tools (Cole, 1995)—in learning processes is often not factored in teacher preparation programs. Further, understandings of the "tool of tools" (if addressed) is too often a monolingual, monologic conceptualization "encapsulated" (Engeström, 1991) in conventional and restrictive schooling and classroom practices.

The implications for teacher learning are profound. We call on teacher educators to expand how we conceptualize the everyday resources youth develop to include expansive socio-spatial repertoires in which youth assert their roles, their practices, and their "right to the city" —more broadly understood as their right to the spaces they inhabit literally and figuratively (Lefebvre, 1996). Here we take Lefebvre's (1996) call for the right to the city to include one's right to one's language, as well as the right to live with dignity, socio-spatially, educationally, and economically (Anzaldúa, 2012; Espinoza & Vossoughi, 2014). Thus, the practices of everyday resistance should be leveraged, not only to expand students' linguistic repertoires or to open new academic and career pathways, but as centrally important to helping youth expand repertoires that can help them develop sociocritical literacies fundamental to designing equitable spaces in new futures.

Our work has shown (Gutierrez, 2016; Gutierrez & Jurow, 2016; Gutierrez & Vossoughi, 2010) the importance of designing robust ecologies for teacher learning, saturated with a range of tools and forms of assistance; the same design principles we have for robust student learning. We have called attention to leveraging nondominant people's everyday practices (Gutiérrez et al., 2017) and to the use of youths' full linguistic tool kits to expand opportunities for meaning making and consequential learning—practices that disrupt the encapsulation of schooling (Engeström, 1991). This approach stands in contrast to those that use "everyday knowledge" to move youth from everyday understandings to school-based understandings, notably moving emergent bilinguals to English-only designations, independent of what we know about how people learn expansively, as well as the cognitive and social affordances of translingualism. Such reductive practices fail to incorporate the linguistic knowledge that is richly available in youths' repertoires into substantive meaning-making practices in school-based learning (Gutiérrez, 2014).

Finally, we argue that teacher learning opportunities must be remediated to create learning systems in which teachers develop deep understandings of youths' cultural, linguistic, and socio-spatial repertoires. This would involve engaging teacher learners in practices that highlight the idea that youth learn in their movement across the practices of everyday life, thus, expanding teachers' occasions to learn how socio-spatial repertoires of practice are constituted and made consequential in school and in the city space in which youth live, play, study, and work (Gutiérrez & Jurow, 2016).

Toward this end, we look to new ways of designing teacher education courses where teachers can expand their pedagogical tool kit through reflection and the application of sociocultural explorations of learning, alongside opportunities to reimagine the larger institutional demands of schooling, including how policies and practices can constrain opportunities to engage in consequential and respectful forms of learning where youth can become designers of their own futures (Gutiérrez, 2008).

ACKNOWLEDGMENTS

We wish to thank the editors for their help in reviewing this manuscript as well as the significant insight provided by Ramón Antonio Martínez and José Ramón Lizárraga.

NOTES

1. We use translingual (Canagarajah, 2013; García, 2009) to describe the everyday linguistic practices of bilingual youth. In other instances, we use emergent bilingual or bilingual to describe youth more broadly.
2. We join a growing number of scholars who adopt the term Latinx to advance a nonbinary approach to describing Latinidad, particularly with regard to gender categories.
3. While the names of the companies and employees are part of public record, we use pseudonyms to focus on how neoliberal policies and practices support dominant linguistic, sociocultural, and racialized ideologies.

REFERENCES

Alim, H. S. (2016). *Raciolinguistics: How language shapes our ideas about race.* London, England: Oxford University Press.

Anzaldúa, G. (2012). *Borderlands/La frontera: The new Mestiza.* San Francisco, CA: Aunt Lute Books.

Barton, D. [MissionCreekVideo]. (2014, September 25). Mission playground is not for sale [Video file]. Retrieved from https://www.youtube.com/watch?v=awPVYlDcupE

Blommaert, J., & Rampton, B. (2011). Language and superdiversity. *Diversities, 13*(2), 1–22.

Canagarajah, S. (2013). *Translingual practice: Global Englishes and cosmopolitan relations.* London, England: Routledge.

Cole, M. (1995). A conception of culture for a communication theory of mind. In D. Vocate (Ed.), *Intrapersonal communication: Different voices, different minds* (pp. 77–98). Hillsdale, NE: Erlbaum.

Cruz, C. (2001). Toward an epistemology of a brown body. *International Journal of Qualitative Studies in Education, 14*(5), 657–669.

Engeström, Y. (1991). *Non scolae sed vitae discimus:* Toward overcoming the encapsulation of school learning. *Learning and Instruction, 1*(3), 243–259.

Erickson, F. (2004). *Talk and social theory.* Malden, MA: Polity Press.

Espinoza, M. L., & Vossoughi, S. (2014). Perceiving learning anew: Social interaction, dignity, and educational rights. *Harvard Educational Review, 84*(3), 285–313.

García, O. (2009). Education, multilingualism and translanguaging in the 21st century. In T. Skutnabb-Kangas, R. Phillipson, A. K. Mohanty, & M. Panda (Eds.), *Social justice through multilingual education* (pp. 140–158). Bristol, England: Multilingual Matters.

García, O. (2014). U.S. Spanish and education: Global and local intersections. *Review of Research in Education, 38,* 58–80.

Gulson, K. N. (2011). *Education policy, space and the city: Markets and the (in)visibility of race.* New York, NY: Routledge.

Gutiérrez, K. D. (2008). Developing a sociocritical literacy in the Third Space. *Reading Research Quarterly, 43*(2), 148–164.

Gutiérrez, K. (2014). Integrative research review: Syncretic approaches to literacy learning. leveraging Horizontal knowledge and expertise. In P. Dunston, L. Gambrell, K. Headley, S. Fullerton, & P. Stecker (Eds.), *63rd Literacy Research Association Yearbook* (pp. 48–61). Alamonte Springs, FL: Literacy Research Association.

Gutiérrez, K. D. (2016). 2011 AERA presidential address: Designing resilient ecologies: Social design experiments and a new social imagination. *Educational Researcher, 45*(3), 187–196. Retrieved from https://doi.org/10.3102/0013189X16645430

Gutiérrez, K. D., Cortes, K., Cortez, A., DiGiacomo, D., Higgs, J., Johnson, P., . . . Vakil, S. (2017). Replacing representation with imagination: Finding ingenuity in everyday practices. *Review of Research in Education, 41,* 30–60. doi:10.3102/0091732X16687523

Gutiérrez, K. D., & Jurow, A. S. (2016). Social design experiments: Toward equity by design. *Journal of the Learning Sciences, 25*(4), 565–598. Retrieved from https://doi.org/10.1080/10508406.2016.1204548

Gutiérrez, K. D., & Rogoff, B. (2003). Cultural ways of learning: Individual traits or repertoires of practices. *Educational Researcher, 32*(5), 19–25.

Gutiérrez, K. D., & Vossoughi, S. (2010). Lifting off the ground to return anew: Mediated praxis, transformative learning, and social design experiments. *Journal of Teacher Education, 61*(1–2), 100–117. doi:10.1177/0022487109347877

Hamilton, M. (1997). Keeping alive alternative visions. In J. P. Hautecoeur (Ed.), *Alpha 97: Basic education and institutional environments* (P. Sutton, Trans.). Hamburg, Germany: UNESCO Institute for Education.

Harvey, D. (2005). *A brief history of neoliberalism.* Oxford, England: Oxford University Press.

Hoffman, A. (2012, October 1). Petitioner fights 'pay to play' in Mission soccer. *Mission Local.* Retrieved from https://missionlocal.org/2012/10/petitioner-fights-pay-to-play-in-mission-soccer/

Hutson, M. A. (2015). *The urban struggle for economic, environmental and social justice: Deepening their roots.* New York, NY: Routledge.

Lefebvre, H. (1991). *The production of space* (D. Nicholson-Smith, Trans.). Malden, MA: Blackwell.

Lefebvre, H. (1996). *Writings on cities* (E. Kofman & e. Lebas, Trans., & Eds.). Oxford, England: Blackwell.

Lipman, P. (2011). *The new political economy of urban education: Neoliberalism, race, and the right to the city.* New York, NY: Routledge.

Martínez, R. A. (2013). Reading the world in Spanglish: Hybrid language practices and ideological contestation in a sixth-grade English language arts classroom. *Linguistics and Education, 24*(3), 276–288.

Pacheco, M. (2012). Learning in/through everyday resistance: A cultural-historical perspective on community resources and curriculum. *Educational Researcher, 41*(4), 121–132.

Soja, E. W. (1989). *Postmodern geographies: The reassertion of space in critical social theory.* London, England: Verso.

Soja, E. W. (1996). *Thirdspace: Journeys to Los Angeles and other real-and-imagined places.* Malden, MA: Blackwell.

CHAPTER 8

TRANSFORMING TEACHING IN MULTILINGUAL COMMUNITIES

Towards a Transcultural Pedagogy of Heart and Mind

Marjorie Faulstich Orellana[1]
*University of California,
Los Angeles*

Krissia Martinez
*University of California,
Los Angeles*

Janelle Franco
*University of California,
Los Angeles*

G. Beatríz Rodríguez
*Travis Early College High School
San Antonio Independent
School District*

Sarah Jean Johnson
*University of Southern
California*

Andréa C. Rodríguez-Minkoff
Chapman University

Lilia Rodríguez
University of California, Los Angeles

Transforming Schooling for Second Language Learners, pages 143–158
Copyright © 2019 by Information Age Publishing

ABSTRACT

This chapter outlines six principles that characterize the language(s) and literacy(ies) pedagogy enacted in an after-school program serving children in a historically immigrant community in the heart of Los Angeles. These principles draw from sociocultural theories of learning and Orellana's "pedagogy of heart" tenets; they are additionally informed by ethnographic studies of the pedagogy enacted across 7 years of the club's existence. Each principle is illustrated using examples from the program and contrasted with dominant approaches to pedagogy for emergent bilinguals in U.S. schools. The analysis suggests possibilities for the transformation of teaching, especially for students living in increasingly diverse, multicultural, multilingual, immigrant communities.

In this chapter we provide an overview of the principles that guide our language(s) and literacy(ies) pedagogy and research in B-Club (a pseudonym), an after-school program serving children of a richly diverse and multilingual, immigrant community in central Los Angeles. We begin with an overview of theory that undergirds our "transcultural pedagogy of heart and mind," which we define as an approach to teaching and learning that crosses cultural and linguistic borders and that unites intellectual and affective engagement. We compare this philosophical approach to teaching and learning with more typical approaches enacted in modern Western schools. We then outline six core principles through which we connect our theory to practice in B-Club, illustrating with examples from our club activity. Drawing from our experiences in designing the club activities, enacting them, and studying what happens upon implementation, we consider how community processes of values development and implementation could transform our ways of working with and building on the strengths and experiences that emergent bilinguals bring to school, in ways that contrast with predominant "standards-based" educational practices. In offering a framework based on our own pedagogical values, and illustrating how our practices flow from and align with those values, our intention is to suggest possibilities for innovative pedagogy in other settings serving emergent bilinguals, as well as ways in which teachers could develop pedagogical practices that are aligned with their own community-determined values.

THE AFTER-SCHOOL PROGRAM

B-Club is part of a larger network of community partnerships established by Mike Cole in the 1980s, referred to as the "Fifth Dimension" (Cole & the Distributed Literacy Consortium, 2006). La Clase Mágica is a bilingual extension of this model developed by Olga Vásquez (2003). B-Club is the direct descendent of a program called "Las Redes" run by Kris Gutierrez at UCLA for many years (Gutiérrez, Baquedano-López, Alvarez, & Chiu, 1999).[2] The first author of this chapter took over the direction of this program in 2010 and has worked continuously in it since then with an evolving group of undergraduate, graduate, and post-graduate students including the coauthors.

Like these other programs, B-Club offers a dynamic setting for thinking about how people learn and how to support that learning. University students—both graduate and undergraduate—come together with transitional kindergarten to fifth grade students to play with learning, and learn while playing. An important set of participants at the club has been preservice teachers, who use the informal learning environment as a space to see children in ways that are often not evident in classroom settings and to try on new practices themselves. They also consider what they can take from this experience into their future classrooms. The authors of this chapter participated in various roles, including as researchers, club coordinators, and course instructors for the graduate and undergraduate service-learning courses connected to B-club.

Fifth Dimension programs are guided by sociocultural principles of learning, which highlight the interlinkages between social, cultural, and cognitive processes. Sociocultural theory (Vygotsky, 1978)[3] thus undergirds the "cultural" and "mind" dimensions of our transcultural pedagogy of heart and mind. Sociocultural theory centers on the notion that people learn and develop through their engagement in activities, in interaction with others, and using tools of all kinds, with language as "the tool of tools" (Vygotsky, 1978). Sociocultural theory illuminates how people learn through experimentation and play, and by solving real problems that they *want* to solve. Sociocultural theory also informs our flexible notion of expertise as we create room for people of diverse ages, language competencies, and experiences to learn with and from each other.

The "heart" dimensions of our pedagogy expand on sociocultural theory by emphasizing the social and relational nature of learning (Orellana, 2016), and by challenging Western notions that divide brains from bodies, intellect from affect, mind from spirit. We are inspired by Laura Rendón's (2009) "sentipensante pedagogy;" this "feeling-thought" approach to teaching and learning is "unitive in nature, emphasizing the balanced, harmonic relationship between . . . intellectualism and intuition, teaching and learning, the learner and the learning material, and Western and non-Western ways of knowing" (p. 1).

At B-Club, adults and children work together to create a "community of learners" (Rogoff, 2003) in which all participants—children and adults of varied ages—have a say in the activities we develop and share in responsibility for what transpires in our time together, following a set of agreements that we generated together and revisit each year. The values that guide B-Club are inspired by philosophers and educators who argue that learning can be fun, not drudgery, and that we learn best when we put our whole bodies, minds, and hearts into what we do. Centering our approach around kids' natural love for and expertise in play, we animate kids' curiosities for connecting with others and use this as the driving force for learning at our club. One of our most-cited maxims draws from the "intellectual emancipation" method of the 1700s French educator, Joseph Jacotet, which was brought to light in recent years (Rancière, 1991). In this method, the task of the educator is simply to create the conditions for the desire to learn to emerge—to spark an interest in learning.

By using the term "transcultural" rather than "multicultural," our pedagogy treats culture as a central, powerful, and dynamic force. Viewing culture as everyday lived activity (Gutierrez & Rogoff, 2003)—a processual approach (González, Moll, & Amanti, 2006) that views culture not as a reified, unified, static and unchanging "thing" that people "have," but as processes and practices through which we organize for everyday activity. The specific ways that people organize vary across cultural contexts and activity settings; in our approach we recognize that people learn from direct engagement in tasks and activities, some explicit instruction, as well as from seeing activities modeled by others (Rogoff, 1990; Lave & Wenger, 1991). We recognize that culture shapes all human activity even as humans continue to transform cultural processes as they interact with others in a changing world.

Transculturality emphasizes seeing from divergent perspectives as we adapt our ways of being, thinking, doing, and speaking in interaction with different people. Transculturality includes the disposition to be open to other points of view: the willingness to reflect on and reconsider our own ideas. Our approach to language development follows from this emphasis on transculturality, as we modify our language forms and styles for different contexts, purposes, activities, and relationships, and reflect on the choices we make. We use meaningful, purposeful, relationship-driven activities to expand our individual and collective repertoires of cultural and linguistic practice. Our aim is not just to help English learners learn English, or even just to "emerge" bilingualism or plurilingualism—but to create room for all participants to grow their linguistic repertoires in new and perhaps surprising ways.

OUR PEDAGOGICAL PRINCIPLES

To anchor this general approach to our transcultural pedagogy of heart and mind in pedagogical practice, we have developed a set of six principles. These pedagogical principles are guidelines that we developed through dialogue with B-Club research team members and are informed by our study of 7 years of experimental play with children. A set of principles is quite different from a set of "standards"—the *standardized* approaches to learning that are common in today's public schools, which focus on narrow, quantitative measures, outcomes or goals.[4] Ours are a set of core beliefs and values that shape the decisions we make, as we continually (re)design the activities and space in response to participants' needs and interests.

In what follows, we illustrate each of these pedagogical principles in turn with examples of our pedagogy-in-practice, focusing especially on what they mean for working with our emergent bi- or multilingual students:

1. follow kids' interests while helping to expand their linguistic and cultural repertoires,
2. nurture buds of development that can grow in different ways,
3. create room for shifting and shared expertise,
4. create opportunities to connect across cultural and linguistic borders,
5. cross borders *playfully*—experimenting with the forms/functions of language, and
6. developing under/overstanding as we see from different perspectives.

Follow Kids' Interests

The starting point for our pedagogical approach is simple: We aim to follow kids' interests and support their learning by looking for where their interest is sparked. This follows from sociocultural theory, and our belief that learning happens best when people *want* to learn. This is quite different from dominant approaches to education, which start with a set of adult-defined standards and focus on "getting kids" to meet objectives determined by teachers or curriculum designers.

This doesn't mean that adults abdicate all responsibility for supporting children's growth, or for shaping its direction. We recognize that kids may not want to learn many things that we (adults) think are important for them, either now or in the future. But we try to create conditions for kids to *want* to learn the things that we believe are important. And we challenge ourselves to consider other possibilities that emerge from seeing what sparks kids' interests, following their lead, and weaving that together with the things we believe are important.

Let's consider this in relation to language learning for emergent bilinguals. In doing so we will explicitly address the tricky issue of balancing following kids' leads with helping to expand their possibilities beyond what they might freely choose.

Like other teachers and researchers, we have found that many kids in bilingual communities in the United States, if given a choice, will opt for

English as their preferred spoken language. After all, kids very quickly internalize dominant ideologies about the prestige value of English, and they often begin to reject their home language as soon as they feel some small measure of confidence in English (Fillmore, 1991; Monzó & Rueda, 2009). So if we simply follow kids' leads, won't this reinforce English dominance? Might this get in the way of supporting bilingual development? This is a concern that prompts many dual language programs to mandate and enforce particular times, spaces, or relationships for speaking in the nondominant language.

But even if we wanted to, it would be nearly impossible to enforce particular language practices at B-Club, because participants in our program have varied linguistic repertoires, and different degrees of comfort and competence in common languages. Our child participants bring varying degrees of experience with English, Spanish, Korean, Tagalog, Mam, Zapotec, Nahuatl, and Bangladeshi. None of us speak all of those languages, and while many of us are emergent or competent bilinguals in English and Spanish, not all are. So rather than trying to control language practice, we model and create room instead for participants to embrace all of their linguistic knowledge, and to shift languages fluidly and comfortably in ways that are appropriate for different speakers. We aim to make using different languages—and learning about them—normal, valued, accepted, playful, and fun.

Another way we support language development is to create the conditions for participants to try on different identities and engage in many kinds of linguistic and cultural practices. Kids can be architects building cardboard worlds from discarded boxes, drummers pounding out the pulses of their desires, talent show hosts judging aspiring dancers and singers, orators or politicians "speechifying" from atop a soapbox, scientists making explorations about bugs in the grassy field outside, or reporters speaking to the public on "B-Club TV." These activities give kids many opportunities to hear and try on different voices, language forms, and discourse styles as they express themselves in various genres and mediums.

For example, a popular activity at our club has involved creating videos together. In this work, children find affinity with different aspects of the production process. Some take interest in acting or storytelling or videography, so we provide opportunities for people to engage different aspects of the work. They collaborate with others in the movie-making process, using a range of specialized language and adapting their language to communicate with each other. Although English sometimes dominates, collaborations in the process are multilingual, with children often "directing" or summarizing their plot in languages other than English.

Nurture Buds of Development

Following kids' interests in these ways allows us to nurture what Vygotsky (1978) referred to as "buds of development"—buds that can grow in many different ways. In this sense, a sociocultural view of learning and development stands in contrast with the standardized approaches to learning that currently shape practice in U.S. schools. These assume that development unfolds along a more-or-less predetermined trajectory, and that learning proceeds incrementally. Experts determine what "should" be learned by children at each grade level, and decide whether kids are "ahead" or "behind." These normative guidelines generally presume a monolingual speaker, not emergent bilinguals, nor children who are growing up exposed to the sights and sounds of many languages. Children living in multilingual communities actually have a head start on important linguistic and cultural competencies for life in an increasingly interconnected world (Orellana & D'warte, 2010). But the capacities of emergent bilinguals may be missed—and therefore not nurtured—if we insist on comparing them with monolingual English speakers, or if we start with a standard set of outcomes based on monolingual norms.

Our approach aims to nurture the buds of development that will help people thrive in a rapidly changing, multimodal and multilingual world: flexibility, versatility, and at least some familiarity with different language forms. We also consider the directions in which kids want to grow—alternative or additional directions to the ones that we (adults) view as more important. For example, we may want them to become competent speakers of standard academic English and standard academic Spanish—but perhaps *they* want to learn or use Spanglish, Tagalog, Korean, Chinese, Zapotec, or Nahuatl.

And what if kids claim they *only* want to speak English, or only use English in their interactions at our club? Once again, we ask: "How can we create the conditions for the desire to use other languages to emerge?" and "What are *authentic* ways of using different languages, as they speak, read, and write for audiences of their parents, neighbors, friends?" We stimulate interest by offering materials in different languages (ones they are familiar with as well as ones they may be curious about), such as personalized multilingual letters and signs. Sometimes, too, we just step out of the way, and marvel at what kids do on their own. We are inspired by a story recounted by Perry Gilmore (2015) in her book, *Kisisi (Our Language): The story of Colin and Sadiki*. Gilmore tells of how her son, Colin, and a Samburu boy, Sadiki—both 5-years-old at the time—developed their own pidgin language as neighbors in postcolonial Kenya. Colin and Sadiki's pidgin language would have no measurable value in school-based assessments. It is not something that we as adults could *teach* to kids. It was created by the youth themselves, motivated by their own intrinsic desire to communicate with each other.

B-Club offers similar authentic challenges such as these boys faced, and freedom to innovate. Our task, as adults, is to respect what kids create rather than suggest that their innovations are "wrong." We support the growth of these buds of development not by *teaching* per se, but by asking questions that give room for children to display and share their expertise. This supports kids in expanding development in new directions—even when these directions live in their imaginations.

Create Room for Shifting and Shared Expertise in Collaborative and Intergenerational Learning

As we work together to nurture children's buds of development, we try to remember that we are not just the nurturers, nor are children the only ones with buds to be nurtured. We can *all* expand our repertoires of cultural and linguistic practice; we can *all* grow and learn in new ways. Teachers can and do learn from their students every day. Recognizing this, we create room for collaboration, and for the shifting and sharing of expertise. When we pool our knowledge and skills, our individual and collective potential increases. At our club we often see kids and adults working together, recognizing and building on each other's linguistic repertoires by asking such questions as "What does that mean?"; "How do you say this in your language?"; and spontaneously translating for others.

In this collaborative learning, kids are cultural producers, not just consumers of knowledge, and not just recipients of instruction (Cook-Gumperz & Corsaro, 1986). We recognize that kids will draw from the practices and knowledge they see modeled around them—by peers as well as adults. At the same time, kids will reformulate and transform what they learn so as to create their own meaningful and creative cultural practices (Johnson, 2015), and this should be celebrated, too.

For example, when asked to create her own club name (and pseudonym for research purposes), one girl claimed "Treeflower Quince One Hundred Thousand" as hers. This unique combination of English, Spanish, and numbers builds on practices this 6-year-old has likely seen modeled in the world around her (e.g., in environmental print and usernames) even as it expresses something unique about what she knows and loves: the fact that trees and flowers are usually found in groups, as she explained in her own words. In selecting her name, Treeflower Quince One Hundred Thousand chose to use both of the languages that she speaks, and math notations as well. Seeing this as an expression of Treeflower Quince One Hundred

Thousand's expertise—and honoring her choices for her own name—is quite different than seeing this as a sign of confusion.[5]

Indeed, children may be more expert on many matters than the adults with whom they work: their home languages, music and other expressions of popular culture, everyday cultural practices, games and activities, the specialized language of youth culture, technology, and more. Many participants in B-Club speak particular varieties of Spanish (e.g., with origins in southern Mexico, Honduras, Guatemala, El Salvador). This can lead to lively exchanges as we discuss different ways of saying things—building our transcultural understandings as we pool the rich collective linguistic and cultural expertise that conjoins in our club.

Create Opportunities to Connect With Others

One of the ways we encourage expanding our linguistic and cultural tool kits is by creating opportunities to connect in and through language, in both its oral and written forms. Literacy serves as a tool for building relationships, and those relationships motivate the use of language and thus its development. This kind of situated and relational literacy is quite different from the "autonomous" (Street, 2006) views of literacy that predominate in schools, where texts are divorced from contexts, relationships, and lived practices. Here the "heart" of our transcultural pedagogy drives us: our relationships are driven by love for each other and for the things that connect us.

Martin (2013) defines relational literacies as "practices through which we learn to exist differently and simultaneously, practices through which we make our differences recognizable and valuable to one another ... third spaces in and through which communities produce, circulate, value, and recognize community knowledges" (p. 137). Building on the notion of centering and valuing community knowledge and practice, within our community of learners model (Rogoff, 1994), we build relational literacies into our practices. We have interactive dialogue journals, where kids and university students write to each other. We have a letter-writing system, where we offer stationery and paper of many kinds. Kids love writing and receiving letters from their friends of all ages. Another popular activity involves posting signs about the activities created by the kids (talent shows, running clubs, a beauty salon, stores, and banks are a few of the things that participants were invited to at our club by means of wall postings). Kids' fascination with signage may reflect their immersion in a multilingual, print-rich neighborhood environment—an important point to consider in relation to current debates about the supposed "word gap" between dominant and nondominant cultural groups (see Orellana, 2016).

As Powell and Davidson (2005) assert, schooled literacies often privilege dominant discourses, neglecting to consider the "funds of knowledge" of English learners and other students from nondominant cultural groups (González et al., 2006). They also strip language from its context: from the relationships, purposes and values that give it meaning. The concept of being in community—seeing, hearing, listening, being with one another, and inviting everyone to participate in the community in different ways—exists in radical contrast with the rugged individualism and competition that shapes most of the U.S. educational systems and society at large. At B-Club, we put relationships, purpose, and values at the center of all our language and literacy practices, and inspire organic opportunities for connection.

Cross Linguistic and Cultural Borders, Playfully

In the ways we have detailed above, we create many opportunities for participants to cross the linguistic and cultural borders that so often divide us. At B-Club kids of different ages mix with younger and older adults from diverse language backgrounds, and we celebrate the creativity that crossing language borders can facilitate. We do not act as bilingual border patrol (Zentella, 1997); we have fun creating names like Treeflower Quince One Hundred Thousand and Baby Corazón. We also take pride in knowing that sounds can be spelled in different ways in different languages; thus Cutie Pie sometimes chose to spell her club name with Spanish phonetics or a mix of English and Spanish spelling-sound correspondences (Curi Pai; Cutie Pi).

Knowing even just a little about different languages can be a source of fun and creative meaning making. For example, one day, Bo, a child whose family immigrated to the United States from Bangladesh, saw the word "gota" written in a bilingual book about rain. ("Gota" is the Spanish word for raindrop.) She and her friend Dolphin giggled hysterically as they looked at the book. Following their lead, we asked what was funny. We learned that "gota" means "pimple" in Bangladeshi. We laughed together with Bo and Dolphin about this multilingual play on words.

Developing Under/Overstanding as We See From Different Perspectives

From these interactions across cultural and linguistic borders that are often used to divide people, we develop what we call "overstandings" as well as deeper *under*standings of the tremendous complexity of human experience. *Overstanding* is a Hip Hop cultural term for learning that occurs through explicit engagement in cultural practice (KRS-One, 2009). As kids write letters, post signs, create clubs, make movies, talk with different people, and flow from one activity to the next thing that lights them up, each child develops personal experience with tools and possibilities of play. Their overstandings are the knowledges built and gained from *doing* language: from speaking, saying, singing, writing, dancing, moving, gesturing, and whatever else is required for participating with others in play.

When participants grow awareness of what it *feels* like to learn while having fun they also develop practice-based compassion for their playmates. Our overstandings of what it means to play is encapsulated in our group agreement to "give everyone a chance." In other words, assume the best in people. Give them an opportunity to show their best selves. Try to understand how they see the world, and not judge them without understanding.

Put another way, the principle of developing overstanding to and through play reflects our community values of and methods for developing participants' transculturality. In this sense overstanding is much more than understanding. It involves going "over" as well as under the words that people use, in order to connect with our hearts, bodies, minds, and spirits, not just words. It is not easy to cultivate over/understanding; we are continuously learning and reflecting on how to respond when empathy is lacking. The important thing is that we continuously model it and model our reflections as well.

BEYOND B-CLUB: A TRANSCULTURAL PEDAGOGY OF HEART AND MIND AND THE TRANSFORMATION OF SCHOOLING FOR EMERGENT BILINGUALS

Our pedagogy is enacted in an after-school program. Some might wonder: Could this be done in K–12 classrooms? How might our pedagogical approach serve to transform education for emergent bilingual students in public schools—or for all students who are growing up in multilingual worlds? To conclude this chapter, we want to suggest how the principles we have outlined here, or others like them, might be used to transform policy and practice at different levels, in ways that shift the educational landscape for language learners in public schools.

Transformative Classroom Practices

First, we want to emphasize that our principles are not a rigid set of prescriptions: They are guidelines that can be adapted to different contexts, activities, and circumstances—as a truly transcultural pedagogy should be.

They *inform* our pedagogical practices rather than dictate them. How they play out both can and should change over time and across contexts. Certainly, every learning context has particular affordances and constraints, and what "works" in one may not always be directly applied to another.

Perhaps, for example, teachers cannot "follow kids' interests" all day, every day. But there could be particular times of day or times in the week when kids have freedom to choose what they do. This might also be an aim that can grow over time. Teacher education students who have worked at the club and have tried to bring our principles into their classrooms describe feelings of uncertainty when following children's leads, especially in terms of meeting the goals and standards that schools set forth for emergent bilinguals. But with experience they report a greater ability to do this, attuning their "internal GPS" so they can support rich language learning experiences and meet grade level "standards" *while* following kids' interests. They also often find that "detours" from particular lessons actually enrich everyone's learning and secure students' deeper engagement with the work.

What about the idea of creating space for children to play with language mixings and remixings? Do we do a disservice to emergent bilingual students by suggesting that it is okay to mix language forms? Surely students will encounter many people who try to enforce "purity" in both English and Spanish, and who may judge them negatively for code-switching. But just as teachers work with children's invented English spellings in developmentally appropriate ways, we might allow room for bi- and multilingual developmental processes to unfold naturally, even as we help students to deploy their linguistic resources in conscious ways. This could include thinking about where and when linguistic borders can be crossed, in what ways, for what purposes, at what cost—and where, when, and how they might choose to stay safely on one side or the other of bilingual borders. Together, teachers and students might establish their own classroom language policies that explicitly connect pedagogical principles to practice.

Certainly, there is growing awareness of the pedagogical power of "translanguaging" in classroom contexts (García, 2009; Gort, 2017): pedagogical practices that allow students to use all the tools in their linguistic tool kits as resources for learning, rather than constraining students' thinking by forcing them to work in only one language. And, if our literacy practices are driven by purpose, audience, and context, we will naturally produce language forms that are appropriate for different audiences: sometimes in standard academic English or Spanish, sometimes with code mixing, sometimes other combinations.

Transformative Institutional Policies

Because classrooms are typically age segregated, the kind of intergenerational learning we have detailed here is hard to create in most public schools. But there *are* ways to build in age mixing in ways that expand the diversity of classrooms and build a larger sense of community. Older students, siblings, grandparents, and other family or community members could be invited in (whenever they are available—ideally during free choice activity sessions) to create some spaces for shifting and shared intergenerational expertise. Such community members would also provide additional language models; as Naqvi, McKeough, Thorne, and Pfitscher (2013) have shown, kids can learn from listening to community members read stories in their own languages, or tell stories using their own language styles.

The pedagogical principles we have outlined here certainly contrast with the prevailing values that permeate education within the contemporary neoliberal context, which are focused on measuring children against singular, narrow, monocultural standards of success, orienting all students toward a defined "common core," and keeping things and people "in their place." We argue for the value of curiosity, for finding pleasure in learning, for pushing and crossing boundaries, and for stimulating our individual and collective creativity. "Achieving outcomes" should not always be the driving force of school.

At the same time, we are not advocating a particular, singular approach to instruction for emergent bilingual and multilingual students. Instead we are suggesting that teachers can work with their own students in their own classroom and institutional contexts, to devise their own pedagogical principles for transformative education. In this chapter, we have shared how our own principles arise from our values and how they in turn shape teaching and learning in our club. Developing principles for their own classrooms may allow teachers to reframe narrow understandings of linguistic competence and to celebrate the wide range of ways in which their students develop and express their linguistic abilities.

Transformative Teacher Preparation

In our work with teacher education students, we grapple with the question of how to support both in- and preservice teachers in this growth process and to prepare them for the diverse populations of students they will serve. A transcultural pedagogy of heart and mind may seem misaligned with the prevailing "lock step" approach to teacher development and credentialing requirements where teachers learn about curriculum content, standards, and isolated teaching practices. We view our approach as an important counterbalance against the press to focus on predetermined standards and outcome measures, and instead to notice and respond to *children, their languages,* and *their communities.* We train teachers in using anthropological tools (e.g., fieldnotes and video analyses) to "see learning" and "see children" (Orellana, Johnson, Rodriguez, Rodriguez, & Franco,

2017) so as to better connect theory and practice. In ongoing research, we consider how this approach prepares teachers to build principled and transformative pedagogy that responds to the needs and interests of their students and the communities they are working in.

As well, we advocate training teachers in the kinds of critical examination researchers do of their "positionality," or orientation to the world and their biases, as a way to help teachers to better understand and be empathetic to children's lives and how their lives may affect their schooling. We probe the meanings of social justice and divergent ways of working towards it. In other words, we do not suggest that a transformative pedagogy of heart and mind is simple or straightforward work, but one that requires an ongoing reflective engagement with the complexities of teaching, learning, culture, and social processes.

As the field of teacher education develops the ways in which it supports teachers of students who are identified as emergent bilinguals (as well as other students who live and learn alongside bilingual or multilingual peers), we offer our principles in the hopes of expanding the dialogue around loving ways to honor and respect children's linguistic development. While sociocultural approaches have long valued the "funds of knowledge" that exist in nondominant communities, often the focus is on practices that are handed down to children by adults in these spaces. Our principles seek to recognize and build from *children's* wealth of knowledge and interests. It is our hope that engaging principles like these will not simply promote language and learning for emergent bilinguals, but that by enacting a more loving and transcultural paradigm, we will create conditions that prepare us all to teach and learn in the richly diverse, multilingual and transcultural contexts of the contemporary world, and of the future.

NOTES

1. The first author is the principal investigator and director of this program, and took the lead in the development of this chapter. She has been involved in the program from its inception in 2010, working with a revolving team of graduate and undergraduate student researchers. The remaining authors all participated in designing, running, and researching in the program for several overlapping years, as well as in our articulation of our values and practices in this report. We have listed their names in alphabetical order.
2. See http://uclinks.berkeley.edu/ for more information about the network of university–community partnership programs that began in California and now spreads around the world.
3. See Vygotsky (1978) for the foundations of sociocultural learning theory, and especially his theorizing about play as a primary mover of development for children. See Cole and the Distributed Literacy Consortium (2006) for illus-

trations of how these theories are applied in Fifth Dimension programs, and Orellana (2016) for more detailed applications of the theory to the work at B-Club.

4. See Orellana and Rodriguez (2013) for a discussion of standardization in relation to the new Common Core State Standards.
5. See Martínez (2013) for discussion of deficit views about code-mixing that many professionals—and even young bilinguals themselves—often hold.

REFERENCES

Cole, M., & the Distributed Literacy Consortium. (2006). *The fifth dimension: An after-school program built on diversity.* New York, NY: Russell Sage.

Cook-Gumperz, J., & Corsaro, W. (1986). Introduction. In J. Cook-Gumperz, W. Corsaro, & J. Streeck (Eds.), *Children's worlds and children's language* (pp. 1–11). Berlin, Germany: Mouton.

Fillmore, L. W. (1991). When learning a second language means losing the first. *Early childhood research quarterly, 6*(3), 323–346.

García, O. (2009). Education, multilingualism and translanguaging in the 21st century. In A. K. Mohanti (Ed.), *Multilingual education for social justice: Globalising the local* (pp. 128–145). New Delhi, India: Orient Blackswan.

Gilmore, P. (2015). *Kisisi (our language): The story of Colin and Sadiki* (Vol. 6). Hoboken, NJ: Wiley-Blackwell.

González, N., Moll, L. C., & Amanti, C. (Eds.). (2006). *Funds of knowledge: Theorizing practices in households, communities, and classrooms.* New York, NY: Routledge.

Gort, M. (2017). Language ideologies in bilingual education policy and practice. *Texas Education Review, 5*(1), 67–75.

Gutiérrez, K. D., Baquedano-López, P., Alvarez, H. H., & Chiu, M. M. (1999). Building a culture of collaboration through hybrid language practices. *Theory into practice, 38*(2), 87–93.

Gutiérrez, K. D., & Rogoff, B. (2003). Cultural ways of learning: Individual traits or repertoires of practice. *Educational Researcher, 32*(5), 19–25.

Johnson, S. J. (2015). *The social and cognitive worlds of young children reading together* (Unpublished doctoral dissertation). University of California, Los Angeles.

KRS-One. (2009). *The gospel of hip hop.* Brooklyn, NY: Power House Books.

Lave, J., & Wenger, E. (1991). *Situated learning: Legitimate peripheral participation.* Cambridge, England: Cambridge University Press.

Martin, L. T. (2013). *The spatiality of queer youth activism: Sexuality and the performance of relational literacies through multimodal play* (Unpublished doctoral dissertation). University of Arizona, Tucson.

Martínez, R. A. (2013). Reading the world in Spanglish: Hybrid language practices and ideological contestation in a sixth-grade English language arts classroom. *Linguistics and Education, 24*(3), 276–288.

Monzó, L. D., & Rueda, R. (2009). Passing for English fluent: Latino immigrant children masking language proficiency. *Anthropology and Education Quarterly, 40*(1), 20–40.

Naqvi, R., McKeough, A., Thorne, K., & Pfitscher, C. (2013). Dual-language books as an emergent-literacy resource: Culturally and linguistically responsive teaching and learning. *Journal of Early Childhood Literacy, 13*(4), 501–528.

Orellana, M. F. (2016, May 19). A different kind of word gap. *Huffington Post.* http://www.huffingtonpost.com/marjorie-faulstich-orellana/a-different-kind-of-word-_b_10030876.html.

Orellana, M. F., & D'warte, J. (2010). Recognizing different kinds of "head starts." *Educational Researcher, 39*(4), 295–300.

Orellana, M., Johnson, S. J., Rodriguez, A., Rodriguez, L., & Franco, J. (2017). An apprentice teacher's journey in "seeing" learning. *Teacher Education Quarterly, 44*(2), 7–26.

Orellana, M. F., & Rodríguez, G.-B. (2013). When standards mean standardization: Where does innovation go? In Patrick Shannon (Ed.), *E/LA Common Core Standards: Compliments, complexities and concerns.* Portsmouth, NH: Heinemann.

Powell, R., & Davidson, N. (2005). The donut house: Real world literacy in an urban kindergarten classroom. *Language Arts, 82*(4), 248.

Rancière, J. (1991). *The ignorant schoolmaster: Five lessons in intellectual emancipation.* Stanford, CA: Stanford University Press.

Rendón, L. I. (2009). *Sentipensante (sensing/thinking) pedagogy: Educating for wholeness, social justice, and liberation.* Sterling, VA: Stylus.

Rogoff, B. (1990). *Apprenticeship in thinking: Cognitive development in social context.* New York, NY: Oxford University Press.

Rogoff, B. (1994). Developing understanding of the idea of communities of learners. *Mind, culture, and activity, 1*(4), 209–229.

Rogoff, B. (2003). *The cultural nature of human development.* New York, NY: Oxford University Press.

Street, B. (2006). Autonomous and ideological models of literacy: Approaches from new literacy studies. *Media Anthropology Network, 17,* 1–15.

Vásquez, O. A. (2003). *La clase mágica: Imagining optimal possibilities in a bilingual community of learners.* Mahwah, NJ: Erlbaum.

Vygotsky, L. S. (1978). *Mind in society: The development of higher psychological processes.* Cambridge, MA: Harvard University Press.

Zentella, A. C. (1997). *Growing up bilingual.* Malden, MA: Blackwell.

CHAPTER 9

PEDAGOGY IN HYPER-DIVERSE CONTEXTS

Educating Newly Arrived Immigrant Adolescents in a Science Class

Christine Malsbary
Vassar College

Jordan Wolf
Flushing International High School

In this chapter, we share some strategies we have accumulated as teachers, researchers, and observers of a particular type of cultural context. Between us, we have spent upwards of 25 years working in high school classrooms serving young people from a multitude of national origins speaking multiple languages. I (Christine) characterize these spaces as "hyper-diverse" (Malsbary, 2016). In the first part of the chapter, I share some of the principles I have noted as important to teaching and learning in hyper-diverse settings. In the second part of the chapter, Jordan, a science educator, describes a science curriculum project he created and articulates the processes that

Transforming Schooling for Second Language Learners, pages 159–178
Copyright © 2019 by Information Age Publishing
All rights of reproduction in any form reserved.

went into planning it as a model for new teachers. We conclude with implications for classrooms and schools that serve emergent bilingual students.

THE HYPER-DIVERSE CONTEXT

Twenty percent of the world's immigrants live in the United States, although the United States accounts for less than 5% of the world's population (Zong & Batalova, 2015). The origins of contemporary immigration lie in the 1965 reform of immigration law, which not only changed the proportion of immigrants but also the diversity of transmigration as the origins of immigrants shifted from Northern Europe to Africa, Latin America, and Asia. In 1960, the top ten immigrant groups came from Poland, Austria, United Kingdom, Soviet Union, Canada, Germany, Hungary, Ireland, Italy, and Mexico. In 2012, the top ten immigrant groups came from Mexico, Korea, India, Guatemala, Philippines, Vietnam, China, Cuba, Dominican Republic, and El Salvador (Zong & Batalova, 2015). As Portes and Rumbaut (2006) explain,

> contemporary immigration features a bewildering variety of origins, return patterns, and modes of adaptation to the United States. Never before has the United States received immigrants from so many countries, from such different social and economic backgrounds, and for so many reasons. Although pre-World War I European immigration was by no means homogeneous, the differences in successive waves of Irish, Italian, Jews, Greeks, and Poles pales in comparison with current diversity. (p. 13)

With the diversification of the United States through more groups from a broader swath of nations comes more linguistic, ethnocultural, and racial diversity as well. Given new constellations of ethnic concentrations, bilingual students may come into greater contact with differing cultural and linguistic flows and their linguistic repertoires may be diversifying as bilinguals make sense of a globalized world (Creese & Blackledge, 2010; García & Flores, 2014).

I (Christine) was one of these students: a young person who came of age as a result of the global shifts described in the preceding paragraph. I became interested in cultural diversity as a child, living in Toronto, and later as a young adult in London, New York, and Los Angeles. As a researcher, I conducted 6 years of ethnographic fieldwork across two cities. I visited classrooms in schools serving primarily recent-arrival immigrant young people and from dozens of varying national origins speaking multiple languages. I documented a particular kind of social world organized by the participants of such classroom spaces that I conceptualized as *hyper-diverse cultural contexts* (Malsbary, 2014; Malsbary, 2016; Malsbary, Espinoza, & Bales, 2016). I had been a teacher in such schools from 2003–2007 in New York City and, upon attending graduate school in 2008, found that my teaching context, and indeed my childhood and life, was not represented in scholarship on schools.

Within the hyper-diverse context, I found that education practices—teaching, learning, languaging, and policy-making—took on new forms. In response to the cultural foment produced by concentrated diversity, I found teachers and students to be imaginative and creative. Amid what could have been a dizzying chaos, *regularities* emerged—consistent, predictable ways in which teachers and students responded to the hyper-diverse context. I documented youth and educators taking particular actions—actions that I turn to describe next—that led to opportunities for learning. Indeed, despite their location on different U.S. coasts with differing immigrant histories and differing language groups, the high school classrooms I observed faced the same kinds of pedagogical issues and challenges, engendering particular modes of response. Like anthropologists before me, I urge the reader to consider these similarities as *sets of fluid practices* that hold possibilities, not a strict or prescriptive recipe for development.

PEDAGOGY IN THE HYPER-DIVERSE CULTURAL CONTEXT

As I use it here, pedagogy refers to the actions teachers take to create opportunities for youth to learn. In the seven classrooms I observed at length over 6 years of fieldwork in two cities, I have found threads of continuity characterizing teachers' work, which I term:

- Improvisational. Teachers continuously respond to the changing linguistic and cultural moments in front of them rather than holding to a static and prescribed lesson plan.
- Cocreative and thus, democratic. Teachers recognize that students are also teachers, and that they themselves are students. Everyone creates the educative act together.
- Planned using both content and language. Teachers thoughtfully consider language and content together, as language is the vehicle of the content.

I will illustrate and clarify each of these in turn.

Pedagogy in the Hyper-Diverse Context is Improvisational

Here, I use an observation from a freshman language arts classroom. One particular day, the teacher (Lucia) read aloud from Hemingway's

(1952) *Old Man and the Sea*. She animated the text loudly as she read to the class: "And the old man saw flying fish spurt out over the water . . . 'dolphin,' the old man said aloud, 'big dolphin.'" As she read, students repeated the word aloud: "dolphin." At a table, a young Spanish-speaking woman leaned over to the Chinese speaker next to her: "What's that?" she asked. "Dolphin? I don't know," her classmate responded hesitatingly. At the same time the teacher was asking the class: "What is dolphin, do you know?" "Na-oo," a bilingual (Chinese-English) young woman said emphatically. The teacher smiled and said, "Dolphins are beautiful." She encouraged students to look through the cards on their tables that had pictures of the various fish featured in *Old Man and the Sea*. While she spoke, another student whispered, "This is mahi mahi."

Lucia then noticed that a student had pulled out the wrong picture. Lucia selected a dolphin card and walked around the various group tables to reinforce understanding of the word. She encouraged the students to write the word in their native languages. Lucia suggested, "You might write the word in your native language which is. . . . ?" Then, Jin Li, a Chinese emergent bilingual, responded "Hii-twwuuuhhhn [Hǎitún]." Lucia repeated, "Hii-twwuuuhhhn" but Jin Li corrected her teacher by raising her finger in a wide swinging arc to emphasize the pronunciation "Hii-twwuuuhhhn." The rest of the class chorally repeated "Hii-twwuuuhhhn" and by then, the teacher and students were laughing. Lucia then asked, "And how do you say dolphin in Spanish?" Some students shouted out "Dolph-EEE-n!" which other students repeated. Lucia, like an orchestra conductor, continued, "And how do you say it in Tagalog?" The sole Tagalog speaker in the class laughed and added, "Lumba-lumba!" This word really got the class going as they chorally repeated, "Lumba-lumba! Lumba-lumba!" around the room with much hilarity. "Any other languages we've forgotten?" Lucia asked. "Alright, that was fun. And while we were saying dolphin in other languages, I know that you wrote dolphin down, with the page number."

One of the things that I noticed immediately about the way in which Lucia brought multilingual student identity into the learning practices in the classroom was her sense of ease with time, particularly during an educational era in which many lessons are scripted and scheduled, lessons broken down to the minute. Lucia noticed her students' need to clarify a word that was important to accessing the text. She took her time to allow and then capitalize on the multilingual moment into a transnational engagement in which students were positioned as linguistic experts. As Canagarajah (2011) explains, "shuttling between the languages brought by the other to co-construct meaning" is a matter of "affirmative action" in a linguistic society that views language competence as "innate, monolingual, and arising from a homogeneous environment" (pp. 4–5). Lucia reflected on her translanguaging work in the following way:

I feel like here there's maybe more acceptance of who you are outside of school, ya know? That you can be yourself and speak your native language and be academic and be successful. You don't have to change who you are. You don't have to leave everything at the door.

For Lucia, working with youth in the transnational social field was no longer about assimilating youth into speaking English, but rather about leveraging youths' cultural lives as "transnational sojourners" (Zúñiga & Hamann, 2009).

Transnationalism studies in education have found that immigrant youth do not merely subjectively experience globalization, but actively create globalization through their practices in transcultural spaces (Lam, 2006; Malsbary, 2014; Orellana, 2009; Pennycook, 2007). Youth are "forging new diaspora and hybrid spaces of social and cultural activities through their growing economic and demographic presence and the use of instantaneous forms of communication" affecting how they "learn, play, work, and interact with the world around them" (Lam, 2006, p. 214). This repositioning of youth as agentive recognizes the work they do as empowered "cultural workers" who reshape and recontextualize global materials in their local communities (Lam, 2006, p. 223).

Pedagogy in Hyper-Diversity is Cocreated and Creative

The Russian psychologist Vygotky (1978) formulated human development as a process that is mediated by the cultural context. The culture of the classrooms I studied was one of every imaginable form of difference: youth from various ethno-racial backgrounds, with far-ranging repertoires of linguistic practices, with varying amounts of schooling preparation and subject-matter knowledge, and familiarity with and mastery over school-valued English and cultural associations. To reach students, all of the teachers I observed across three schools formally enrolled in my studies set up their instructional environments to be *cocreative* and *democratic*. By which I mean, students taught one another, translated for one another, and gave teachers frequent feedback as to the relevancy or use of the learning materials they had been handed. In this way, following Vygotsky, the learning context mediated the development of learning opportunities through interaction for students and teacher alike.

In one study, Malsbary, Espinoza, and Bales (2016) examined closely youths' interaction in a group context. The following classroom scene was representative of youth interaction around content and language. This particular group included two Chinese speakers, two Spanish speakers, and a Tagalog speaker. As they dissected owl pellets, they spoke to each other in English while translating for their same-language peers, as described in this vignette:

> The youth were preparing to dissect pellets of owl vomit, some enthusiastically, some with visible disgust. A Spanish-speaker busily handed out equipment to her group members. Before they could begin, each young person had to have a hypothesis written out concerning what they believed would be in the vomit—and why. As the teacher pinned a picture of an owl on the board as a visual aid to support understanding of the English word, the Tagalog-speaker turned to her Chinese-speaking classmate, pointed at the picture, and asked: "Him, what do you think he will eat?" The Spanish-speaker swiftly interrupted: "Mouse!" The Tagalog-speaker turned to her and asked, "Mouse, ok why?" The Spanish-speaker declared that the mouse would "be eaten by" the owl because it was much bigger. "Eaten by" was a language structure the youth had been practicing all week. Gesticulating, Spanish-speaker mimicked an owl eating a mouse, and asked the Tagalog-speaker for guidance, saying: "I don't know how to write it."

What is apparent in the vignette is how learning was codirected and co-constructed by the youth themselves. The Tagalog-speaking young woman engaged her resources as a peer teacher, engaging her classmates' learning through a question and answer series. The youth were comfortable supporting each other in this way, and in the study, we repeatedly saw youth actually teach one another and ask questions about content to one another.

My coauthors and I termed youths' group work *autonomous* to highlight the ways in which youth ran their groups independently. Each autonomous learning group had two or three students who acted as experts and two or three students who were positioned as novices in that they were still learning the culture of the classroom, emergent bilinguals newly acquiring English, and were experiencing the "looped concepts," discussed below, for the first time. In autonomous learning groups, youth who were emergent bilinguals were almost always paired with a student from their language group better versed in discipline-specific English. Linguistic diversity in the community was extensive and included various dialects of Spanish from the Caribbean Islands and Central American plains as well as Bengali, Fijian, Mandarin, Cantonese, Arabic, Haitian Creole, French, and Tagalog. In groups, students relied on one another, asking each other more questions than the teacher. The collaborative negotiation around curricular tasks spurred interest in subject matter, and more student talk was related to subject matter than any other topic. These sociocultural practices all occurred across intense diversity: peer translators supported youths' access to curricular tasks, and peers also spoke in English with youth who did not share their language backgrounds. Indeed, autonomous learning groups functioned to mediate interaction between peers who shared ethnolinguistic affinities and peers from non-similar ethnolinguistic groups almost equally.

While youth were in their groups, teachers were free to focus on creating curriculum that acted as a stable system through which all youth could access content. Teachers explained to me that they "looped" or cycled the same concepts over 2 years in extended, multi-week, inquiry-based projects. For instance, the science teacher (Jordan Wolf, from whom we will hear later in this chapter) taught the concept "food webs" through an interdisciplinary project with the literature teacher one year, and through a DNA project the next. This meant that expert students who read more independently in English, or who were on their second year of the concept, could assist novices who were not yet able to access content in grade-level English given their emergent bilingualism. Looping also prepared tenth graders to take the state assessment in biology.

Teachers thought deeply about which students should be grouped together, describing their decision as a lengthy, intensive process during which they took into account language, national origin, student personality, prior schooling, grade point average, leadership ability, and many other factors in order to make effective groups that could autonomously support all students' learning. Second, autonomous learning groups supported teachers during in-class time. With youth directing each other's learning, teachers were free to engage in intensive interventions with individual students, in what Wolf called his "rounds." Given the diversity of academic needs across myriad languages, it could take time for a teacher to clarify conceptual and linguistic difficulties and make pedagogical adjustments when necessary; time teachers don't have when they are at the front of the classroom instructing or managing classroom flow.

It is not new to consider the social environment and social interaction as generative to learning. Anthropologists who study learning view it as a collaborative, social event, where emphasis is not only on content learned ("things learned"), but also on the processes and practices which organize learning ("the learning itself;" Erickson, 1982; Wolcott, 1982). What *is* new here is the aspect of necessity. There is a central fact to teaching in hyper-diversity, and that is the *absolute necessity* of employing youths' assets, prior knowledge, and skills in cocreative learning. While teachers working in non-hyper-diverse settings might *choose* to implement collaborative structures out of their progressive belief in the ethics of democratic participation, working within a hyper-diverse context means the choice to foster student democratic participation is made *for* teachers. In order for learning to occur *at all*, teachers had to lean on students to translate and mediate for one another.

In the following section, Jordan explains our last proposition: that pedagogy in hyper-diversity is planned using both language and content to mutually affect student learning.

Pedagogy in Hyper-Diverse Contexts Is Planned With Language and Content Goals

With language learners, there is significant pressure to teach vocabulary before content. It becomes a bit of a chicken-and-egg scenario when you dig down deeper. Do we learn the word *rain* before we see a drop, or do we ascribe a name to that water from the sky because we are getting wet and have an innate human need to name things? In this section, I (Jordan) argue the latter, that experience precedes vocabulary, and in fact the two are mutually reinforcing. I will present an approach to planning that integrates content (what students need to know), and language (the words and structures they need in order to express what they know). In my high school for recent immigrants, we say that every teacher is an English teacher, no matter the subject they teach. I teach science, but along the way I am also teaching my students English through the science content.

Planning a period, a week, a semester, or year-long class all start with the question "What should I teach?" Every teacher struggles with this question. One has to consider what is in the state standards and therefore likely to show up on the state exam. If the students are never likely to see the content, it does not mean it is not important, but it certainly is not going to help you or them when it comes time for accountability on an exam. Next, and this is another important step, is considering "What am I interested in?" Great teachers bring passion to their work because they teach what they are passionate about. I am passionate about the environment and protecting wildlife, which is what led me to care so much about our overexploited oceans. The topics that get the teacher excited are likely the topics that will motivate and engage the students.

Finally, "What's doable and appropriate in the time period I am thinking about?" If you have to pack in ten disparate topics in a year, that gives less than a month per topic. While I would argue good projects can extend the narrative throughout the year, linking topics through content or themes, a class is still limited in its scope by the reality of limited time. This is the hard part: editing down what you think you should teach in favor of the most important topics. And, lest one forget, there needs to be time for students to prepare and present the topic they are learning. Creating a presentation, writing a scientific paper, drafting an essay, or designing a webpage—all of these products require time for process, editing, revision, and reflection.

When I started teaching, this all seemed daunting, and it still does. Thinking about planning this way and giving adequate time for students to engage in processes means that something will not get taught, which is fine. I prefer depth rather than breadth: better they learn a few things well than a great deal of information poorly, especially in a classroom where sometimes the most basic aspects of language are also being taught.

Notice I said nothing about language until the very end of my planning. Planning content has to come first, because only now that I know what I want to teach do I know what language needs to be taught. When teaching native speakers, the planning focus can stay mostly around content. With language learners however, this is where effective planning leads to outcomes students can realistically achieve. At the international high schools in New York City where I teach, this approach is simply called the *Internationals Approach.* We consider content and language as two sides of the same coin. I will do my best to elucidate the thought processes that go into planning a project integrating both language and content. As an example, I will use a biology project on marine ecology, human impacts, and DNA, as taught through *The Old Man and the Sea* by Ernest Hemingway (1952). It was taught over 3 months in two classes: science and English language arts. While this interdisciplinary approach is convenient and ideal, I have done it all by myself in the past. A project like this can be done by any teacher and it can be scaled up or down depending on how much time is available. Most importantly, it is rich in both content and language, making it a wonderful project for the hyper-diverse context.

One thing this way of teaching does require is a break from the more traditional model of teaching found in many schools. If you are trying to race through the ten units of the year, this will not work. If you are stuck teaching the curriculum handed down to you and you are not allowed to deviate, then read no further. If, however, you are at a school that encourages teachers to work together and to design your own curriculum to solve the problems unique to your students, and if you are given the space to do so, then this may work. The only risk in using the old curriculum that does not work is that you will continue to achieve the same results.

What Are They Going to Learn?

My high school only accepts recent immigrants for whom English is not the native language, and who have been in the country less than 4 years. We are a public school, so our students are whoever the city enrolls with us and fit the criteria. Despite English being their second language, these students do not get many breaks. Our students need to pass five state exams in the same 4 years as native English speakers. This timeline necessitates teaching content and language simultaneously because students cannot afford a year in remedial English learning the basics.

In my subject area, biology, deciding what to teach starts with analyzing the Living Environment State Regents exam (basically biology that focuses on processes as much as form). It is an annual practice for my colleagues and I to do an item analysis on the most heavily tested topics. At the top of the list of the most frequently tested key ideas every year are ecology, human impacts on ecosystems, and DNA as the genetic molecule. This is a huge spread of topics. It ranges from teaching how energy flows through photosynthesis from plants to other organisms, to what happens when humans overfish, to biodiversity at the taxonomic species level. Here I will speak mostly to the planning of the ecology section of the project.

While the content is daunting, the vocabulary needed is more so. Take ecology by itself. Subject-specific vocabulary such as "predator" and "autotroph" are likely new words for most students. To understand those content-specific words though, they need to understand everyday words such as hunt, kill, feed, and synthesize or build. From just two vocabulary words, there are already seven that realistically need to be taught. Here is the place to scaffold your instruction for newer speakers, as well as for more fluent ones: How many other words are there in the thesaurus that have the same or similar meanings?

In addition to the vocabulary of interaction, students need organisms to populate the ecosystems they are studying. This is where the imagery of *The Old Man and the Sea* (Hemingway, 1952) gives us something to talk about. Students are driven to read by the suspense of the plot and theme of struggle in the book, and along the way encounter a whole ocean of life to study—in the book there are four types of sea turtles, two types of sharks, and several species of fish, algae, and other sea life. In one quote, there is quite a bit of biodiversity—three sea turtles and a jellyfish:

> He loved green turtles and hawk-bills with their elegance and speed and their great value and he had a friendly contempt for the huge, stupid loggerheads, yellow in their armour-plating, strange in their love-making, and happily eating the Portuguese men-of-war with their eyes shut. (Hemingway, 1952, p. 40)

Now consider how students will structure their speaking and writing using these words. "A lion eats an antelope" is a lot different than, "A lion is eaten by an antelope," yet students produce both of these forms almost interchangeably when I do pre-assessments. To talk about an ecosystem, I need to teach subject–verb agreement and active and passive voice, or grammar that is essential. These are "the basics."

TABLE 9.1 Teaching for Language Learning	
Content Focus	**Skills and Language Addressed**
Food Chains and Webs	• Active and passive voice (is eaten by, eats) • Standard conventions of food chain diagrams (the arrow indicates "is eaten by," or movement of energy and materials) • Order of events (First plankton . . . Next zooplankton . . .) • Ordinal numbers (primary, secondary, tertiary . . .)
Energy Pyramids	• Comparisons: Greater than/less than; more/fewer • Annotating diagrams
Material Cycles	• Directionality ("Carbon moves from . . . to . . .") • Process and structure or verb and noun: "By the process of photosynthesis, carbon becomes part of the structure of sugar in plants"
Ecosystem structure	• Living/nonliving • Levels of organization: "A community is made up of many populations, a population is made of many organisms of the same species"

Just as the content was considered in the planning of this project, so now is language. Table 9.1 presents a chart adapted from a planning document as part of the planning process used for this ecology project.

Within each topic, there is a litany of everyday vocabulary I have chosen to omit here for the purpose of highlighting skills and academic language. For a native speaker, all of these grammatical conventions do not pop into the forefront when considering the content of an ecology unit. Just by looking at the state exams, the textbook, and even Hemingway, all of these implicit language skills begin to jump out. They need to be taught just as explicitly as any of the content, and in fact can be assessed themselves. It is handy to know when students are struggling with the content or just struggling with how to say what they know. Now that the language of the topic is as explicit as the content, the next step is to consider the framework of the project, precisely, what driving questions keep the students invested in learning about any of this.

Why Learn It?

Once you know what content and language is to be taught, how then to decide how to teach? This is where personal interest and passion come into play. My own background is that of a scientist, particularly one who fell in love with nature. I am an avid birdwatcher, an entomologist, and a runner who likes to be in green places. What drove me into the oceans was a gap in my own knowledge about the marine environment and an opportunity provided by another teacher.

One of my colleagues was an established marine biologist by training and a voracious reader and admirer of Hemingway. He needed to plan an interdisciplinary project with his apprentice, a new ESL-licensed teacher. The apprentice handled the literary elements of the project, teaching three classes of 25 multilingual students each how to read what was for many their first book in English. Interspersed with literature classes, every other day was a biology class where students learned the nuts and bolts of ecology and ecosystem function. I inherited the project the next year when the ESL apprentice became the full-time humanities teacher on my interdisciplinary team. Add to all of this that students just seem to have an affinity for all things aquatic, many have grown up in nature and small towns or near aquariums in big cities, and we had a project. Other considerations were what resources we could draw on in the community. We are close to many marine resources in New York City, including museums, aquariums, parks, and whale watching tours, but if we were located elsewhere this just as easily could be a project on forests through Jack London's (1914) *White Fang*, prairies via Aldo Leopold's (1966) *Sand County Almanac*, or desert canyons through Edward Abbey's (1985) *Monkey Wrench Gang*.

Now that the theme of the project is set, the depth of the project and the investment of students—given that our context is hyper-diverse and multilingual—depends on the driving question. If it is truly an open-ended question, then students across ability and language levels should be able to access it. According to the Common Core State Standards (CCSS), open-ended questions that involve problem solving are the best driving questions. In this ecology project, the question I presented to my students was, "Can we save the oceans?" The project begins with a discussion about images of destruction in marine ecosystems, from bleached coral reefs, decks of trawling boats packed bow to stern with tens of thousands of fish and other sea life, even New York City underwater in a global warming scenario. In both English and native languages, students wrote about environmental destruction in their own home countries. When I hit them with the driving question, they are then hooked.

There are many benefits to making this or any project interdisciplinary: By learning the same vocabulary in two classes and two disciplines, they are reducing by 25% the number of different narratives they must understand in their four core classes each day. They are also being given vocabulary that becomes lingua franca for 2 hours a day versus only one. Relevant to engagement, inclusion of Hemingway's (1952) *The Old Man and the Sea* presents them with a story about struggle, another hook they all can relate to. What they learn throughout that story is what a romanticized, pristine ecosystem could look like. This sets the stage for them to learn what a healthy, functioning ecosystem looks like, in contrast to those they will encounter later in the project when they research the challenges facing marine ecosystems. Oceans are shared by the whole world, and this generation of teachers and students is at a tipping point for environmental stewardship or destruction, as is every country and culture that is connected to the seas.

Next, and most importantly, I address how students demonstrate their learning.

How Are They Going to Show It—Collaborative Projects

How and when will students use the language we are teaching? Project-based group instruction is the cornerstone of success. The key to this approach is that language and content will be retained and owned by students if they have many opportunities to use them. More importantly, students will take ownership of their learning when they are asked to work collaboratively to make and share authentic products that address a relevant problem. Every teacher sees when some content clicks more than other content; it is because students are making a personal connection to it and they have a personal interest in learning about it.

The challenge for the teacher is now how to plan a project so it meets a few requirements:

1. The product feels authentic. Does it have a real audience such as another class, parents, or the community outside the school? Does it contribute to a grander effort such as a citizen science project?
2. Students can be assessed individually on their contribution to a group effort. The peer pressure and collaboration of being part of a group will motivate and provide support for many students, but it should not allow students to use someone else's work as a substitute for their own assessment. Students need to have accountability for their own slice of the project.
3. There are many checkpoints for understanding along the way. Nothing is worse for a teacher than dedicating days or weeks to student work, only to realize at the end that the product has missed the mark. Every day or two, students should be assessed, even if it is informally, to make sure they are making progress. The summative assessment should be one of many chances to demonstrate understanding, not the only chance.
4. Collaboration is necessary, not optional. For language learners, this is essential. Many times, I have realized that I did not make a project truly collaborative when I noticed that no one was talking to one another. It was usually because I had failed to give them something to talk about, and they can do the worksheet or the poster section on their own. Designing a project so each student is responsible for an integral piece is one way to avoid this. For ex-

ample, if each student presents one section of the scientific method in an experiment, it is nearly impossible to not talk to one another and still present a cohesive product. Practicing new language with one another increases by several-fold the number of opportunities they will have to use new vocabulary and structures.

All of these keys to projects went into the planning of The Old Man and the Sea (Hemingway, 1952) ecology project. Now in its third iteration, products students have made include:

- Ecosystem Voicethread: Interactive narrated PowerPoints called Voicethreads (Voicethread.com) teaching about one slice of the food web in Santiago's Sea. These also included students using the organisms to explain a literary element of the book.
- Sixty Years After Santiago Pamphlets: Pamphlets about the impacts on ecosystems of human activities like greenhouse gas production, offshore oil drilling, and agricultural run-off.
- "It's Your World" Video: Persuasive videos contrasting the "pristine" ecosystems of the 1950's to the impacted ecosystems of today.
- "What's on Your Plate?": A traditional lab report and science symposium on seafood mislabeling detection in our local food markets, as determined using DNA barcodes.[1]

All of these projects required students to work with one another to create the final product, and to listen to one another to do the final reflection and feedback. At all points of the project, students were teaching each other and using the vocabulary and grammar identified earlier. For instance, in the first project, "Ecosystem Voicethread," individuals were assessed on their representation of one aspect of an ecosystem such as a food web or material cycle while the group product was united by the fact that they were all presenting about the same organisms. In the "What's on Your Plate?" science fair, groups of four to five students chose one type of organism, then each researched and answered one or two questions agreed upon by the group as the most important for their organism. While the questions were as disparate as "What is the endangered status of squid?" or "What eats squid in the ocean?" these groups were united by a common organism, as well as a single experiment they all contributed to, where they identified several types of squid using DNA they themselves extracted.

Ongoing Assessment of Both Content and Language

During the course of these projects, assessments of both content and language are constantly happening, albeit in different forms. Sure, there is

▼ 🔖 Bio Outcome 35: Identify relationships among organisms as they interact in food chains and webs.	2.7
✓ OMS 5-2 - Food Chain Exit Ticket - 2013-03-04	M
✓ OMS 5-3 - Santiago's Food Web Exit Ticket - 2013-03-08	3.0
✓ OMS Quiz 5-1 - 2013-03-12	1.0
✓ OMS Ecology Study Guide Packet - 2013-03-14	4.0

Figure 9.1

a quiz every once in a while, but those count just as heavily as an exit ticket for any one outcome being assessed. For example, while the first ecology quiz assessed two outcomes (food webs and energy flow), and the second one assessed those two plus two more (material cycles and human impacts), those outcomes could be assessed several times before and after the quiz. Figure 9.1 is an excerpt from my grade book for one student (4 = high proficiency, M = missing).

In the course of 10 days, I generated four assessment scores for this student, just on food webs. When it came time several weeks later for the final assessment, the Voicethread, she had accumulated five or six total scores. She also had the opportunity to demonstrate the outcome during the project reflection when she reported back on what another student presented about a different part of the food web. At the heart of these assessments is the content, but also, the language she was using to communicate what she understood. The scores reflect as much: two is the minimum passing grade, and what a student receives if they can show the food web, but still have difficulty using the active and passive voice to demonstrate it ("the Galano shark eats the marlin" versus "the Galano shark is eaten by the marlin"). A score of four is mastery, when a student can use both language and content correctly.

When I approach a project, my grading system takes two models. The simplest is to link language and content outcomes. A student is showing mastery (4 out of 4 on the scale we use) if they consistently use the language correctly and can master the content. They are only about 2/4 (equivalent to a 70% or C in our system) if they can do one, but not both the language and content correctly. The second model is unlinked, where language is given its own outcome separate from the content and a student can generate two separate scores. The difference in the rubric for these models would look something like Tables 9.2 and 9.3.

Perhaps it is a matter of preference, or ease of use, but I use the combined single-outcome model more frequently in my classes. In either case, students can see from start to finish during the project that their language is expected to conform to a standard, just as their content mastery.

For example, verb conjugation in the following sentences matter: "I eat pizza" and "I am eaten by pizza." When teaching food chains and food

TABLE 9.2   Single-Outcome (Language + Content) Model

	Proficient	Highly Proficient
Outcome 35: Identify relationships among organisms as they interact in food chains and webs.	Mostly correct use of arrows in diagrams. Niche correctly used for most organisms. Uses one of the active and passive voices correctly.	All diagrams use correct arrow conventions. Labels all organisms with niche ("-ivore" words, producer, etc.). Consistently uses active and passive voice to describe trophic relationships.

TABLE 9.3   Two-Outcome Model

	Proficient	Highly Proficient
Bio Outcome 35: Identify relationships among organisms as they interact in food chains and webs.	Mostly correct use of arrows in diagrams. Niche correctly used for most organisms.	All diagrams use correct arrow conventions. Labels all organisms with niche ("-ivore" words, producer, etc.).
Language Outcome 1: Writes using active and passive voice.	Uses one of the active and passive voices correctly.	Consistently uses both active and passive voice.

webs, it must be connected to student experience to practice with constant examples from a text, or of the same old organisms (in New York, it is always rabbits, deer, and red-tailed hawks). So, with the inception of *The Old Man and the Sea* (Hemingway, 1952) project, we realized very quickly that students could have an ecosystem they are invested in, if only on paper. Hemingway includes distinct references to at least 37 different organisms throughout the book. With a little help from the *Encyclopedia of Life* (http://eol.org) and Wikipedia, I created a referenced card for every organism, making sure to include text about its diet.

After we did an example or two as a class and learned that the arrow in a food web always means "is eaten by," students received the set of cards, one set per group, a sheet of paper filled with one-directional arrows, and a pair of scissors. Their task was to create, using the text in front of them, the complete *The Old Man and the Sea* (Hemingway, 1952) food web to the best of their abilities. Next, as a group, each person had to describe at least one interaction with the correct passive or active voice, and why they think it is accurate using evidence from the text (a Common Core staple). We then start a scavenger hunt of sorts, asking groups to use their food web and that of the class to find examples of all pertinent vocabulary, including *carnivore*, *producer*, and *niche*.

This adaptation of my old paper-and-pencil worksheets on food webs was a revelation. It activated all of the grammar and vocabulary necessary for the project. Not only that, but making it a group activity forced students to collaborate and practice the language I wanted them to know. Having a small sample of text with a narrow focus also served as a precursor for later in the project, when students conducted broader research on the life history of one marine species.

I try to use and reuse vocabulary throughout the school year. If a word was useful in October, but useless in April, I need to ask myself why I taught it in the first place. This certainly helps a teacher focus on what the essential vocabulary is: what is going to give the most bang for the buck, so to say, and allow students to feel like they are really mastering and owning new language throughout the year.

In the most recent version of this project, I stretched the theme of *The Old Man and the Sea* (Hemingway, 1952) well beyond the ecology of the book into other essential topics in biology. We used the environmental impact angle of the project to bridge it to DNA barcoding, a relatively new technique for identifying species through a short sequence of their DNA. Combined with overfishing and other traditionally recognized environmental problems caused by humans, the DNA aspect led us to connect *The Old Man and the Sea* (Hemingway, 1952) to the fish we saw on sale in our local markets. We tested whether market substitution was happening with our seafood through a lab experiment and student interpretation of the data. In order to understand the impact of the results we got from our labs, students needed to reach back into the ecology content we had just learned and reengage with the vocabulary to speak about how their fish sample connected to a whole ecosystem and the behavior of humans impacting it.

While this was an extremely ambitious series of projects, I hope that it can serve as a model for any project in a hyper-diverse and multilingual classroom. The elements of language and content integration and project-based instruction are the cornerstones of empowering education. Immigrant youth can do anything native speakers can, provided they are given more explicitly taught objectives for language and more deliberately planned opportunities for practicing what they have learned.

IMPLICATIONS: TRANSFORMATIVE PEDAGOGY

In sum, we have shared three principles of successful pedagogies in hyper-diversity: that it is improvisational, it is cocreative and democratic, and the planning process has to include simultaneous language and content planning. To conclude, we want to make a few points about how these principles are transforming schooling as it exists for emergent bilingual students.

In many classrooms around the United States, emergent bilinguals (EBs) are pulled out of content area classes into separate English language skills classes or ESL. Likewise, in bilingual classrooms, only two languages are present, like English-Spanish or Russian-English. Neither of these approaches address the realities of classrooms that are multilingual. Multilingual classrooms might need to have a lingua franca, like English, to provide a vehicle for instruction that multilingual, multicultural students understand. But they must, at the same time, promote the tenets honored by dual language and bilingual education programs and research that the native language is critical for English development and honors the soul of students and their cultural lives. We have suggested a way forward here, one that involves clear structure through careful planning and creative improvisation that allows for moments of surprise in the classroom. These two pillars—the static and the fluid, the clear and the messy, are not easy to enact—but they are important. Just as important, we believe, is opening up space for student participation in their own learning.

In the 15 years that I have worked in teacher education across three states—California, New York, and Hawaii—I have seen very little in the way of clearly informed instruction for hyper-diverse classrooms. Arguably, the three states mentioned are among the most diverse contexts in the globe. Jordan's work stands apart. In teacher education programs, addressing intense hyper-diversity is pushed into courses that call themselves "multicultural" but are really geared towards bicultural/bilingual contexts. Teachers like Jordan, who actually know what to do and do it well, must be given the financial resources and the time allotment they need to share their expertise with teacher education programs. Once that structure is put in place, it needs to be scalable so that teacher education programs around the country can give beginning and continuing teachers the expertise they need to effectively instruct in hyper-diverse contexts.

Along with hyper-diversity come opportunities to transform classrooms as we know them. Relying on students to act as teachers—a move which decenters traditional power relations and naturally leads to democratic voice—is not just an option in hyper-diverse spaces, but is demanded by the nature of the space. No one teacher will speak all the languages of his or her students. Rather than eschew multilingual explosiveness due to vibrant migration, rather than build a wall, rather than concede to white hegemonic politics—let us use hyper-diversity as an opportunity to transform schooling into what we have dreamt it could be.

NOTES

1. This one is a bit more complex. For more information on how to do this in your classroom, see http://www.dnabarcoding101.org/ (Cold Spring Harbor, 2013) and http://www.ibol.org (International Barcode of Life, 2013).

REFERENCES

Abbey, E. (1985). *The monkey wrench gang*. Salt Lake City, UT: Dream Garden Press.

Canagarajah, S. (2011). Codemeshing in academic writing: Identifying teachable strategies of translanguaging. *The Modern Language Journal, 95*, 401–417.

Cold Spring Harbor. (2013). www.dnabarcoding101.org. Retrieved September 15, 2017.

Creese, A., & Blackledge, A. (2010). Translanguaging in the bilingual classroom: A pedagogy for learning and teaching? *The Modern Language Journal, 94*, 103–115.

Erickson, F. (1982). Classroom discourse as improvisation: Relationships between academic task structure and social participation structure in lessons. In L. C. Wilkinson (Ed.), *Communicating in the classroom* (pp. 153–181). New York, NY: Academic Press.

García, O., & Flores, N. (2014). Multilingualism and Common Core State Standards in the United States. In S. May (Ed.), *The multilingual turn: Implications for SLA, TESOL, and bilingual education* (pp. 147–166). New York, NY: Routledge.

Hemingway, E. (1952). *The old man and the sea*. New York, NY: Scribner.

International Barcode of Life. (2013). www.ibol.org. Retrieved September 15, 2017.

Lam, W. S. E. (2006). Culture and learning in the context of globalization: Research directions. *Review of Research in Education, 30*(1), 213–237.

Leopold, A. (1966). *A Sand county almanac*. New York, NY: Oxford University Press.

London, J. (1914). *White fang*. New York, NY: Grosset & Dunlap.

Malsbary, C. B. (2014). "It's not just learning English, it's learning other cultures": Belonging, power, and possibility in an immigrant contact zone. *International Journal of Qualitative Studies in Education, 27*(10), 1312–1336.

Malsbary, C. B. (2016). Youth and schools' practices in hyper-diverse contexts. *American Education Research Journal, 53*(6), 1491–1521.

Malsbary, C. B., Espinoza, S., & Bales, L. (2016). Liana's learning in a democratized classroom. *Pedagogies: An International Journal, 11*(3), 249–269.

Orellana, M. F. (2009). *Translating childhoods: Immigrant youth, language, and culture.* New Brunswick, NJ: Rutgers University Press.

Pennycook, A. (2007). *Global Englishes and transcultural flows.* New York, NY: Routledge.

Portes, A., & Rumbaut, R. G. (2006). *Immigrant America: A portrait* (3rd ed.). Berkeley, CA: University of California Press.

Vygotsky, L. S. (1978). *Mind in society: The development of higher psychological processes.* Cambridge, MA: Harvard University Press.

Wolcott, H. (1982). The anthropology of learning. *Anthropology & Education Quarterly, 13*(2), 83–108. Retrieved from www.jstor.org/stable/3216624

Zong, J., & Batalova, J. (2015). Frequently requested statistics on immigrants and immigration in the United States (Migration Policy Institute). Retrieved from https://www.migrationpolicy.org/article/frequently-requested-statistics -immigrants-and-immigration-united-states

Zúñiga, V., & Hamann, E. T. (2009). Sojourners in Mexico with U.S. school experience: A new taxonomy for transnational students. *Comparative Education Review, 53*(3), 329–353.

SECTION IV

TRANSFORMATIVE PRACTICES

CHAPTER 10

TRANSLANGUAGING AND THE TRANSFORMATION OF CLASSROOM SPACE

On the Affordances of Disrupting Linguistic Boundaries

Ramón Antonio Martínez
Stanford University

Michiko Hikida
Ohio State University

Leah Durán
University of Arizona

ABSTRACT

This chapter explores how emergent bilingual children and youth engage in everyday forms of translanguaging within the context of classroom interactions. Drawing on ethnographic and interactional data from three urban schools, it highlights the ways in which these students transform the social

Transforming Schooling for Second Language Learners, pages 181–198
Copyright © 2019 by Information Age Publishing

space of their respective classrooms by disrupting supposed linguistic boundaries and generating novel opportunities for learning and social interaction. These findings point to the need to follow the lead of emergent bilingual students in the development and implementation of translingual policies and pedagogies. The ways students normalize translanguaging in their everyday expressions of bilingualism can be leveraged in classrooms to prepare them to engage with multiple communities.

These are troubling times for emergent bilingual students in U.S. schools. This is a point that we wish to underscore precisely because there have been some promising signs with respect to the direction of policy and pedagogy for these students in recent years—signs that might easily obscure persistent problems and concerns. The reauthorization of the Elementary and Secondary Education Act as the Every Student Succeeds Act (ESSA) near the end of the Obama administration, for example, marked an unprecedented step towards greater accountability for meeting the needs of those emergent bilingual students officially classified as "English learners" (Council of Chief State School Officers, 2016). Dual language bilingual programs are proliferating nationwide (U.S. Department of Education, 2015), and there is a growing body of research suggesting that such programs lead to better long-term academic outcomes for these students than does English immersion instruction (Umansky & Reardon, 2014). And California, which led the way, ushering in an era of restrictive language policy in the late 1990s, has done an about-face on bilingual education with the recent approval of Proposition 58, the so-called "multilingual education initiative" (California Secretary of State, 2016). Taken together, this turn of events might be interpreted as a prelude to greater educational *opportunities* (including increased access to dual language and other bilingual programs) and improved educational *outcomes* for emergent bilingual students.

These positive signs notwithstanding, there are some very troubling indicators and some very serious reasons for concern. No sooner had the Trump administration taken office than Republican lawmakers began the process of repealing the Obama-era regulatory guidance around ESSA implementation (Brown, 2017). Despite mounting evidence on the benefits of bilingualism and bilingual education, most emergent bilingual students nationwide are *not* enrolled in bilingual programs (National Center for Education Statistics, 2017). Although California's recent move to reverse English-only legislation marks an important turning point in the history of bilingual education, similarly restrictive language policies are still in place in 28 states (Center for Applied Linguistics, 2017). Across various policy contexts and instructional arrangements, emergent bilinguals are often misunderstood and/or underserved. For example, some of these emergent bilinguals are initially *misclassified* as "English learners" as a result of flawed and/or inconsistent criteria, instruments, practices, and procedures used for the identification and classification of such students (Linquanti, Cook, Bailey, & MacDonald, 2016). In addition, those emergent bilingual students officially classified as "English learners" disproportionately attend under-resourced schools characterized by unequal opportunities to learn (Callahan, 2005; Gándara, Rumberger, Maxwell-Jolly, & Callahan, 2003; Umansky, 2016). Even in dual language settings, which arguably offer some of the most promising pedagogical possibilities for emergent bilingual students, official policies and practices of *language separation* often end up marginalizing and stigmatizing these students and their linguistic competencies (Martínez, 2017). All things considered, there is a dire need for transformation of both policy and pedagogy for emergent bilinguals.

As the chapters in the previous two sections of this book have revealed, policies and pedagogies can have a transformative impact on schooling for emergent bilingual students. Even in the absence of such policies and pedagogies, however, emergent bilingual children themselves engage in everyday language and literacy practices that transform the space of the classroom. In this chapter, we focus on *translanguaging* (García, 2009)—students' flexible use of their full linguistic repertoires—as one way in which these children transform classroom space. Drawing on ethnographic and interactional data from our research in three different urban schools, we highlight the ways in which students transform the social space of their respective classrooms by disrupting supposed linguistic boundaries and generating novel opportunities for learning and social interaction.

TRANSLANGUAGING

Translanguaging is an English translation of the Welsh term *trawsieithu*, which was first coined in the 1980s by Welsh educator and bilingual activist Cen Williams (1994; Lewis, Jones, & Baker, 2012). Williams originally defined translanguaging as "the planned and systematic use of two languages for teaching and learning in the same lesson" (Lewis, Jones, & Baker, 2012, p. 643). Baker (2001) subsequently popularized the term for an international scholarly audience, developing Williams' conceptualization of translanguaging as a pedagogical approach for bilingual settings. García (2009) has revived the term in recent years, extending it beyond classroom contexts and pedagogical practices to refer to a speaker's flexible use of linguistic resources across everyday settings. For García (2009), then, translanguaging is not simply how students and teachers use language flexibly for the specific purposes of teaching and learning, but rather how all speakers use language flexibly across everyday contexts more generally. Otheguy, García, and Reid (2015) clarify this notion of translanguaging by defining it as "the deployment of a speaker's full linguistic repertoire without regard for watchful adherence to the socially and politically defined boundaries of named (and usually national and state) languages" (p. 283). We draw on this definition of translanguaging in the remainder of this chapter.

As Otheguy, García, and Reid (2015) note, this view of translanguaging differs from the way that mainstream linguists have historically conceptualized the phenomenon known as *code-switching*. Whereas code-switching has been defined as the alternation of two distinct languages (Gumperz, 1982), a translanguaging perspective rejects the premise that a bilingual speaker's languages exist as two separate and separable codes in favor of the premise that speakers who engage in this practice are drawing flexibly on a single linguistic repertoire. According to Otheguy, García, and Reid (2015), *all* speakers—including monolinguals—engage in translanguaging when they combine in their speech linguistic elements that are typically assumed to belong to distinct linguistic *varieties* (i.e., languages, dialects, registers, and styles). The key distinction is that monolinguals are typically not recognized as translanguaging and are, therefore, allowed to do so without sanction. In contrast, bilinguals are explicitly marked when they draw flexibly on their linguistic repertoires, and their translanguaging is, therefore, often explicitly stigmatized, actively discouraged, and effectively restricted by policies and practices of language separation (Martínez, 2017). Although there has been a recent move towards translanguaging pedagogies (García & Kleyn, 2016; Palmer, Martínez, Mateus, & Henderson, 2014; Pontier & Gort, 2016), the fact of the matter is that most emergent bilinguals are in classrooms where the official policies and practices both assume and reinforce the supposed boundaries between languages.

DISRUPTING BOUNDARIES, TRANSFORMING SPACE

In this section, we present data from our respective research studies in three different urban schools to highlight the ways in which emergent bilingual students transformed the social spaces of their classrooms by disrupting linguistic boundaries and generating novel opportunities for learning and social interaction. These settings include a Spanish-English dual language classroom, an ESL/English-only classroom at a school that was transitioning towards a bilingual model, and a more typical ESL/English-only classroom. Despite these different instructional arrangements, students in all three classrooms drew flexibly on their linguistic repertoires in their everyday classroom interactions. This flexible use of language, we argue, mattered for the social construction of classroom space. Although two of these classrooms were spaces in which English was meant to be privileged, and all three classrooms were spaces in which linguistic boundaries were meant to be enforced, students' everyday translanguaging effectively transformed these classrooms into more flexible and dynamic spaces for learning and social interaction.

We draw on *spatial theory* (Lefebvre, 2005) to frame classroom space as socially constructed. Although we do not enjoy the luxury of an in-depth discussion here (see Gutiérrez & Cortez chapter in this volume for a more detailed treatment of spatial theory), we draw on the notion that space is *produced* through human action, and that how humans live *spatially* is both constitutive of and constituted by space. As sites that both reflect and constitute the broader spatial contexts in which they are situated, classrooms are spaces where dominant language ideologies and restrictive language policies get inscribed, enacted, and contested (Martínez, 2009; Martínez, 2013). The three classrooms that we studied were sites in which students' flexible use of language conflicted with official language policies and contributed to the production of qualitatively different spaces than those prescribed by said policies. Below we share a brief example from each classroom to illustrate how these emergent bilingual students transformed classroom space through their everyday translanguaging.

Classroom 1: Dual Language Kindergarten/First Grade

The first example comes from a study that Ramón conducted in a multi-age Kindergarten/first grade classroom that was part of a Spanish-English dual language program at a K–12 public school in southern California. All of the students were emergent bi/multilinguals, but some were officially classified as "English Learners" while others were classified as "Initially Fluent English Proficient." One student was of Sudanese ancestry, two were of Filipino ancestry, and the remaining 17 students were of Latinx ancestry. The classroom teacher, Ms. Birch, was a White woman who spoke both Spanish and English fluently. Like most dual language programs, the program at this school prescribed separate times for the use of each language. Approximately 90% of instructional time was meant to be in Spanish, while the remaining 10% of instructional time was meant to be in English. Despite this official policy of language separation, and despite the fact that Ms. Birch did allot separate blocks of time for each language, students in this class often disrupted linguistic boundaries within these instructional blocks. In fact, Ms. Birch herself sometimes translanguaged, modeling for students, if only inadvertently, that it was possible to draw flexibly on one's linguistic repertoire.

In the following example, two students, Laura and Samantha, were working together at the science center. Their assigned task was to observe butterflies that were inside a collapsible, mesh viewing chamber, and then draw a picture documenting their observations. As Ramón approached the girls, they were both very animated as they leaned forward in their chairs to get a closer look at the butterflies. The following interaction[1] ensued:

01	Laura:	¡Se pegaron juntos!
02	Samantha:	*((turning to her classmates at a nearby table))* ¡Se pegaron juntos!
03		*((turns towards Ramón, who is approaching the science center))*
04		**Mister!** Se pegaron juntos y después éste se- hizo otra
05		vez de- *((flaps arms behind back as if to imitate butterfly wings))*
06		de volar.
07	Laura:	*((to Samantha))* Se metió allí abajo. (3.0) Estaba subiendo aquí.
08		*((points with finger, then sits down and grabs marker to draw))*
09		Yo ya sé, una mariposa **purple.** *((grabs purple marker))*
10	Samantha:	Yo ya hice un **pink.**
11	Laura:	**What?!?**
12	Samantha:	*((stands up and grabs a blue marker))* Ahora un **blue.**
13	Laura:	**What?!?!**
14	Samantha:	Y de és- éste, éste. *((exchanges one blue marker for one that is a*
15		*slightly different shade of blue))*
16	Laura:	¡Ay, está uno arriba! *((stands up and uses purple marker to point*
17		*at butterfly))* Est- está moviendo su cola en la misma. ¡Ay!

In this 38-second strip of dialogue, Laura and Samantha draw flexibly on both English and Spanish to share their observations with each other and to discuss what they are going to document in their drawings. Laura initiates the interaction in Line 01 by noting in Spanish that two of the butterflies inside the viewing chamber have stuck to each other ("¡Se pegaron juntos!"). In Line 02, Samantha turns to inform classmates at a nearby table, repeating Laura's utterance verbatim. Then, as Ramón approaches the science center, Samantha turns to him and says (in Lines 04–06), "**Mister!** Se pegaron juntos y después éste se- hizo otra vez de- de volar," flapping her arms behind her back as if to imitate a butterfly flapping its wings. At this point, Laura, who is still intently observing the behavior of the butterflies, informs Samantha (in Line 07) that one of the butterflies has moved down to the very bottom portion of the viewing chamber ("Se metió allí abajo"). She then pauses for 3 seconds before showing Samantha where the butterfly in question had been climbing prior to hiding at the bottom of the viewing chamber ("Estaba subiendo aquí").

Up until this point, the conversation between Laura and Samantha has proceeded entirely in Spanish.[2] This changes in Line 09, when Laura announces that she now knew what she is going to draw—a purple butterfly:

"Yo ya sé, una mariposa *purple*." Note that Laura's utterance includes a single lexical switch in the word final position. Instead of saying *morada*, she uses the English equivalent. As she grabs a purple marker and sits down to begin drawing, Samantha informs her (in Line 10) that she has already drawn a pink one: "Yo ya hice un *pink*." Note that, like Laura, Samantha includes a single English lexical item in the word final position of her translingual utterance. Laura responds with apparent surprise—and in English— in Line 11 (*"What?!?"*). Samantha then stands up and grabs a blue marker as she declares (in Line 12) that she is now going to draw a blue one: "Ahora un *blue*." Apparently incredulous, Laura again replies in English in Line 13: *"What?!?!"* Without replying directly to this utterance, Samantha speaks entirely in Spanish (in Lines 14–15), identifying additional colors that she is going to use to color butterflies. Laura then proceeds to speak entirely in Spanish (in Lines 16–17) as she notices and comments on the behavior of one of the butterflies.

With respect to this translingual interaction and the individual translingual utterances of which it was comprised, some questions emerge about which we can only speculate: For example, did Laura deliberately switch to English for *purple* in Line 09? Did this lexical switch somehow prime Samantha's subsequent switch to English for *pink* in Line 10? Did Samantha's switch to English, in turn, prime Laura's subsequent English utterance (*"What?!?"*) in Line 11? Did Samantha's switch back to a monolingual Spanish utterance in Line 14 prime Laura's switch back to a monolingual Spanish utterance in Line 16? Of course, all of these questions beg the larger question of whether or not these girls were conscious of their translanguaging within this interaction. If we challenge the premise that a bilingual speaker's languages exist as two separate and separable codes, and begin instead, as Otheguy, García, and Reid (2015) suggest, from the perspective of the individual bilingual speaker, then this question becomes difficult to answer. On the one hand, these instances of translanguaging did not appear to be particularly salient for either Laura or Samantha. Indeed, their translingual talk seemed to be unmarked and perfectly normalized. On the other hand, the sequential organization of their interaction, including the syntactic shape of their respective utterances, suggests that each girl's translanguaging may have influenced the other girl's translanguaging. Of course, it is altogether possible that some of these translingual utterances may have been more salient to them than others. And even if some instances of unmarked translanguaging functioned below the level of explicit consciousness, it is still possible to understand them as examples of *tactical* talk (Erickson, 2004; Martínez, 2014)—talk that may not necessarily involve full reflective awareness, but that nonetheless involves "tactical attention to and appreciation of the affordances available in the circumstances" (Erickson, 2004, pp. 167–168) of a given interaction.

All speculation aside, what we can say empirically is that Laura and Samantha both engaged in translanguaging within the context of this brief interaction—that they combined in their speech linguistic elements typically understood as belonging to two separate languages. They were disrupting the supposed boundaries between English and Spanish in a space where those boundaries were meant to be enforced, and they were doing so in ways that normalized this flexible expression of bilingualism and contributed to the transformation of their classroom space. This dual language classroom was certainly intended to be a bilingual space, but the policy of language separation framed it as a *diglossic* (Ferguson, 1959) space—one in which Spanish and English were functionally separate. This functional separation of the two languages was something that the enactment of the official policy perpetuated within this classroom. By translanguaging, however, Laura and Samantha (like most of their classmates) were helping to transform what was this bilingual (but diglossic) space into a *translingual* space—one in which students drew flexibly on their linguistic repertoires and in which the boundaries between languages were not enforced.

To be sure, this is not something that students did alone. Although Ms. Birch enacted the official policy of language separation in various ways, she also sometimes engaged in translanguaging herself, and she did not actively discourage students from translanguaging. Her pedagogical practices both converged with and deviated from official policy. In this sense, she, too, contributed to the social construction of a space that was more flexible than it was officially intended to be. Together, these students and their teacher transformed a bilingual classroom into a translingual space.

Classroom 2: English-Only First Grade (in Transition)

The second example presents evidence of bilingual children's dexterity and playfulness with language. The data shared here are taken from a larger study of children's writing that Leah conducted within a first-grade ESL/English-only classroom on the outskirts of a large urban area in central Texas. In this classroom, all of the children were bilingual, spoke Spanish and English, and were of Mexican and Central American heritage. The teacher, Ms. Barry, was a White woman who spoke Spanish and had a master's degree in bilingual/bicultural education. The district had in the past offered bilingual programs, moved to an English-only model, and was in the first year of transitioning back to a bilingual program. At the time of the study, students in kindergarten were provided with bilingual instruction, but teachers in older grades (including Ms. Barry's first grade classroom) were directed to provide instruction only in English. The administration permitted teachers to use Spanish out loud to clarify, but the curricular materials were only in English, and teachers in older grades were expected to teach reading and writing in English only. The district's handbook for the bilingual program also, like many bilingual programs, specified that languages should be kept separate.

Although the district had a restrictive language policy, Ms. Barry expressed an asset-based orientation towards her students' everyday language practices and consistently encouraged and modeled the use of Spanish, English, and translanguaging as valuable tools for learning. Although translingual practices are often discouraged by teachers (Walsh, 1991), Ms. Barry viewed these practices as important resources for learning. She often modeled and explicitly invited children to write and talk in Spanish, English, or both, with the understanding that children could and should choose whichever mode of expression best suited their purpose and audience.

Children frequently combined both Spanish and English in their talk with each other, particularly in conversations without adults participating. As an example, the following brief exchange during writing time highlights how both languages were unmarked:

> **Yamilet:** Yo lo voy a pintar. Mira, tengo blanco.
> **Eric:** ¿Qué hace negro con *white*?
> **Victor:** Se hace *grey*.

As for Laura and Samantha, described above, linguistic boundaries did not appear to be particularly salient to these children: both *white* and *blanco* seemed to be easily understood and communicatively effective. While different students were observed using Spanish and English in differing proportions, depending on the context and interlocutors, neither language nor the use of both together seemed to be marked. This unmarkedness of both languages has elsewhere been shown to be a critical component in fostering both linguistic play and literacy learning (de la luz Reyes, 2012). Indeed, over the course of the year, children began to experiment with Spanish in their writing. This occurred in a variety of ways, from using the occasional word in Spanish to writing all in Spanish to writing in parallel translation. During a poetry unit, several students used Spanish and English together in writing in ways that echoed their seamlessly translingual talk. This may have been perhaps influenced by genre conventions, as poetry seems to invite more translanguaging than prose (Callahan, 2004). One such example is shown in Figure 10.1.

In this poem, the author, Kelsey, moved between named languages: Spanish ("está como brillando") and English ("and brighter/ than the treasure box") and back again ("y brillante como un diamante"). The poem also makes use of rhyme ("brillante como un diamante") figurative language ("brighter than a treasure box") and direct reader address ("como tú"), all

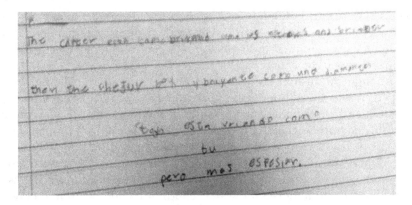

Figure 10.1 Translanguaging in poetry.

The glitter está como brillando como las estrellas and brighter
than the treasure box y brillante como un diamante
todo está brillando como
tú
pero más especial.

features which Ms. Barry had taught as part of the poetry unit. While the use of both languages together was discouraged by the official district language policy, Kelsey's translingual composing made for a stronger poem than might have been possible in just one language. Her disregard for linguistic boundaries allowed for new opportunities for cross-linguistic alliteration (brighter/brillando/brillante) and allowed her to engage in variation on a theme rather then direct repetition. Often it is precisely the unexpected or unusual word or turn of phrase that makes a piece of writing memorable (Bomer, 2010). Moreover, in conversation with Leah, Kelsey reported intensely enjoying the experience of writing translingual poetry, "feeling just like, I want to make a lot of poems and have more time."

This creative writing attests to a linguistic dexterity that is both valuable in its own right and reflects the literary skills that schools and standards point to as desirable. By disrupting the boundaries between English and Spanish within the context of the language arts classroom, Kelsey and her classmates were developing their literary skills, enjoying the creative potential of language arts, and generating new meanings for what it means to be a bilingual writer.

Classroom 3: English-Only Fifth Grade

The third example highlights two ways that bilingual fifth graders translanguaged in the everyday interactions within a fifth-grade classroom at a public elementary school in central Texas where Michiko conducted a study of literacy and identity. The classroom was designated an ESL classroom, which required that all of the instruction be delivered in English. The teacher, Mr. Peterson, had an endorsement in English as a second language instruction, but he did not consider himself bilingual. As an ESL teacher, he was charged with teaching in English while also supporting bi/ multilingual students' English language development. Despite the explicit policy of English-only instruction and his self-described lack of proficiency, Mr. Peterson often sprinkled Spanish words and phrases into his talk. Within the classroom, the de facto language policy seemed to be more flexible as evidenced by the teacher's use of Spanish and his permissiveness when students used Spanish. Of the sixteen fifth graders, six lived in Spanish-English bilingual homes, and for four of those students, the year of this study was their first year in an English class after transitioning from bilingual classrooms.

Despite the official designation as an English-only classroom, these students effectively transformed this space into a translingual classroom through their translanguaging practices. Within this classroom, translanguaging helped students make sense of English words and draw fine semantic distinctions between those words. In one example, Mr. Peterson read aloud from the Grimm brothers' version of Cinderella. One page in the text stated that the stepmother threw lentils into the ashes of the fireplace and told Cinderella to pick them out. Mr. Peterson then paused and asked if students knew what lentils were.

Mr. Peterson: *((to the class))* Do you know what lentils are?
Ida: Yeah. ***Lenteja.***
Mr. Peterson: What? *((sounds intrigued, not like he didn't hear))*
Ida: ***Lentejas.*** They're like beans.
Mr. Peterson: Yeah. *((and he continued to read))*

Here, Ida, a student in her first year outside a designated bilingual classroom, drew on her knowledge of Spanish to directly translate a vocabulary word. She then elaborated and compared lentils to beans in English. Ida's use of the Spanish word *lentejas* made the information available to her bilingual peers, while her comparison to something in English supported her English-speaking peers' understanding of the vocabulary as well.

In another example, Ida and two of her classmates, Caroline and Blu, who had also recently transitioned from bilingual classrooms, used Spanish to draw a fine semantic distinction between the words *soft* and *smooth*. The distinction was relevant to science content that they were discussing in class. The class had finished watching a short video about erosion and deposition, and as a group they were completing the quiz at the end of the video.

01	Mr. P:	((*reading the question*)) How would a sandblasted rock differ from a rock that hasn't been sandblasted? Sandblasted, like sandpaper, what's it going to do to a rock? ((*Rubbing his hands together*))
02	Caroline:	It would make it soft.
03	Marley:	No. It makes it smooth.
04	Mr. P:	It would make it soft?
05	Ss:	Smooth. Smooth.
06	Caroline:	Smooth.
07	Mr. P:	So, use smooth. Be careful, um. I think in Spanish "smooth" and "soft" might be similar or something? I don't know. I was talking with [the bilingual teacher] once ...
08	Blu:	Smooth?
09	Caroline:	**Suavecito y::**
10	Blu:	**No, liso.** It's **liso.**
11	Caroline:	**Liso y suavecito**
12	Mr. P:	But in English smooth and soft ...
13	Ida:	((*quietly and to Caroline and Blu*)) **Suavecito** is more like (inaudible)
14	Mr. P:	... Soft means squishy and smooth means no friction.

In Line 02, Caroline used the word *soft* and was quickly corrected by Marley, a correction she took up. In Line 07 the teacher invited the students to draw on their knowledge of Spanish by asking if the translations for *soft* and *smooth* were similar in Spanish. Then, in Lines 08 through 13 Blu, Caroline, and Ida moved fluidly between English and Spanish to distinguish between these two words. In this example and the previous example, these fifth-grade students drew flexibly on their bilingual repertoires in order to make sense of words within the context of literacy and science learning. Their translanguaging served as a tool that enabled and facilitated their learning within these respective interactions. Again, these were students who had recently transitioned from a bilingual classroom. By translanguaging while they were learning, these students effectively transformed this ESL classroom into a translingual space in which it made sense to draw flexibly on their full linguistic repertoires.

DISCUSSION AND IMPLICATIONS

The three classrooms that we described above represent three somewhat distinct instructional arrangements. The first classroom was a dual language classroom in which both English and Spanish were official languages of instruction, but in which the official policy was one of language separation.

Despite this official designation, the teacher in this classroom sometimes drew flexibly on her own linguistic repertoire by translanguaging within the context of instruction. The second classroom was an English as a second language classroom at a school that was transitioning to a bilingual model, but it was still officially a monolingual classroom. However, the teacher in this classroom was bilingual, and she actively supported and promoted students' translanguaging. The third classroom was in some ways a more typical English as a second language classroom. While the teacher in this classroom was not bilingual, he did sometimes engage in translanguaging himself. Across all three classrooms, however, students drew flexibly on their bilingual repertoires in ways that seemed to normalize translanguaging. They disrupted the boundaries between English and Spanish in their everyday talk, and by doing so, they challenged the official language policies at their respective schools.

As the examples from these classrooms illustrate, these children's everyday translanguaging functioned as a tool that enabled and facilitated learning and social interaction. In the first classroom, translanguaging enabled Laura and Samantha to engage in a playful conversation at the science center. They drew flexibly on their linguistic repertoires as they commented on the butterflies and as they narrated their own actions documenting what they observed. In the second classroom, Yamilet, Eric, and Victor engaged in a similarly translingual conversation about mixing colors, while Kelsey drew flexibly on her linguistic repertoire to produce a translingual poem. In Kelsey's case, translanguaging afforded novel opportunities related to the aesthetics of composition while also enabling her to redefine what it meant to be a bilingual writer. And in the third classroom, Blu, Caroline, Ida, and the teacher drew on their knowledge of both Spanish and English to make sense of literary texts and science content. Across all three classrooms, translanguaging enhanced and facilitated learning and interaction, enabling these emergent bilingual students to construct identities for themselves as literate and capable learners.

We also argue that these students' engagement in translanguaging functioned to normalize this flexible expression of bilingualism, and that this normalization of translanguaging effectively transformed these bilingual and monolingual classrooms into translingual spaces. Although two of these classrooms were spaces in which English was meant to be privileged, and all three classrooms were spaces in which linguistic boundaries were meant to be enforced, students' everyday translanguaging transformed these classrooms into more flexible and dynamic spaces. We are not suggesting that these students were deliberately or intentionally seeking to transform their classrooms in this way. We simply argue that the transformation of these classrooms into translingual spaces is an inevitable outcome of the normalization of this flexible use of language. By using language flexibly, they transformed their classrooms into more flexible contexts than they would otherwise have been.

Again, the teachers in all three classrooms also contributed to the transformation of their respective classrooms into translingual spaces. By not discouraging students from translanguaging, by actively encouraging their translanguaging, and/or by engaging in translanguaging themselves, these teachers allowed for a more flexible space than would have been possible without their intervention. Although these teachers were not necessarily informed by the scholarship on translanguaging, some of their instructional moves overlapped with the principles and teaching practices described in the emergent literature on *translanguaging pedagogies* (García & Kleyn, 2016; Palmer et al., 2014; Pontier & Gort, 2016).

We would like to suggest that what we observed in these three classrooms (from both students and teachers) has important implications for understanding and enacting translanguaging pedagogies across multiple program models and instructional arrangements, especially within the current educational context for emergent bilingual students. The first classroom that we described is typical of dual language programs in that its official policy emphasized the separation of languages. Whereas the language separation policies and instructional practices characteristic of dual language education often marginalized and stigmatized emergent bilingual students' everyday forms of translanguaging, the space that these particular students and their teacher co-constructed was one in which translanguaging was accepted and unmarked. If more dual language programs similarly normalized translanguaging, this would represent an enormous step in the right direction. However, if translanguaging were deliberately, explicitly, and systematically encouraged, we suspect that this would create even more opportunities for students to display and cultivate their linguistic competencies. In fact, Ms. Birch and her colleagues have recently expressed an interest in more deliberately implementing translanguaging pedagogies in their classrooms.

The second and third classrooms that we described offer a glimpse of what is possible even in restrictive language policy contexts. Whereas English-only education officially marginalizes languages other than English, the students and teachers in these two classrooms' co-constructed spaces in which it was possible and sometimes preferable to draw flexibly on their full linguistic repertoires. Given that most emergent bilinguals in this country are learning in ESL/English-only settings, where they are often misunderstood and underserved, and where their linguistic competencies are not always recognized, these two examples seem particularly relevant. They suggest that English-only contexts can potentially reinvent themselves to be more flexible spaces. Again, however, if translanguaging were even more deliberately, explicitly, and systematically encouraged in these instructional settings, we suspect that this would create even more opportunities for emergent bilingual students to display and cultivate their linguistic competencies. Across all three of these classrooms, dynamic and flexible learning contexts were created by students and their teachers, but this was not always necessarily done with full or deliberate awareness. We suggest that more deliberate efforts could be made to further promote students' translanguaging, and that such efforts would likely yield tremendous benefits for students and teachers alike.

CONCLUSION

The emergent bilingual students that we have described in this chapter drew flexibly on their linguistic repertoires in their everyday classroom interactions, disrupting the supposed linguistic boundaries between English and Spanish as they talked, learned, and made meaning. These everyday examples of translanguaging afforded unique opportunities for learning and social interaction, and they effectively served to transform a bilingual classroom and two monolingual classrooms into more flexible and dynamic learning contexts—into *translingual* spaces.

By highlighting the transformative impact of emergent bilingual students' everyday translanguaging, our intention is neither to downplay the dire need to transform policies and pedagogies nor to romanticize the possibilities for student agency. We absolutely need transformation at the level of both policy and pedagogical practice precisely because the current state of schooling for emergent bilinguals constrains their agency and limits their opportunities. In our experience, however, such change is slow and often meets with significant resistance. Our argument is that regardless of how long it takes (and we know that meaningful transformation can take a very long time), emergent bilingual students are not necessarily going to wait for such transformation. More to the point, these children and youth will never be completely constrained or empowered by what adults do for them. As the examples above have illustrated, emergent bilingual students will continue to disrupt linguistic boundaries and thereby transform classroom space regardless—and sometimes in spite—of the policies and pedagogies that adults imagine, enact, and impose on their behalf.

In each of the classrooms that we have described in this chapter, the teachers clearly played an important role in allowing for the construction of translingual spaces. However, it was ultimately the students themselves who engaged in and normalized translanguaging. Needless to say, their spontaneous translanguaging is not, in and of itself, sufficient to transform schooling in ways that lead towards equity. One overarching implication, though, is that we can and should look to emergent bilingual students and follow their lead as we seek to develop and implement translingual policies and pedagogies. We would do well to learn from these students' everyday expressions of bilingualism as we prepare them to engage with multiple communities, including those that look and sound like them. More deliberate efforts to enact and implement translanguaging pedagogies could create conditions conducive to recognizing, sustaining, and cultivating emergent bilingual students' dynamic expressions of bilingualism and expansive linguistic competencies in the service of robust learning, meaningful interaction, and educational equity.

APPENDIX A
TRANSCRIPTION CONVENTIONS

In all of the transcripts featured in this chapter, **bold italics** are used to mark the switch from the "matrix language" (i.e., the language in which each interaction begins). In the transcripts from Classrooms 1 and 2, Spanish is the matrix language. In the examples from Classroom 3, English is the matrix language. Below is a list of other transcription conventions used throughout this chapter:

    : A colon immediately following a letter indicates that the speaker has noticeably lengthened or drawn out that sound. Additional colons indicate further lengthening of that sound.

    - A dash indicates a sudden cut-off of a given word or sound

(1.5) Numbers in parentheses indicate silences or pauses in seconds and tenths of seconds.

(( )) Double italicized parentheses enclose material that is not part of the talk being transcribed.

NOTES

1. Throughout all transcripts, we leave the so-called "matrix language" (i.e., the language in which the interaction begins) unmarked, explicitly marking with **bold italics** the places where students switched into the other language. We do this not in order to reify Spanish and English as separate codes, but rather to highlight the precise points in each interaction where students disrupted the supposed linguistic boundaries between the two. Please see Appendix A for a description of additional transcription conventions.

2. Samantha did utter the English word "Mister!" in line 04, but this was when addressing the researcher and not part of her conversation with Laura.

REFERENCES

Baker, C. (2001). *Foundations of bilingual education and bilingualism* (3rd ed.). Clevedon, England: Multilingual Matters.

Bomer, K. (2010). *Hidden gems: Naming and teaching from the brilliance in every student's writing.* Portsmouth, NH: Heinemann.

Brown, E. (2017, March 27). Trump signs bills overturning Obama-era education regulations. *Washington Post.* Retrieved from https://www.washingtonpost.com/news/education/wp/2017/03/27/trump-signs-bills-overturning-obama-era-education-regulations/

California Secretary of State (2016). *The statement of vote: State ballot measures (Propositions 51–67) by county.* Retrieved from http://elections.cdn.sos.ca.gov/sov/2016-general/sov/65-ballot-measures-formatted.pdf

Callahan, L. (2004). *Spanish/English codeswitching in a written corpus.* Amsterdam, Netherlands: John Benjamins.

Callahan, R. (2005). Tracking and high school English learners: Limiting opportunity to learn. *American Educational Research Journal, 42*(2), 305–328.

Center for Applied Linguistics (2017). U.S. Educational language policy. Retrieved from http://www.cal.org/areas-of-impact/language-planning-policy/u.s.-educational-language-policy

Council of Chief State School Officers (2016). *Major provisions of Every Child Succeeds Act related to the education of English learners.* Washington, DC: Council of Chief State School Officers.

de la Luz Reyes, M. (2012). Spontaneous biliteracy: Examining Latino students' untapped potential. *Theory into Practice, 51*(4), 248–255.

Erickson, F. (2004). *Talk and social theory: Ecologies of speaking and listening in everyday life.* Cambridge, England: Polity Press.

Ferguson, C. A. (1959). Diglossia. *Word, 15*(2), 325–340.

Gándara, P., Rumberger, R., Maxwell-Jolly, J., & Callahan, R. (2003). English learners in California schools: Unequal resources, unequal outcomes. *Education Policy Analysis Archives, 11*(36), 1–52.

García, O. (2009). *Bilingual education in the 21st century: A global perspective.* Malden, MA: Wiley/Blackwell.

García, O., & Kleyn, T. (2016). Introduction. In O. García & T. Kleyn (Eds.), *Translanguaging with multilingual students: Learning from classroom moments* (pp. 1–6). New York, NY: Routledge.

Gumperz, J. J. (1982). Conversational code-switching. In J. J. Gumperz (Ed.), *Discourse strategies* (pp. 59–99). Cambridge, England: Cambridge University Press.

Lefebvre, H. (2005). *The production of space.* Malden, MA: Blackwell.

Lewis, G., Jones, B., & Baker, C. (2012). Translanguaging: Origins and development from school to street and beyond. *Educational Research and Evaluation: An International Journal on Theory and Practice, 18*(7), 641–654.

Linquanti, R., Cook, H. G., Bailey, A. L., & MacDonald, R. (2016). Moving toward a more common definition of English learner: Collected guidance for states and multi-state assessment consortia. Washington, DC: Council of Chief State School Officers.

Martínez, R. A. (2009). *Spanglish* is spoken here: Making sense of Spanish-English code-switching and language ideologies in a sixth-grade English language arts classroom. Unpublished doctoral dissertation, UCLA, Los Angeles, CA.

Martínez, R. A. (2013). Reading the world in *Spanglish*: Hybrid language practices and ideological contestation in a sixth-grade English language arts classroom. *Linguistics and Education, 24*(3), 276–288.

Martínez, R. A. (2014). "Do they even know that they do it?": Exploring awareness of Spanish-English code-switching in a sixth-grade English language arts classroom. *Bilingual Research Journal, 37*(2), 195–210.

Martínez, R. A. (2017). Dual language education and the erasure of Chicanx, Latinx, and indigenous Mexican children: A call to re-imagine (and imagine beyond) bilingualism. *Texas Education Review, 5*(1), 81–92.

National Center for Education Statistics (2017). *The condition of education 2017 (NCES 2017-144), English language learners in public schools.* Retrieved from https://nces.ed.gov/programs/coe/indicator_cgf.asp

Otheguy, R., García, O., & Reid, W. (2015). Clarifying translanguaging and deconstructing named languages: A perspective from linguistics. *Applied Linguistics Review, 6*(3), 281–307.

Palmer, D., Martínez, R. A., Mateus, S., & Henderson, K. (2014). Reframing the debate on language separation: Towards a vision for translanguaging pedagogies in the dual language classroom. *The Modern Language Journal, 98*(3), 757–772.

Pontier, R., & Gort, M. (2016). Coordinated translanguaging pedagogy as distributed cognition: A case study of two dual language bilingual education preschool coteachers' languaging practices during shared book reading. *International Multilingual Research Journal, 10*(2), 89–106.

Umansky, I. M. (2016). Leveled and exclusionary tracking: English learners' access to academic content in middle school. *American Educational Research Journal, 53*(6), 1792–1833.

Umansky, I. M., & Reardon, S. F. (2014). Reclassification patterns among Latino English learner students in bilingual, dual immersion, and English immersion classrooms. *American Educational Research Journal, 51*(5), 879–912.

U.S. Department of Education. (2015). Dual language education programs: Current state policies and practices. United States Department of Education, Office of English Language Acquisition. Washington, D.C.

Walsh, C. (1991) *Pedagogy and the struggle for voice: Issues of language, power and schooling for Puerto Ricans.* New York, NY: Bergin & Garvey.

Williams, C. (1994). *Arfarniad o ddulliau dysgu ac addysgu yng nghyd-destun addysg uwchradd ddwyieithog* [*An evaluation of learning and teaching methods in the context of bilingual secondary education*] (Unpublished doctoral dissertation). University of Wales, Bangor, Cardiff, Wales.

CHAPTER 11

BILINGUAL YOUTH AND NETWORKS OF SUPPORT

Designing a Formula for Success on the Path to College

Colleen Hamilton
University of Wisconsin-Madison

Mariana Pacheco
University of Wisconsin-Madison

ABSTRACT

This chapter analyzes how Spanish-English bilingual youth leveraged their available networks of family members, teachers, mentors, and counselors to navigate their schooling trajectories toward college. This perspective illuminates how networks of support transformed opportunities for youth by providing key resources and access that youth drew on to prepare for college. As youth leveraged resources for college preparation, they articulated a "formula for success" which included adopting a college-bound mindset and agentically organizing available resources. This analysis demonstrates the ability of bilingual youth to design a formula for success that extends

Transforming Schooling for Second Language Learners, pages 199–216
Copyright © 2019 by Information Age Publishing
All rights of reproduction in any form reserved.

beyond college toward futures in which they, in turn, enhance the networks that supported them.

For emergent bilingual students in U.S. schools, a narrow emphasis on monolingual-like language proficiency and systemic practices such as deficit-oriented race- and language-based tracking continue to limit their educational opportunities (Cook, 2016; Flores & Rosa, 2015; Grinberg & Saavedra, 2000; May, 2014; Ochoa, 2013; Valenzuela, 1999). Disembodied, reductive, proficiency-based views of bilingualism underlying these practices fail to account for the extent of bilinguals' communicative repertoires and the impact of social contexts and identities on situated learning trajectories (Gutiérrez, Baquedano-López, & Tejeda, 1999; Norton, 2000; Norton & McKinney, 2011; Pavlenko & Blackledge, 2004; Rymes, 2010).

Informed by an understanding that bilingualism extends beyond proficiency and even communicative repertoires, the analysis presented in this chapter draws on robust views of bilingualism as a situated resource for learning, schooling, and identity work. In this regard, we re-center cultural-historical contexts, relations of power, and intersecting fluid identities that Spanish-English bilingual youth in this study leveraged to realize their own personal and educational goals. Taking this view of bilingualism as a resource rather than just something they "possess," we analyze how bilingual youth leveraged their available networks of family members, teachers, mentors, and counselors to navigate their schooling trajectories toward college. The college-going identities youth enacted are seen as emerging from cultural-historical contexts of racialized schooling and mediated by their dynamic language practices as they claimed, contested, and shaped powerful routes to college access (Bucholtz & Hall, 2005). That is, their bilingualism shaped the circumstances bilingual youth navigated—with the support of others in their bilingual worlds—to gain access to academic opportunities.

First, this perspective on bilingual youth's schooling trajectories illuminates how networks of support transformed opportunities for youth by providing key resources and access that youth drew on to prepare for college. Second, youth's voices are foregrounded in an analysis of how they humanized stories of bilingual difference through which they were able to access resources for college preparation. They did so by articulating a "formula for success" which included adopting a college-bound mindset and agentically organizing resources available from networks of support. Furthermore, this analysis demonstrates the ability of bilingual youth to design a formula for success that extended beyond college toward imagined social futures (Gutiérrez, 2008, 2016; Gutiérrez & Jurow, 2016) in which they, in turn, enhance the networks that supported them.

LANGUAGE AND LEARNING AT SCHOOL
FOR BILINGUAL YOUTH

Transformative work in bilingualism and bilingual education has document-ed the richly dynamic abilities of bilingual individuals and communities, as well as the ways these abilities have been included and leveraged for learning at school. This research disrupts a legacy of deficit thinking about bilingual students by focusing on how bilingual practices and pedagogies can be lever-aged by teachers for learning at school as well as diverse visions of success.

Valuing Home Languages, Cultures, and Identities

Bridging home and school languages reinforces language and content learning for bilingual students at school. Through strategic use of hybrid home/school language practices that leverages students' full communica-tive resources, educators can create a zone of learning that invites meaning negotiation (Gutiérrez, Baquedano-López, & Tejeda, 1999), mediates and co-constructs understandings (García & Wei, 2014) and increases inclu-sion, participation, and understanding (Creese & Blackledge, 2010). This meaning-making reflects dynamic and recursive translanguaging in which bilinguals move fluidly and strategically across languages, depending on contextual factors, to support and enact bilingual community identities (Zentella, 1997) as well as to enhance learning (Escamilla et al., 2014). In instructional contexts, encouraging translanguaging opens the floor to bilingual voices, engages students across their languages, and promotes metalinguistic awareness, home-school bridges, and student engagement (García & Wei, 2014).

Asset-based views of bilingualism demonstrate that they can promote ac-ademic success through linguistically and culturally responsive pedagogies (Martínez, Orellana, Pacheco, & Carbone, 2008; Orellana, 2009; Zentella, 2005). In contrast, research has consistently demonstrated that when bilin-gual students are required (officially or unofficially) to leave their language and cultural identities at the door, their opportunities for academic success are constrained (García & Wei, 2014). For example, subtractive assimila-tionist practices and ideologies that failed to authentically value Mexican American students' home languages and cultures limited their ability to succeed in school (Valenzuela, 1999). Indeed, home languages, including bilingual language practices, can be leveraged to facilitate a sociocritical literacy, for example, that encourages critical thought through historiciz-ing literacy practices (Gutiérrez, 2008). That is, bilingual youth can come to understand more fully their role as social, agentive actors whose experi-ences are historically constituted but certainly not historically determined.

Likewise, leveraging students' cultural and political-historical knowledge in the classroom can expand students' academic skills and opportunities for success (Gutiérrez, 2008; Ladson-Billings, 1995; Pacheco, 2009, 2012). In sum, bilingual students' languages, cultures, and identities are powerful tools for organizing learning, academic success, and critical awareness of the construction of social contexts over time.

Academic Success for Bilingual Youth

Academic success can be understood as a student's movement through stages of schooling from elementary to secondary and postsecondary despite the deficit perspectives, marginalizing experiences, and low-quality and under-resourced schooling they often confront (Burciaga, 2007; Callahan, 2005; Gándara, Rumberger, Maxwell-Jolly, Callahan, 2003). Bilingual youth overcome these barriers by carefully gathering outside resources, defining their own success stories, and honing tactics of resistance to cultivate strength and succeed academically (Burciaga, 2007; Sandoval, 1991). For example, by reflecting on cultural practices embedded within communities and communicated through *consejos* and *pedagogies of the home*, bilingual youth practiced resisting deficit frames, learning through tension, and uncovering paths to academic success (Delgado Bernal, 2001; González, 2001). Additionally, ethnic studies courses combined with service learning within schooling contexts can support bilingual student academic success at predominantly White institutions by fostering critical reflection and community engagement (Delgado Bernal, Alemán, & Garavito, 2009). This work indicates that the schooling trajectory of bilingual youth seeking college access is imbued with adversity and possibility, particularly where bilingual identities intersect with immigrant, low-income, or first-generation college student status, and highlights the networks of support across in-school and out-of-school contexts that are integral to bilingual youth's academic success.

Success Beyond Academics: Social Mobility and Opportunities

Transforming bilingual youth's schooling trajectories extends beyond college access to broader horizons of possibility. Youth must have opportunities to hone a critical awareness of the historical processes that structure inequitable schooling, that "socialize Mexican American children to take their place in the lower stratum of the social hierarchy and enter the workforce as a source of cheap labor" (Grinberg & Saavedra, 2000, p. 431). In investigating social mobility beyond academic achievement, Villenas (2005; Villenas & Moreno, 2001) found that bilingual youth drew on *mother-daughter pedagogies* of resistance and resiliency to navigate interlocking systems of racism, patriarchy, and exploitation. In these pedagogies, dominant deficit discourses were implicitly critiqued and reinterpreted by mothers, who transcended the historical determinism of these discourses to tell their daughters new stories of strength and opportunity.

Bilingual youth can use these tools to design new social futures and build a sociocritical literacy that reframes everyday and institutional literacy practices and texts as tools for critical social thought (Gutiérrez, 2008, 2016; Gutiérrez & Jurow, 2016). Leveraging these tools both recognizes and builds on the expertise that students bring with them, including their bilingual practices and home-based pedagogies. The resulting repertoire enables bilingual youth to become designers of their own social futures. Hybrid language practices are an integral part of this repertoire (Gutiérrez, 2008; Gutiérrez, Baquedano-López, & Tejeda, 1999), and situating bilingualism as a tool of sociocritical literacy illuminates the conceptual link between what youth speak (a dominant understanding of bilingualism) and how youth organize their lives, shaped by the past and in view of an imagined future.

We can then extend on dreaming and imagination to frame youth as not only future actors, but current designers of their social futures (Gutiérrez, 2008; Gutiérrez & Jurow 2016) as they organize their schooling trajectories by leveraging networks of support for college access. Focusing on the dynamic navigation of this path by bilingual youth challenges deficit perspectives and foregrounds dynamic, asset-based understandings of bilingual students. This perspective builds on transformative work in bilingualism and bilingual education that has highlighted how the bilingual practices of students and their communities can be leveraged for learning at school and beyond (e.g., García & Wei, 2014; Gutiérrez, 2008; Martínez et al., 2008).

Bilingualism as a Borderlands

Bilingual youth in this chapter are seen as navigating a *borderlands* between what is and what could be (Anzaldúa, 1987, 2002; Calderón, Delgado Bernal, Pérez Huber, Malagón, & Nell Vélez, 2012). Reframing bilingualism as a borderlands space borrows understandings of cultural-historical contexts, power relations, and intersectionality implicated in geographic borders to illuminate the hybridity, co-construction, and in-betweenness of bilingual experiences. To navigate these borderlands, bilingual youth draw strength from their hybrid languages, leveraging them for learning (García & Wei, 2014) and building their sociocritical literacy (Gutiérrez, 2008). With these resources, bilingual youth design new trajectories that are situated within cultural-historical contexts and constellated networks of support, which youth organize to achieve their academic goals and broader social opportunities. In turn, bilingual youth integrate reciprocal support for these networks to enhance not only their personal well-being, but that of their families and communities.

This embodied understanding of bilingualism builds on current views in language research. These views call for a multilingual turn and broader considerations of sociocultural processes and intersecting identities in language learning that foreground bilinguals' richly dynamic hybrid language practices, as well as a critique or reductive understandings of language as proficiency that serve to marginalize groups of racialized speakers (Flores & Rosa, 2015; García & Wei, 2014; Grinberg & Saavedra, 2000; Gutiérrez et al., 1999; May, 2014; Norton, 2000; Pavlenko & Blackledge, 2004). This framework re-centers cultural-historical contexts, relations of power, and intersecting fluid identities in order to foreground youth's hybrid language practices and sociocritical literacy.

RESEARCH METHODS

This study took place in a midsize Midwestern community with Bella, Christina, Jacobo, Minnie, Puggs, and Roberta, six Spanish-English bilingual Latinx youth in their first year of college (all names are self-selected pseudonyms; Hamilton, 2018). Ethnographic methods including in-depth individual and group interviews, artifacts of bilingualism (e.g., eyeglasses, graduation pins), and written reflections were utilized to explore the relationships between bilingualism, critical consciousness, and schooling trajectories. These data generation methods reflect the importance of foregrounding participant voices using *testimonio* and *cultural intuition* within a Chicana feminist epistemology (Calderón et al., 2012; Delgado Bernal, 1998), where testimonio seeks to recover silenced stories and cultural intuition builds on participant analysis. Through these methods, bilingual youth reflected on their path to college and the role their languages played in this trajectory.

Data analysis began with the transcription of the audio recordings by the first author to build *data intimacy* (Saldaña, 2011), or familiarity with the words participants chose to describe their experiences. Analytic memos building on researcher fieldnotes and research products furthered the *data analysis spiral* (Creswell, 2007) and were used to track emerging themes, patterns, and categories, as well as to reflexively freewrite. Analytic memos brought to our attention how, while narrating their experiences, youth portrayed themselves as key actors along their college-going pathways, at times utilizing individualistic or meritocratic themes to reconstruct their trajectories over the course of research interviews. Reviewing these memos, we were compelled to return to the data to illuminate the secondary—but vital—roles played by family members, teachers, counselors, and mentors, analyzed here as the networks of support that bilingual youth drew on while uncovering their path to college.

NETWORKS OF SUPPORT LEVERAGED
BY BILINGUAL YOUTH

Drawing on these reported data, this analysis illuminates how youth organized institutional and language-based resources to strategically enhance their schooling experiences and become designers of their own success (Gutiérrez, 2008, 2016). Within their designed futures, youth included a reciprocal investment into the academic and human resources that supported them in their schooling trajectories.

Surrounded by Networks of Support

Data analysis revealed that youth drew on integral connections and resources, conceptualized here as networks of support including teachers, school counselors, family members, and mentors, to enhance their path to college. Explored in detail below, these networks of support appeared across youth's reports of school-based support from bilingual teachers who encouraged and mentored youth; counselors who provided access to advanced coursework, scholarship information, and career counseling; administrators who commended bilingual youth for their contribution to school-community relations; precollege instructors who fostered a college-bound identity; mentors who provided feedback on scholarship and college applications; and family members who supported bilingual practices, educational opportunities including emotional and financial support, and mentorship of younger siblings. Furthermore, bilingual youth leveraged the interconnectedness of this support, for example, where volunteer requirements for scholarship applications could be met by connecting with their local bilingual church, and where parents joined with school counselors to advocate for and organize youth's access to advanced coursework and, thus, postsecondary education.

Youth at the center of these networks were able to advance their educational goals and design new social futures for themselves and their communities (Gutiérrez, 2008, 2016) by countering the historic underrepresentation of Latinx, first-generation, and immigrant students on college campuses. They accomplished this design work by drawing on a critical consciousness, fostered by experiences across these networks, to read situational power dynamics and enact contextualized responses that leveraged available support to resist marginalization (Sandoval, 1991).

Specifically, bilingual practices were integral to building youth's critical consciousness in that they expanded youth's understanding of people, languages, and cultural identities, as well as their interconnection. These understandings echoed the interwoven networks of support that transformed youth's schooling trajectories. One participant, Puggs, reflected,

> I think knowing more of bilingualism, I think it's [the] more you know the history and you know what's happened and their cultures, [then] you can understand more of what's happening, you can understand why a person acts like that, maybe why they get offended, why a person acts the way they do. It tells a story, well, it gives you more of a background of the person even if they don't even know it.

In this excerpt, the idea surfaced of bilingualism as a lens to historicize "what's happening" and "why a person acts the way they do" through an understanding of their stories. Historicizing experiences and practices in this way allowed bilingual youth to build the sociocritical literacy that helped disrupt what is by imagining what could be (Gutiérrez, 2008, 2016). In this sense, language is not only a communicative tool for understanding the world, but is also central to identities through imagination, in that indexing ourselves through language reflects who we understand ourselves and others to be (Weedon, 1997). "Knowing more of bilingualism . . . It tells a story," as Puggs said, even when that story is obscured in hidden historical processes of marginalization. Puggs leveraged her bilingualism to make these histories visible and use them to understand the world around her. By embedding language in culture, history, and practices, bilingual youth demonstrated a vision of themselves as *historical actors* (Espinoza, 2003, as cited in Gutiérrez, 2008) who organized future action by understanding the effects of the past on present conditions. Puggs' historicized knowledge was based on "knowing more of bilingualism," a reflection of the important bilingual and bicultural practices of her networks of support.

Humanizing Stories of Difference to Recruit Resources for College Preparation

Narrow academic emphasis on language proficiency reduces the complexity of hybrid language practices to a focus on what bilingual students are seen as lacking (García, 2009a, 2009b). In light of this monoglossic view of language, which underlay English language support services reported by bilingual youth in this study, youth resisted identifying as *English language learners* at school. They saw it as a stigmatizing label, overly determined by perplexing language assessments that limited their access to upper-level courses—in Minnie's case, by one missed point over three consecutive attempts to exit the ESL program. In avoiding this classification, bilingual youth could access expanded resources for college preparation while humanizing their bilingual differences from the imagined monolingual norm.

Bilingual youth's humanizing stories of difference emerged as they considered language and cultural identities and the roles these identities played in their unique personal histories. Their narratives constituted powerful counter-stories of resistance and resiliency, reinterpreting dominant deficit discourses about bilingualism. In doing so, participants embedded their bilingual differences within larger cultural communities, which they portrayed as networks of support for their language and cultural identities. One participant, Roberta, explained the links among her language, cultural, and national identities by saying,

> Spanish is part of me. Ok, so I know Mexicans and Spanish is related because that's our language, but I feel like for me it's a part of being me. So I feel like if I lose Spanish, I'm losing myself... Mexicans speak Spanish and that's how, in [my hometown] most of them are Mexicans, it's how we, even though they're kind of strangers, I feel like we're kind of like a family, a big family. So it's a part of allowing us to make those bonds.

In portraying herself as a member of a "big family" and using "we," "us," and "our," Roberta evoked an imagined community of nationally and ethnically Mexican people in Mexico and the United States. One of the central practices of this community was speaking Spanish, which Roberta emphasized twice as "part of me...part of being me." The integral practice of Spanish was reiterated when Roberta shared that she would be "losing myself" if she were not bilingual. Moreover, Roberta realized that without a shared language, she would not be able to participate in this community and "make those bonds." She reflected, "I feel like, there's a beauty to our language that relates to our culture. It's my identity. What makes me me is that I'm Hispanic, so I speak Spanish, and I can talk to my people." In identifying Spanish as an integral community identity practice, Roberta utilized a discourse of commonality to humanize the particular source of her difference, voicing the idea that we all have some defining characteristic that "makes me me," without which we would not be ourselves, and would not have access to our "people."

Humanizing stories of difference and depicting their centrality to common human experience supported bilingual youth as they accessed college preparation. Their narratives served to destigmatize their bilingual difference, meaning that their identities as Mexican, Latina, or Hispanic bilingual students should not reduce them to the stigmatized label of *English language learner* and hence prevent them from accessing resources for college preparation. Acknowledging difference in this way allowed bilingual youth to claim legitimate college-bound student identities at school and to access the accompanying resources without erasing the practices of the communities that supported them.

Indeed, the ways in which youth reported humanizing stories of their own difference is reflective of their sociocritical literacy (Gutiérrez, 2008). They understood the cultural-historical, co-constructed nature of difference, which provided "the means for developing a historicizing literacy that links students' historical and immediate past, the present, and the imagined future through social dreaming—a collective dream for a better world" (Gutiérrez, 2008, p. 158). Bilingual youth looked to the past, through stories of difference, and drew on these historicized understandings of their communities to inspire their future plans.

Leveraging Networks of Support Into a Formula for Success

The idea of a "formula for success" is borrowed from Roberta's use of the phrase, which indicated the measures she had taken to access college. The metaphor of a formula underlines how bilingual youth deliberately, methodically, and strategically navigated their college preparation, for example, by tracking their grades and selecting advanced academic tracks, practicing academic literacy skills, preparing for standardized entrance tests, and obtaining mentorship in writing application essays. Throughout these efforts, bilingual youth drew on networks of support across school and community contexts. This formula, representing a tool kit of college preparation strategies, conveys how youth incrementally designed their social futures by drawing on the resources of their networks to construct, piece by piece, a bridge to college. Gutiérrez (2008) explains how such processes constitute learning:

> Learning...cannot be reduced to the appropriation of tools that help enhance personal growth, develop voice, or build skills, although these are arguably important by-products; instead, the object is the constitution of what Gee (1996) calls a "social semiotic toolkit" that extends students' repertoires of practice in ways that enable them to become designers of their own social futures. (p. 156)

Analysis of bilingual youth's schooling experiences shows that their designed college preparation took the form of establishing a college-bound mindset and recruiting necessary resources. That is, youth's efforts to "become designers of their own social futures" and self-directed design work was embedded within a constellation of school-, community-, and family-based resources as well as within unfolding trajectories as new goals emerged.

This embeddedness underscores the extent to which bilingual youth's success in their academic endeavors was not static, individualistic, or meritocratic, but was—like youth themselves—emergent, multi-layered, personal-historical, co-constructed, and contingent upon constellations of factors (Bucholtz & Hall, 2005). Bilingual youth undertook this design work to prepare for college both as a way of fulfilling their families' dreams for them *and* to access opportunities that would allow them to reciprocally invest in their families. Preparatory tools such as good grades represented developing skills *and* a step towards college. College access itself signified personal growth *and* a step toward an imagined social future of financial security. Thus, *success* was fluidly defined by bilingual youth (González, 2001), where success at one stage then became an important resource that was added to their tool kit to prepare for meeting the next goal on an emergent, embedded trajectory.

Adopting a College-Bound Mindset

First, bilingual youth in this study framed their decision to actualize their goal of college enrollment in terms of their own perceived sense of personal motivation, commitment to figuring things out, and intent to realize a specific vision, mentality, or attitude—or what one participant described as a particular "mindset." This commitment to a course of action represented a confluence of college-oriented practices and a realization of agency on the part of bilingual youth at the center of these networks of support and despite institutional constraints. One participant, Jacobo, reported realizing that his parents' dreams had become his own when he reached a turning point late in high school:

> That's when I actually started taking my grades very seriously and pursuing the fact that I could actually go to college. Because, I don't think throughout high school I ever realized how important this would be to not only myself but my parents, just knowing that they only got an elementary school education and the fact that my brother and I can actually pursue careers . . . after gaining that mindset, it instilled a new passion for pursuing of further education past high school that could better my life in the long run and not just my life but my parents' lives.

In this excerpt, Jacobo's "mindset" encompassed college enrollment as an initial step in a larger, lifelong formula for success that would enable him to "better my life in the long run and not just my life but my parents' lives." By completing college and obtaining financial security for themselves and their families, bilingual youth envisioned reciprocally investing in the networks that supported them. Jacobo's college pursuits grew out of this commitment and mirrored the example of his older brother, referenced here. His brother was transitioning to college and modeling this college-bound mindset when Jacobo described realizing his own academic achievement and "taking my grades very seriously." Through his narrative, Jacobo illustrated the constellation of family, academic, and self-efficacy factors that shaped this shift in mindset.

Once Jacobo reached this turning point, he remembered taking pride in having figured out school and undertaking a methodical approach to college and scholarship applications with the goal of obtaining college admission and a full-tuition arts scholarship. He discovered this scholarship through his involvement in a poetry organization, where his writing mentor introduced him to a former scholarship recipient:

> I guess it was kind of fate or something, but once I found out about the scholarship, I kinda built this mindset that I didn't want my parents to pay for school if I could get this scholarship based on my own art...I didn't want them to pay for education, and if there was a way that I could do that, that I would pursue it and then try to build on it, and I did.

Jacobo often described his efforts as self-initiated, conveyed by his repetition of "I" in this excerpt: "I found out," "I built this mindset," "I didn't want my parents to pay," "I worked so diligently," "I didn't slack," and his clear conclusion that "I did." However, in addition to the integral role of his writing mentor, other actors contributed to Jacobo's progress: his mother drove him to the weekly poetry workshop, waiting outside in the car for the duration of the meeting; his brother and writing mentor helped him revise and edit his college and scholarship applications; and Jacobo "worked so diligently" primarily because he refused to oblige his parents to pay for his postsecondary education. Jacobo also evoked the role of "fate," indicating the importance of something (perhaps benevolent others, luck, or coincidence) other than himself and his individual agency that aligned complex factors in his favor. Thus, within youth's individualistic and meritocratic narratives, social networks of support played instrumental roles.

Nevertheless, Jacobo deliberately took advantage of these opportunities and organized these resources into a self-designed formula for success. He reported independently researching colleges, rankings, and programs; setting aside 4 months to draft and revise his application materials; and recruiting others to advocate for him in reference letters. He concluded that, "No one was gonna take me to college if I didn't want to go...it kinda instilled this thing in my mind that I have to be much more independent and pursue what I want to do." Jacobo's feeling of independence echoed the importance of his role as a designer of his own social future, which extended beyond more typical institutional supports, even as he leveraged the networks of support and available resources for college access.

Furthermore, Jacobo's narrative speaks to the role of parents who contributed to bilingual youth's college preparation. Because of parents' admonitions not to follow in their footsteps, youth felt a sense of urgency to access college and alleviate their families' socioeconomic struggles. This backdrop contributed to an understanding of why youth framed their college enrollment as a step in a larger formula for success resulting in financial stability, bringing their families along with them as they designed their social futures. Parents also played an important emotional and financial support role in their children's trajectories, demonstrating the ability of parents to "prepare us for lives that none of them had ever imagined" (Collins, 1999, as quoted in Villenas & Moreno, 2001). This preparation motivated youth to challenge themselves, learn from their mistakes, resist low expectations, and build a college-bound, success-bound mindset.

Recruiting Resources Through Networks of Support

Bilingual youth recognized the important role of networks of support and reported identifying and recruiting key people to support their formula for success. Youth may not have been able to access college without these resources; yet, given the presence of networks of support and the resources they offered, youth were instrumental in organizing and leveraging them to further their goals. Bilingual youth's schooling trajectories were thus dynamically co-constructed by both the youth themselves and the networks of support around them.

Jacobo, Puggs, and Roberta shared that their families encouraged them to aim for a 4-year college degree as the premier symbol of academic success. Puggs, a first-generation college student, received consistent support for academic achievement from siblings, parents, and grandparents and reported that, "I knew that I wanted to go to college basically since I was born." Bilingual youth were encouraged both in broad terms and through specific help, such as keeping track of deadlines and completing applications. In this way, youth relied on their families for the emotional, logistic, and financial support needed to design their college futures and reenvision their families' trajectories.

A second important network of support for bilingual youth in this study were high school teachers and counselors. For example, Minnie credited the preparation of her college application materials to English teachers at her school, who required seniors to complete five college applications by October so that they could help students substantively draft and revise their personal statements. In this way, teachers facilitated youth's college preparation by providing time and resources to enhance a critical component of the college application. Similarly, high school guidance counselors provided support by helping bilingual students strategically choose classes and plan course schedules to allow time to complete specialized certificate

programs or access additional support through study halls. One participant, Bella, planned to study nursing in college and regularly sought out
counselors when exiting the English as a second language program, planning her certified nursing assistant coursework, and finding and applying
for scholarships. Bella consulted her counselor so often, she reported feeling guilty about "having to bother my counselor a lot." This frequent access
undoubtedly enhanced her opportunities for academic progress.

Bella came to understand the strategic role played by guidance counselors. One counselor in particular developed a relationship with her family
beginning in middle school and consequently advocated for her inclusion
in an early, selective scholarship competition. Bella won the scholarship
and proudly wore the scholarship pin at her high school graduation. From
eighth grade to graduation, she and her mother followed the scholarship requirements to achieve academically and volunteer at her bilingual
church. In this way, Bella drew on key people and their connections to
design her own college preparatory program that required her to maintain good grades, volunteer, and plan for college to take advantage of the
scholarship. Bella played a central role in leveraging multiple networks of
support over time, and in and out of school.

The analysis presented here illuminates multiple instances of bilingual
youth's goal-directed behavior, where youth leveraged available resources
and a sociocritical literacy (Gutiérrez, 2008) to create their formula for success and design their social futures. Clearly, bilingual youth's efforts built on
available networks of support, including community-based language and
cultural practices and school-based college preparation, which required
them to interweave supports across contexts and institutions. These bilingual youth inhabited a broad resource landscape, embedded within networks of support, as they creatively built bridges to college while negotiating complex and dominant formulas for success. In this analysis, we have
foregrounded these networks of support, and youth's reciprocal investment
in them, as a way to highlight the specific practices that transformed bilingual youths' schooling trajectories.

IMPLICATIONS AND CONCLUSION

This chapter analyzes bilingual youths' college pathways by illuminating the
transformative practices in which youth engaged to organize their schooling trajectories, by depicting the rich resource landscape they drew on to
achieve academic success, and by foregrounding their humanizing perspectives on their bilingual practices and communities. Their reflections during
their first year of college highlight the important ways they leveraged networks of support to access postsecondary education and imagine new social

futures, which included a commitment to mobilizing their future success to reinvest in these networks.

In the experiences of bilingual youth reported here, it is essential to acknowledge that opportunities for transformation at school were manifestly limited by school policies that reflected a monoglossic view of language (García, 2009a). These policies resulted in the segregation of bilingual youth into English language learner tracks on the basis of what they were seen as lacking (García, 2009b). Bilingual youth were required to resist this academic profiling (Ochoa, 2013) in order to exit this track and access college preparation. The narratives presented in this chapter disrupt this deficit view of bilingual students by emphasizing a view of embodied language within humanized histories and communities, making space for the hybrid language practices of these communities. When home languages are officially welcomed through classroom language policy incorporating translanguaging, learning opportunities are transformed and join the networks of support available to bilingual students (Gutiérrez, Baquedano-López, & Tejeda, 1999; García & Wei, 2014).

More flexible language policies in classrooms can be complemented by transformative pedagogies, including the creation of spaces and discourses dedicated to bilingual students (Delgado Bernal, Alemán, & Garavito, 2009). These spaces help bridge home and school contexts, enhancing the interconnection of resources leveraged by bilingual youth in this study and transforming the way bilingual youth are positioned at school. Drawing on resources across contexts not only bridges and welcomes but also creates a dynamic learning zone utilizing students' full meaning-making repertoires (Gutiérrez, Baquedano-López, & Tejeda, 1999). The creation of dedicated spaces for bilingual students can facilitate their movement through schooling, redefining as possibility the adversity presented by constraints and challenges (e.g., tracking, labels) to academic success and social mobility that they encountered in schools.

The transformative practices explored in this chapter were enacted in support of bilingual youth as well as by youth themselves, illuminating the co-construction of their schooling trajectories at the intersection of networks of support. From this analysis of their experiences of bilingualism and schooling, bilingual youth emerge as primary designers of new social futures. They accomplished this design work with the support of teachers, school counselors, family members, and mentors who provide key resources for their college preparation. Additionally, bilingual youth redesigned stories of difference from a dominant monolingual norm by humanizing and historicizing their bilingual experiences. In doing so, they established a college-bound mindset and gained access to college preparatory resources. Throughout, they planned to reinvest in their networks of support as their paths extended toward future possibilities.

These understandings are brought into focus when bilingualism is viewed as a *borderlands* between what is and what can be, where bilingual in-betweenness is leveraged as a resource for critical consciousness and sociocritical literacy. This stance disrupts proficiency-based, reductive views of language to foreground cultural-historical contexts, relations of power, and intersecting identities. We argue that a transformation of language policies and pedagogies can draw inspiration from the embodied, historicized, dynamic language practices of bilingual youth. This transformation will support students in transcending narrowly defined academic outcomes and definitions of success to reframe them as designers of their own successful paths.

REFERENCES

Anzaldúa, G. (1987/2012). *Borderlands/La frontera: The new Mestiza.* San Francisco, CA: Spinsters/Aunt Lute.

Anzaldúa, G. (2002). Now let us shift... the path of conocimiento... inner work, public acts. In G. Anzaldúa & A. Keating (Eds.), *This bridge we call home: Radical visions for transformation* (pp. 540–578). New York, NY: Routledge.

Bucholtz, M., & Hall, K. (2005). Identity and interaction: A sociocultural linguistic approach. *Discourse Studies, 7*(4-5), 585–614.

Burciaga, R. (2007). Chicana PhD students living nepantla: Educación and aspirations beyond the doctorate (Unpublished doctoral dissertation). University of California, Los Angeles, CA.

Calderón, D., Delgado Bernal, D., Pérez Huber, L., Malagón, M. C., & Nell Vélez, V. (2012). A Chicana feminist epistemology revisited: Cultivating ideas a generation later. *Harvard Educational Review, 82*(4), 513–567.

Callahan, R. M. (2005). Tracking and high school English learners: Limiting opportunity to learn. *American Educational Research Journal, 42*(2), 305–328.

Cook, V. (2016). Where is the native speaker now? *TESOL Quarterly, 50*(1), 186–189. https://doi.org/10.1002/tesq.286

Creese, A., & Blackledge, A. (2010). Translanguaging in the bilingual classroom: A pedagogy for learning and teaching? *The Modern Language Journal, 94,* 103–115.

Creswell, J. (2007). *Qualitative inquiry and research design* (2nd ed.). Thousand Oaks, CA: SAGE.

Delgado Bernal, D. (1998). Using a chicana feminist epistemology in education research. *Harvard Educational Review, 68,* 555–582.

Delgado Bernal, D. (2001). Learning and living pedagogies of the home: The mestiza consciousness of Chicana students. *International Journal of Qualitative Studies in Education, 14*(5), 623–639.

Delgado Bernal, D., Alemán, E., & Garavito, A. (2009). Latina/o undergraduate students mentoring Latina/o elementary students: A borderlands analysis of shifting identities and first-year experiences. *Harvard Educational Review, 79*(4), 560–585.

Escamilla, K., Hopewell, S., Butvilofsky, S., Sparrow, W., Soltero-González, L., Ruiz-Figueroa, O., & Escamilla, M. (2014). *Biliteracy from the start: Literacy squared in action*. Philadelphia, PA: Caslon.

Flores, N. (2013). Silencing the subaltern: Nation-State/Colonial governmentality and bilingual education in the United States. *Critical Inquiry in Language Studies, 10*(4), 263–287. https://doi.org/10.1080/15427587.2013.846210

Flores, N., & Rosa, J. (2015). Undoing appropriateness: Raciolinguistic ideologies and language diversity in education. *Harvard Educational Review, 85*(2), 149–171.

Gándara, P., Rumberger, R., Maxwell-Jolly, J., & Callahan, R. (2003). English learners in California schools: Unequal resources, unequal outcomes. *Education Policy Analysis Archives, 11*(36), 1–54.

García, O. (2009a). *Bilingual education in the 21st century: A global perspective*. Malden, MA: Wiley-Blackwell.

García, O. (2009b). Emergent bilinguals and TESOL: What's in a name? *TESOL Quarterly, 43*(2), 322–326.

García, O., & Wei, L. (2014). *Translanguaging*. New York, NY: Palgrave MacMillan.

González, F. (2001). *Haciendo que hacer*—cultivating a Mestiza worldview and academic achievement: Braiding cultural knowledge into educational research, policy, practice. *International Journal of Qualitative Studies in Education, 14*(5), 641–656.

Gutiérrez, K. (2008). Developing sociocritical literacies in the Third Space. *Reading Research Quarterly, 43*(2), 146–162.

Gutiérrez, K., Baquedano-López, P., & Tejeda, C. (1999). Rethinking diversity: Hybridity and hybrid language practices in the third space. *Mind, Culture, and Activity, 6*(4), 286–303.

Gutiérrez, K. D. (2016). 2011 AERA presidential address: Designing resilient ecologies: Social design experiments and a new social imagination. *Educational Researcher, 45*(3), 187–196. https://doi.org/10.3102/0013189X16645430

Gutiérrez, K. D., & Jurow, A. S. (2016). Social design experiments: Toward equity by design. *Journal of the Learning Sciences, 25*(4), 565–598. https://doi.org/10.10 80/10508406.2016.1204548

Grinberg, J., & Saavedra, E. (2000). The constitution of bilingual/ESL education as a disciplinary practice: Genealogical explorations. *Review of Educational Research, 70*(4), 419–441.

Hamilton, C. (2017). Bilingualism as a borderlands: Spanish-English bilingual youth's bilingual Mestiza consciousness and designed schooling trajectories. Unpublished doctoral dissertation, University of Wisconsin-Madison.

Ladson-Billings, G. (1995). Toward a theory of culturally relevant pedagogy. *American Educational Research Journal, 32*(3), 465–491.

Martínez, R. A., Orellana, M. F., Pacheco, M., & Carbone, P. (2008). Found in translation: Connecting translating experiences to academic writing. *Language Arts, 85*(6), 421–431.

May, S. (Ed.). (2014). Disciplinary divides, knowledge construction, and the multilingual turn. In *The Multilingual Turn: Implications for SLA, TESOL, and Bilingual Education* (pp. 7–31). New York, NY: Routledge.

Norton, B. (2000). *Identity and language learning: Extending the conversation.* Bristol, England: Multilingual Matters.

Norton, B., & McKinney, C. (2011). An identity approach to second language acquisition. In D. Atkinson (Ed.), *Alternative approaches to second language acquisition* (pp. 73–94). New York, NY: Routledge.

Ochoa, G. L. (2013). *Academic profiling: Latinos, Asian Americans, and the achievement gap.* Minneapolis: University of Minnesota Press.

Orellana, M. F. (2009). *Translating childhoods: Immigrant youth, language, and culture.* Piscataway, NJ: Rutgers University Press.

Pacheco, M. (2009). Expansive learning and Chicana/o and Latina/o students' political-historical knowledge. *Language Arts, 87*(1), 18–29.

Pacheco, M. (2012). Learning in/through everyday resistance: A cultural-historical perspective on community resources and curriculum. *Educational Researcher, 41*(4), 121–132.

Pavlenko, A., & Blackledge, A. (Eds.). (2004). *Negotiation of identities in multilingual settings.* Clevedon, England: Multilingual Matters.

Rymes, B. (2010). Communicative repertoires and English language learners. In M. Shatz & L. C. Wilinson (Eds.), *The education of English language learners* (pp. 177–197). New York, NY: Guilford Press.

Saldaña, J. (2011). *Fundamentals of qualitative research: Understanding qualitative research.* New York, NY: Oxford University Press.

Sandoval, C. (1991). U.S. third world feminism: The theory and method of oppositional consciousness in the postmodern world. *Genders, 10,* 1–24.

Valenzuela, A. (1999). *Subtractive schooling: U.S.–Mexican youth and the politics of caring.* Albany: State University of New York Press.

Villenas, S. A. (2005). Between the telling and the told. In J. Phillion, M. F. He, & F. M. Connelly (Eds.), *Narrative and experience in multicultural education* (pp. 71–94). Thousand Oaks, CA: SAGE.

Villenas, S., & Moreno, M. (2001). To valerse por si misma between race, capitalism, and patriarchy: Latina mother-daughter pedagogies in North Carolina. *International Journal of Qualitative Studies in Education, 14*(5), 671–687. https://doi.org/10.1080/09518390110059883

Weedon, C. (1997). *Feminist practice and poststructuralist theory* (2nd ed.). London, England: Blackwell.

Zentella, A. C. (1997). *Growing up bilingual: Puerto Rican children in New York.* Cambridge, MA: Blackwell.

Zentella, A. C. (2005). (Ed.). *Building on strength: Language and literacy in Latino families and communities.* New York, NY: Teachers College Press.

CHAPTER 12

BILITERACY AS EMOTIONAL PRACTICE

Latina/o Children Building Relationship Through Digital Literacy at an Afterschool Technology Program

Lucila D. Ek
University of Texas at San Antonio

Armando Garza
California State University-Fullerton

Adriana García
Northside Independent School District

ABSTRACT

This chapter explores how supportive relationships are co-constructed through language and literacy practices in an after-school technology program serving Latina/o bilingual elementary students. Analysis found three ways in which children and El Maga (the cyber-being who presides over the

Transforming Schooling for Second Language Learners, pages 217–235
Copyright © 2019 by Information Age Publishing

club) build a friendly, caring relationship: (a) through particular Spanish lexicon; (b) through humorous language practices including dichos y refranes, adivinanzas, y bromas humorísticas (cultural sayings, riddles, and humorous jokes); and (c) through multimodal texts. Children produced linguistically complex texts to build relationships in which their bilingual and bicultural practices were validated, highlighting the role of emotion at the center of bilingualism and biliteracy development.

At Los Árboles Elementary, as soon as the bell rings to signal the end of the school day, the emergent bilingual kids in the *La Clase Mágica* [The Magical Class] club walk to the cafeteria for their juice and pretzel snack with their teacher candidate compañera/os [companions]. Munching on their snacks, they anticipate the day's activities. The iPads emerge from their compañeras'/os' backpacks and the learning begins. For half an hour, the cafeteria fills with the sounds of children and teacher candidates playing games or surfing the web as they chat to each other in Spanish and English.

After snacking, the compañera/o and compañerita/o [elementary students] dyads move to the computer lab. They arrange themselves comfortably in front of one of the PC computers, iPads out. They open a website and a couple clicks takes them to a brightly-colored Maze that contains the day's learning activity. The task card guides the dyads to fun science activities. The card may direct them to a particular website or to a YouTube video that will further instruct them to use manipulatives or a hands-on activity to reinforce their learning. Compañero/a and compañerito/a engage in these activities in Spanish and English.

At the end of their session, children click on the mailbox icon to read the email El Maga sent them. El Maga is the mysterious magical being that presides over this after-school club. Children read their email from El Maga and craft their response.

As panic about the literacy crises in the nation's public schools continues unabated (Enright, 2011; Gehsmann & Templeton, 2012; McDougall, 2010), Latina/o emergent bilingual children are engaging in rich language and literacy practices in informal learning contexts that are often overlooked by traditional assessments of children's language and literacy learning. *La Clase Mágica* at the University of Texas at San Antonio (LCM@UTSA), an after-school technology program, exemplifies the robust learning experiences of Latina/o bilingual elementary-aged students in such spaces. Drawing from a larger multi-year qualitative project, we examine how positive, supportive relationships are co-constructed through language and literacy practices in this informal learning space. Our scholarly focus is grounded in *new literacy studies* as these theories counter traditional orientations that view literacy as merely the acquisition of a set of skills including reading and writing (Street, 2001). Rather, literacy is a social practice shaped by social relationships, culture, and ideological values.

This chapter centers on a key language and literacy practice of LCM@ UTSA: the email writing between the children and El Maga. El Maga's emails have been constant for 4 years for a majority of the children. In particular, we focus on how the children's (and El Maga's) language choices and uses within written texts build a caring relationship between the children and El Maga. Our analysis yielded three ways that they built a friendly, caring relationship: (a) through particular Spanish lexicon; (b) through humorous language practices including *dichos y refranes, adivinanzas, y bromas humorísticas* [cultural sayings, riddles, and humorous jokes]; and (c) through multimodal texts. These findings place emotion at the center of children's bilingualism and biliteracy development.

NEW LITERACY STUDIES

New literacy studies (NLS) challenge traditional orientations that view literacy as the acquisition of a set of skills including reading and writing (Gee, 2015; Street, 2001). Rather, NLS argues that literacy is a social practice; moreover, this theory points to the existence of multiple literacies that are cultural and ideological and vary from cultural group to cultural group (Street, 2001). With regards to literacy learning, NLS highlights the importance of context and culture in shaping how literacy is defined, constructed, and enacted. Social relationships constitute a significant component of this context. Part of what makes literacy social are the actors engaged with one another as they create and use texts in particular ways for particular goals. A focus on building social relationships necessitates a discussion of the role of affect. Hence, we look at how affect is co-constructed linguistically in El Maga's and the children's writings to one another. Their email exchanges constitute a biliteracy practice that is reflective of the environment of the after-school technology program. Bilingual Latina/o children develop social and academic skills including their voices (Ek, García, & Garza, 2014). Recognizing literacy as a product of social and cultural practices illuminates these children's own intricate linguistic and literate practices.

Building on the early work in the NLS tradition, researchers have focused on new literacy practices that are mediated by new technologies (Knobel & Lankshear, 2007; Lam & Rosario-Ramos, 2009; Lankshear & Knobel, 2006). These literacy practices have been dubbed "digital literacies" and research in this area acknowledges the complex multimodal, multimedia aspect of these practices (Lewis & Fabos, 2005). Scholarship devoted to understanding how youth engage in digital practices in their daily lives tends to focus on students who are monolingual or whose first language is English (Coiro,

Knobel, Lankshear, & Leu, 2008; Hagood, Leander, Luke, Mackey, & Nixon, 2003). Nevertheless, the studies that examine bilingual students and technology have contributed much to our understandings of how engagement in digital literacies is key to identity formation, maintenance of the heritage language, and acquisition of a second language (Lam & Rosario-Ramos, 2009; Lam & Warriner, 2012; Sánchez & Salazar, 2012).

According to Gee (2015), literacy includes both particular ways of using language to read and write as well as emotions and values. Our study illuminates how emotion is embedded in digital literacies.

BICULTURAL-BILINGUAL LATINA/O CHILDREN'S LANGUAGE PRACTICES, BILITERACY, AND AFFECT

Scholarship focused on students' bilingualism and biliteracy highlight the significance of language as a resource (Bauer & Gort, 2012). Researchers have documented Latina/o bilinguals' code-switching (Zentella, 1997), hybrid language use (Gutiérrez, Baquedano-López, Alvarez, & Chiu, 1999), and translanguaging (García, 2009).

Significant sociocultural work which examines the hybrid language and literacy practices—that is, the strategic use of multiple codes and registers—of bilingual (English/Spanish) students includes studies of an afterschool computer club (Gutiérrez, Baquedano-López, Alvarez, et al., 1999) and of an elementary classroom (Gutiérrez, Baquedano-López, & Tejeda, 1999). These studies reframe the role of language in the formal and informal classroom from the object of instruction to a tool for learning. Gutiérrez, Baquedano-López, Alvarez et al.'s (1999) study demonstrates the importance of language as a central mediating tool in fostering the learning and socialization of Martha, a third-grade bilingual Latina. In an exchange of email letters with El Maga (the cyberspace entity who presided over the computer club), Martha drew upon a repertoire of codes (English and Spanish) and registers to accomplish particular goals including building a relationship with the cyber being. This repertoire of codes represents a rich corpus of linguistic and literacy tools that serve as means of communication and production of understandings (Ek et al., 2014).

In a similar way, our study builds on research on Latinos'/as' productions in hybrid language and literacy practices (de la Piedra, 2009; González, 2001; Gutiérrez, Baquedano-López, Alvarez et al., 1999) and/or translanguaging practices (García, 2009), where affect, conveyed through language, mediates social relationships. Gutiérrez Baquedano-López, Alvarez, and Chiu (1999), in particular, laid the theoretical groundwork for our analytical focus here given that its setting is similar to our site. LCM@UTSA is a flexible learning space that celebrates biculturalism and bilingualism.

As such, bilingual children and teacher candidates have the freedom to use all their linguistic resources at their disposal to foster biliteracy development. Using these ideas, LCM@UTSA provides a context to build a translanguaging space that "allows multilingual individuals to integrate social spaces (and thus 'language codes') that have formerly practiced separately in different places" (García & Li Wei, 2014, p. 24). In this learning space, those linguistic codes are observed as formal and informal use of Spanish and English, linguistic borrowings from either language, specific anglicisms, and other types of linguistic registers.

Affect and Language and Literacy Practices

As Ochs and Schieffelin (1989) and González (2001) have demonstrated, emotion is inextricably connected to language. Highlighting the role of emotion in the language practices of bilingual Latinas/os, González writes that emotion is "the infrastructure for child language socialization, a processual and dynamic locus for constructing meaning and identity. Emotion to the child is ubiquitous. Language does more than index prefabricated affective structures, and emotion does not have to be contextualized" (p. 49). Using these ideas, we claim that any examination of bilingual children's biliteracy must also be an investigation of their language practices which are interconnected with affect to convey specific meanings.

Because literacy is multidimensional, language and literacy development go hand in hand with children's social and emotional growth (Figueroa-Sánchez, 2008). In fact, emotional development has a crucial impact on children's cognitive and interpersonal skills (Hirsh-Pasek, Golinkoff, & Eyer, 2003). Thus, along with the development of their emotional literacy, Latino/a children need to have a space and opportunities to engage in activities that foster their language and literacy development (Ek et al., 2014)—activities in which children are able to reflect their own sociocultural community contexts.

Cultural tools such as *dichos y refranes, adivinanzas, y bromas humorísticas* [cultural sayings, riddles, and humorous jokes] have been present among Latina/o communities for generations and are constantly used to express love, strength, friendship, and playfulness. Teachers and educational researchers, trying to promote reading and writing skills of this student population, have been interested in using and exploring these cultural linguistic practices (e.g., Espinoza-Herold, 2007).

Researchers have examined *dichos y refranes* as linguistic and cultural resources to explore print-literacy skills between Latina/o parents and their children (Espinoza-Herold, 2007; Sanchez, Plata, Grosso, & Leird, 2010; Smith & Riojas-Cortez, 2010). For instance, Smith and Riojas-Cortez (2010) documented how parents expressed love and caring to their children through *cartitas de cariño* [little notes to say you care]. Through *cartitas,* they realized that researchers and teachers can learn from writing experiences that are full of emotional creativity and powerful words—*cartitas,* as the product of writing with love, showed "a meaningful and meaning-laden form of literacy" (p. 131). Indeed, the participants of this study used their own knowledge and the linguistic and cultural tools they had at their disposal to express love and caring. In addition, Smith and Riojas-Cortez reported that the *cartitas* are both effective and affective tools to socialize children—and excellent resources to create letters of love and endearment as a meaningful activity.

Writing letters is an opportunity to engage Latina/o children in language and literacy development. Bilingual Latina/o children use their own ways of speaking to communicate with peers, friends, and family (Ek et al., 2014; González, 2001). In the effort to convey their own meaning, bilingual Latina/o children extend their cultural and linguistic repertoire by incorporating specific lexicons that they capture from the media or from their immediate social and cultural environments. Moreover, when they communicate using written text, their choices of specific signs or symbols are based on their lived experiences (Janks, 2001), and comprehension will depend on the shared understandings of those specific signs, symbols, and/or rules (Fairclough, 2000).

METHODS

For this paper, we draw from a larger ongoing qualitative research study of LCM@UTSA which is a partnership between the Academy of Teacher Excellence at UTSA and Los Árboles Elementary[1] (Ek, Machado-Casas, Sánchez, & Alanis, 2010). LCM@UTSA is designed to promote the academic achievement of bilingual Latina/o elementary-aged students, particularly in the areas of bilingualism, biliteracy, and technology (for a detailed description of LCM@UTSA see Bustos Flores, Vásquez, & Riojas Clark, 2014). The project was modeled on the original *La Clase Mágica,* an award-winning afterschool program (Vásquez, 2003) as well on UCLA's Las Redes project (Gutiérrez, Baquedano-López, Alvarez et al., 1999). The project is now in its fifth year, and its team includes several professors and doctoral students. Following a "social design experimentation" framework (Gutiérrez, 2016; Gutiérrez & Jurow, 2016) to promote equity and learning for nondominant students, LCM@UTSA is committed to improving the educational and social circumstances of Latina/o communities mainly composed of bilingual teacher candidates, K–12 bilingual students and their parents, and teachers.

Each semester, a cohort of 20–25 bilingual teacher candidates—primarily Latinas/os—enroll in classes that include fieldwork at LCM@UTSA once a week for 2 hours (typically 8 to 11 weeks). Every Tuesday, bilingual teacher candidates, called "compañeros/as" (companions) meet their "compañeritos/as" [little companions], the school-aged children who eagerly await them to engage in that day's learning activities. UTSA students are provided with iPads to use with Los Árboles Elementary school students; the school provides a computer lab. Each bilingual teacher candidate is paired with one child with whom to engage in various online activities, write digital stories, use mobile device apps, and explore other educational software.

For this paper, we analyzed data collected in the spring of 2013. During this semester, there were 22 bilingual elementary school Latino/a students who participated in LCM@UTSA. All attended Los Árboles Elementary and were enrolled in the school's dual-language program; 21 were of Mexican origin and 1 was of Honduran origin in Grades PK–5.

Although the new teacher candidates enroll in LCM@UTSA each semester, the children can stay in the program until they graduate from fifth grade (or leave the school). During this semester, unbeknownst to the children, teacher candidates, and some of the professors, Garza and García were both El Maga. Garza and García always attended each of the LCM@UTSA sessions as part of the UTSA-team—children considered them as teachers most of the time. Their roles had specific purposes; however, they were always observing the students' and teacher-candidates' work so they could use those literacy events as potential topics for their exchange of emails. Given their key role in developing children's writings, we include a brief description of Garza's and García's backgrounds.

Garza was born and raised in Monterrey, México. His education was in the public school system from kindergarten to college. He attended a state university that included high school. He began learning English as a teenager and studied English in Monterrey. At 25 years of age, he began studying English in the United States, obtained his master's degree in Georgia, and returned to Mexico for a couple of years. In fall of 2010, he moved to San Antonio, eventually completing his PhD. He is now an assistant professor of elementary and bilingual education in Southern California.

García was educated in public schools in San Antonio, Texas, and transitioned from her native Spanish to English upon entering first grade. She left Spanish in her public life, speaking it at home and translating for her parents when they needed it, and in college she began to realize and appreciate the value of her bilingualism. She quickly grew enamored with the intricacies of the Spanish language, and majoring in English and Spanish, committed to never forgetting her bicultural background. She is a bilingual education and language support teacher in San Antonio.

DATA COLLECTION AND ANALYSIS

The larger corpus of data that has been collected includes: weekly field-notes written by the teacher candidates (in either English or Spanish), demographic and technology surveys from the families of each elementary school student, digital and print artifacts produced by the children and family members, children's and El Maga's emails, digital self-narratives, and video recordings of children's presentations of their projects. For this paper, we analyzed the children's and El Maga's emails collected in the spring of 2013 guided by the question: How do children and El Maga construct an affective social relationship with one another through their email exchanges? Because we did not want García's and Garza's experience as El Maga to influence our analysis, Ek conducted the analysis of the emails. She read through them several times, coding to identify salient themes, patterns, and relationships. Multiple codings challenged initial interpretations of themes and helped refine later interpretations.

Central to our analysis was a focus on the discourse found in the children's and El Maga's correspondence. We looked at the children's choice of code and variety of code, lexicon, and how these indexed particular emotions. In addition, we examined children's innovative uses of text that included emoticons. We also considered how children and El Maga co-constructed affective stances in their emails to each other. Stances can be either epistemological or affective positions in an exchange between participants (Ochs, 1993). The process of analyzing the emails prompted Ek to ask Garza and García to reflect on their own cultural and linguistic backgrounds. Ek's identification of the analytical themes also prompted her to ask García and Garza several questions about their language choices and uses when writing to the children. Centering our analysis on language and literacy practices and emotions, findings are grouped into the following categories (a) co-constructing friendship through Spanish lexicon, (b) co-constructing play through humorous language practices, and (c) the use of multimodal texts to convey fondness.

CO-CONSTRUCTING FRIENDSHIP
THROUGH SPANISH LEXICON

El Maga and the children were very friendly to each other in their emails and they explicitly referred to each other with " *amig@*," " *amiguis*," " *cuate*" to signal their affiliation. The following example comes from one of El Maga's emails to Andrea (pseudonym), a first-grade student:

Hola Andrea, {Hi Andrea,

¿Cómo estás amiguis? Yo estoy muy {How are you friend? I am very

bien porque estoy feliz como una lombriz.	{well because I am happy as a tapeworm.
Qué bueno que te gusta leer, estudiar, eres	{How good that you like to read, to study, you
una niña inteligente. Ya me platicó [Mariana]	{are a smart girl. [Mariana] already told me
que hicieron para su cumpleaños suena que	{what you did for her birthday it sounds like
se divirtieron mucho.	{you (pl.) had a lot of fun.
Un chiste para ti:	{A joke for you:
-Un/a niñ@ está haciendo su tarea y	{-A girl/boy is doing her/his homework and
pregunta a su padre:	{asks her/his father:
-Papá ¿Cómo se escribe campana?	{-Dad, how do you write bell?
-Campana se escribe "como suena"	{-You write bell how it sounds.
-Entonces ¿Escribo "talán-talán"?	{-Then, do I write, "ding-dong"?
¡Como dijo el cirujano, parto sin dolor!	{Like the surgeon says, I split without pain.
El Maga	{El Maga

Here, El Maga referred to Andrea with the endearment "*amiguis*" [friend] which comes from "*amiguita*" [little female friend]. García learned the word from a Mexican soap opera that used "*amiguis*" to address a female friend so she only used it to address the girls while speaking sweetly or in a playful manner. Although El Maga referred to himself/herself as amig@ to maintain the mystery around his/her gender, some students referred to him/her as "*cuate*" which is a Mexican idiomatic expression or slang for *amigo* (masculine). *Cuate* is used very informally among young people, especially children and teenagers (mostly male). Taking up the use of *cuate*, El Maga began referring to the boys as *cuates*.

The children also signaled their caring for El Maga through terminology that directly expressed their feelings. Linda, for example, often closed her email to El Maga with the phrase, "*Con cariños tu amiga, Linda*" [With fondness your friend, Linda]. Smith and Riojas-Cortez (2010) define *cariño* as "the notion of fondness or tenderness expressed through words and actions" (p. 128). As such, they explored how Latino/a parents express love and caring for their children through *cartitas de cariño*. In these letters, parents described a variety of actions that demonstrated *cariño* towards their children. Though *cariño* is considered a singular noun, when it is utilized in a plural form, as Linda used it, it signals the possible existence of several manifestations of love and tenderness towards someone.

CO-CONSTRUCTING PLAY THROUGH HUMOROUS
LANGUAGE PRACTICES

As exemplified in El Maga's email to Andrea above, El Maga was often play-ful and humorous with the students through language practices including *dichos* (cultural sayings) such as *feliz como una lombriz* [happy as a tapeworm], *chistes* [jokes] such as *¡Como dijo el cirujano, parto sin dolor!* [Like the surgeon says, I split without pain], and *adivinanzas* [riddles]. The children of LCM@ UTSA also displayed their sense of humor and knowledge of these linguis-tic practices. An extended example of the children's uptake of El Maga's humor occurred with Ernesto.

Hola Ernesto,	{Hi Ernesto,
Suena muy interesante tu fotonovela espero	{Your fotonovela sounds very interesting I hope
leerla muy pronto. Qué buena pregunta	{to read it very soon. What a good question,
me haces, fíjate que Los Magas comemos	{notice that we Magas eat
muchas frutas y verduras para mantenernos	{many fruits and vegetables to be
sanos e inteligentes. . . .	{healthy and intelligent. . . .
¡Como dijo el gran queso al rato regreso!	{Like the great cheese said I'll be back later!
El Maga	{El Maga
——	——
Hola maga!	{Hi Maga,
A mi tambien me encanta la fruta, como las	{I too love fruit, like
manzanas y las naranjas y peras pero a mi	{apples and oranges and pears but they don't
no me da poderes magicos.	{give me magic powers.
abamos [sic] *al rato*	{we'll talk later
Este osito de peluche, ya se va para su	{This teddy bear is now going to his
estuche!	{box!
ernesto	{ernesto

Because *dichos*, or cultural sayings, are usually transmitted orally, they are part of the culture of some Latina/o families. One of the characteristics of these sayings is their rhythmic and playful tone which instills in children a desire for repetition and memorization framed under play pedagogies (Ger-villa Castillo, 2006). After one person, perhaps an adult, utters a *dicho*, the child is prompted to respond back by providing another one—sometimes children use their creativity and invent one. And in turn, children create a repertoire of cultural sayings that will be used throughout the years and generations. This cultural and pedagogical practice is present in Mexico's PK–6 school curriculum (http://www.curriculobasica.sep.gob.mx).

The exchange between Ernesto and El Maga is an example of this linguistic and cultural practice. El Maga was providing a cultural saying with, *"¡Como dijo el gran queso, al rato regreso!"* and when analyzing this *dicho,* questions were raised among other Latina/o Spanish speakers about it as written by El Maga. They remembered the saying as *"Como dijo el ratón al queso, al rato regreso"* [Like the mouse said to the cheese, I'll be back later]. García explained that her father would tell her the saying every morning before he left for work thus making the language practice more applicable to that specific context of a father telling his daughter he will see her later. As in English, in Mexican Spanish, the *"gran queso"* [big cheese], using the superlative, refers to someone important.

As the exchange shows, Ernesto clearly understood El Maga's saying and responded to her/him with the goodbye phrase *"abamos* [sic] *al rato"* (we'll talk later). This signals that within these biliteracy practices, cultural understandings (Ek et al., 2014) were constantly present. In addition to this playful cultural dialogue, Ernesto finished his email by adding *"Este osito de peluche, ya se va para su estuche!"* [This teddy bear is now going to his box!]. Basically, Ernesto was saying goodbye by using the cultural linguistic practice that El Maga modeled before. Furthermore, Ernesto was using his funds of knowledge (González, Moll, & Amanti, 2005) to effectively communicate through bicultural linguistic practices.

In a similar way, El Maga made use of riddles that are common in Mexico and other Latin American countries. As pointed out earlier, the use of *adivinanzas* [riddles] is another cultural and pedagogical tool that is commonly utilized to enhance language and literacy development. The following email is an example of how El Maga made use of these kinds of riddles.

Hola [Ernesto,]	{Hi [Ernesto,]
Que buen chiste Ernesto se los conté a mis	{What a good joke Ernesto I told it to my
amigos Magas y se carcajearon de la	{Maga friends and they chuckled with
risa . . . Te mando unos chistes de	{Laughter . . . I send you some funny
adivinanza espero que te gusten.	{riddles hope you like them.
¿Cuál es mayor la luna o el sol?	{What is older the moon or the sun?
Respuesta: La luna, porque la dejan salir	{Answer: The moon, because they let her go out
de noche.	{at night.
¿Qué le dijo un ojo al otro ojo?	{What did one eye say to another eye?

Respuesta: Tan cerquita y no nos vemos.	{Answer: So close and we don't see each other.
Tu amig@,	{Your friend,
El Maga	{El Maga

The sharing of *dichos, chistes,* and *adivinanzas* between El Maga and Ernesto took place over several weeks as Ernesto provided wittier and wittier jokes. One of Ernesto's last jokes was in the following email:

Hola Maga	{Hi Maga,
En spring break mi familia y yo ivamos [sic]	{During Spring Break my family and I were
a ir a la playa, pero estubo [sic] *lloviendo*	{going to go to the beach, but it was raining a lot
mucho y no pudimos ir.	{and we couldn't go. . . .
Me gustan tus chistes pero yo tengo uno	{I like your jokes but I have one
para ti	{for you
ABUELA, ABUELA	{GRANDMOTHER, GRANDMOTHER,
TENGO UN IPOD,	{I HAVE AN IPOD,
Y LA ABUELA LE RESPONDE-	{AND THE GRANDMOTHER RESPONDS-
TRANQUILO CON UN VASO DE	{CALM DOWN WITH A GLASS OF
AGUA Y UN SUSTO SE TE QUITA	{WATER AND A SCARE IT'LL GO AWAY.
Adios	Good bye
Ernesto	Ernesto

Although El Maga's and the children's emails were primarily in Spanish, as we have demonstrated in other work (Ek et al., 2014), the use of translanguaging practices (García, 2009) was common and considered a resource for developing children's biliteracy. In the email above, the English word, "IPOD" pronounced with Spanish phonology is the key to the joke in that it sounds like the word *hipo* [hiccup]. That the grandmother in the joke confuses the word IPOD signals a generational digital gap, where the older generation may not be familiar with newer technology. Once again, Ernesto was responding to the prompts that El Maga was giving, and he was using cultural and linguistic resources to enact biliteracy emotional practices.

USE OF MULTIMODAL TEXTS TO CONVEY FONDNESS

We found that children's and El Maga's use of multimodal texts helped construct high emotional intensity through different font sizes, capital letters, and multiple exclamation points, among other markers. For example, El Maga greeted Elena with: *¡¡¡Holaaaaaaaaaa Elenaaaaaaaaaaa!!!* [Hellooooooooooo Elenaaaaaaaaaaa!!!]. Multimodal text is defined as those texts that have more than one "mode" so that meaning is communicated through a synchronization of modes (Gee, 2003; Kress, 2003; Kress et al., 2005; Kress & Van Leeuwen, 2001; Lankshear & Knobel, 2006). Similar to de la Piedra's (2013) study which documented how the genre of *consejo* draws from diverse forms of multimodal literacies such as expression, including verbal, print, aural, visual, spatial, and behavioral forms of communication, El Maga drew on a mix of print language as well as other multimodal resources in order to provide "*consejo*" and "*cariño*" to the children.

At LCM@UTSA the children interact with El Maga through a digital medium that allows them to do so in multimodal ways. Hence, children's literacy resources include not only words but also pictures, photos, and emoticons. Moreover, the visual images "show" interpersonal meaning that is developed through a visual "voice" (Bearne, 2003; Kress, 2003). Emoticons are defined as "[a] sequential combination of keyboard characters designed to convey the emotion associated with a particular facial expression" (Crystal, 2004, p. 39). As such, children used emoticons to express their emotions such as in this email from Elena to El Maga:

Hola Maga,	{Hi Maga
Es bien te gusto mi fotonovela. Me disgusta	{It's good that you like my *fotonovela*. I dislike
que ya se acabe la clase magíca, yo quiero	{that *clase magica* is ending, I want
que continue. Pero ya voy a la secundaria	{it to continue. But I am going to middle school
año quentra [sic]. *Bueno ya me tengo que*	{this next year. Well I already have
despidir [sic], *nunca me olvidare de la clase*	{to say goodbye, I will never forget *la clase*
mágica :(*	{*mágica :*(*
Elena Rodriguez y Dianela Ramos (teacher candidate)	{Elena Rodriguez and Daniela Ramos (teacher candidate)

Fifth-grader Elena expressed her sadness about having to graduate from LCM@UTSA with the usual open parenthesis but she intensified the motion by adding a tear represented by an asterisk. Emoticons such as :O and ;(were often used by children. Emoticons transcend languages and are used to clarify meaning and show emotions without providing lengthy explanations (Kruger, Epley, Parker, & Ng, 2005). In addition to emoticons, several compañeritas/os used photographs or images that they collected from the educational software they were using. Though the scope of this chapter does not include the analysis of such visual representations, we mention them here as a way to extend our discussion of multimodal texts to convey fondness.

The emails gave children more freedom to move away from using standard orthography. Even though El Maga provided a model for standard grammar and spelling, he/she did not correct children's grammar, syntax, or spelling. Perhaps because of this, children felt free to resist conventional ways of writing.

CONCLUSIONS

We have focused on one of the language and literacy practices in an after-school technology program designed to develop emergent bilingual Latina/o children's bilingualism, biliteracy, and digital literacies. We analyzed emails written by the children and El Maga, a magical being who resides in cyberspace. We found that El Maga and the children co-constructed a caring and supportive relationship that nurtured the children's use of their linguistic repertoires including Spanish, specific Latina/o language practices such as *dichos y refranes, adivinanzas, y bromas humorísticas* [cultural sayings, riddles, and humorous jokes]. In addition, the use of digital media afforded children the freedom to use multimodal texts including emoticons. That El Maga is bilingual and bicultural was also key to developing the children's biliteracy, particularly in Spanish. The bilingual Latina/o children in this study produced a variety of linguistically complex texts to produce certain affective stances that built the relationship with El Maga, who not only recognized but also validated students' bilingual and bicultural practices.

TRANSFORMATIVE PRACTICES IN OTHER CONTEXTS

Informal learning spaces like LCM@UTSA are key sites for emergent bilingual children both to demonstrate and to acquire language and literacy skills. LCM@UTSA is also a significant space that addresses the growing digital divide where working-class Latina/o children and their families have limited access to technology and to developing digital literacies. It is imperative that scholars and educators continue to address issues of bilingualism and biliteracy and how these are mediated by new technologies for Latina/o bilingual students.

As we described in this chapter, the use of multimodal literacy practices influenced how culturally and linguistically diverse students developed biliteracy skills. It is important for school administrators and educational advocates to be aware of these types of literacies and to envision how such practices can be implemented in school settings. In addition, we urge teacher educators to include the broad array of NLS in their curriculum; we join the body of researchers (e.g., Bauer & Gort, 2012; Martinez-Alvarez, Cuevas, & Torres-Guzman, 2017; Martínez-Roldán & Smagorinsky, 2011; Molle, Sato, Boals, & Hedgspeth, 2015; Téllez & Varghese, 2013; Wiemelt & Welton, 2015) advocating for a more encompassing training of a new generation of teachers of bilingual and emergent bilingual students. We strongly believe that programs such as LCM@UTSA can be implemented in other settings where biculturalism, bilingualism, and biliteracy are pursued in a variety of languages and cultures (e.g., Bigelow, Vanek, King, & Abdi, 2017; Gynne & Bagga-Gupta, 2015; Honeyford, 2014; Martinez-Alvarez et al., 2017).

TRANSFORMATIVE POLICIES

The lessons learned from the LCM@UTSA project also have implications for educational policy particularly as the Latina/o population continues to grow. As our project has shown, Latina/o students' use of Spanish is key to their learning and development. Thus, policymakers must champion and increase bilingual education programs for both English learners and heritage language learners to counter the constant attacks on bilingual education. Policymakers can address the digital divide by recognizing schools as key spaces for providing working-class students access to technology and supporting the creation of additional programs such as LCM.

TRANSFORMATIVE PEDAGOGIES

Rather than focusing on what children cannot do, researchers and practitioners must learn to see the complex language and literacy practices that bilingual and emergent bilingual children engage in, particularly in informal contexts. The cultural and linguistic practices of culturally and linguistically diverse students are rich funds of knowledge (González et al., 2005) that need to be utilized in formal and informal school settings to promote language and literacy development. Teacher educators must take into account these practices and train their pre- and in-service teachers so they conceive culture and language varieties as powerful tools for learning (e.g., Durán & Palmer, 2014; Ek & Domínguez Chávez, 2015; Garza, 2017; Garza & Langman, 2014; Orellana, Martínez, Lee, & Montaño, 2012).

IMPLICATIONS FOR FUTURE RESEARCH

Latina/o bilingual children should receive validation and *cariño* not only from cyber beings in after-school technology clubs, but from teachers, administrators, and policymakers. There is a need for more research into how affect is being utilized in formal school settings. Furthermore, we invite practitioners to observe how such emotional practices develop literacy and biliteracy skills and how emotional literacies are embedded in cultural and linguistic practices.

As we described in this chapter, bilingual and emergent bilingual students' use of visual images to convey meaning requires more research to leverage these multimodal literacy practices as important pedagogical tools. Ultimately, the use of multimodal texts—where different codes, language variations, and hybrid practices are represented—need to be studied as positive ways to promote biculturalism, biliteracy, and bilingualism.

NOTE

1. All names (school, children, and teacher candidates) are pseudonyms.

REFERENCES

Bauer, E. B., & Gort, M. (Eds.). (2012). *Early biliteracy development: Exploring young learners' use of their linguistic resources*. New York, NY: Routledge.

Bearne, E. (2003). Rethinking literacy: Communication, representation and text. *Reading, 37*(3), 98–103. doi:10.1046/j.0034-0472.2003.03703002.x

Bigelow, M., Vanek, J., King, K., & Abdi, N. (2017). Literacy as social (media) practice: Refugee youth and native language literacy at school. *International Journal of Intercultural Relations, 60,* 183–197. doi:10.1016/j.ijintrel.2017.04.002

Bustos Flores, B., Vásquez, O. A., & Riojas Clark, E. (Eds.). (2014). *Generating transworld pedagogy: Reimagining la clase mágica.* New York, NY: Lexington Books.

Coiro, J., Knobel, M., Lankshear, C., & Leu, D. J. (Eds.). (2008). *Handbook of research on new literacies.* Mahwah, NJ: Erlbaum.

Crystal, D. (2004). *A glossary of netspeak and textspeak.* Edinburgh, Scotland: Edinburgh University Press.

de la Piedra, M. T. (2009). Hybrid literacies: The case of a Quechua community in the Andes. *Anthropology & Education Quarterly, 40*(2), 110–128. doi:10.1111/j.1548-1492.2009.01031.x

de la Piedra, M. T. (2013). Consejo as a literacy event: A case study of a border Mexican woman. *Language Arts, 90*(5), 339–350.

Durán, L., & Palmer, D. (2014). Pluralist discourses of bilingualism and translanguaging talk in classrooms. *Journal of Early Childhood Literacy, 14*(3), 367–388.

Ek, L. D., & Domínguez Chávez, G. (2015). Proyecto bilingüe: Constructing a figured world of bilingual education for Latina/o bilingual teachers. *Bilingual Research Journal, 38*(2), 134–151. doi:10.1080/15235882.2015.1064834

Ek, L. D., García, A. S., & Garza, A. (2014). Latino children: Constructing identities, voices, linguistic, and cultural understandings. In B. Bustos Flores, O. A. Vásquez, & E. Riojas Clark (Eds.), *Generating transworld pedagogy: Reimagining la clase mágica* (pp. 129–142). New York, NY: Lexington Books.

Ek, L. D., Machado-Casas, M., Sanchez, P., & Alanis, I. (2010). Crossing cultural borders: La Clase Mágica as a university–school partnership. *Journal of School Leadership, 20*(6), 820–848.

Enright, K. A. (2011). Language and literacy for a new mainstream. *Part of a special section on Social and Institutional Analysis, 48*(1), 80–118. doi:10.3102/0002831210368989

Espinoza-Herold, M. (2007). Stepping beyond 'sí se puede: Dichos' as a cultural resource in mother–daughter interaction in a Latino family. *Anthropology & Education Quarterly, 38*(3), 260–277.

Fairclough, N. (2000). Multi-literacies and language: Orders of discourse and intertextuality. In B. Cope & M. Kalantzis (Eds.), *Multi-literacies: Literacy learning and the design of social futures* (pp. 162–181). London, England: Routledge.

Figueroa-Sánchez, M. (2008). Building emotional literacy: Groundwork to early learning. *Childhood Education, 84*(5), 301–304.

García, O. (2009). *Bilingual education in the 21st century: A global perspective.* Malden, MA: Wiley-Blackwell.

García, O., & Li Wei. (2014). *Translanguaging: Language, bilingualism and education.* New York, NY: Palgrave Macmillan.

Garza, A. (2017). Negativo por negativo me da dar un . . . POSITIvo: Translanguaging as a vehicle for appropriation of mathematical meanings. In J. Langman & H. Hansen-Thomas (Eds.), *Discourse analytic perspectives on STEM education: Exploring interaction and learning in the multilingual classroom* (pp. 99–116). Cham, Switzerland: Springer.

Garza, A., & Langman, J. (2014). Translanguaging in a Latin@ bilingual community: Negotiations and mediations in a dual-language classroom. *Association of Mexican-American Educators, 8*(1), 37–49.

Gee, J. P. (2003). *What video games have to teach us about learning and literacy* (1st ed.). New York, NY: Palgrave Macmillan.

Gee, J. P. (2015). *Social linguistics and literacies: Ideology in discourses* (5th ed.). New York, NY: Routledge.

Gehsmann, K. M., & Templeton, S. (2012). Stages and standards in literacy: Teaching developmentally in the age of accountability. *Journal of Education, 192*(1), 5–16.

Gervilla Castillo, Á. (2006). *Didáctica básica de la educación infantil: Conocer y comprender a los más pequeños.* Madrid, Spain: Narcea, S. A. de Ediciones.

González, N. (2001). *I am my language: Discourses of women & children in the borderlands.* Tucson, AZ: University of Arizona Press.

González, N., Moll, L. C., & Amanti, C. (Eds.). (2005). *Funds of knowledge: Theorizing practice in households, communities, and classrooms.* Mahwah, NJ: L. Erlbaum.

Gutiérrez, K. D. (2016). Designing resilient ecologies: Social design experiments and a new social imagination. *Educational Researcher, 45*(3), 187–196.

Gutiérrez, K. D., Baquedano-López, P., Alvarez, H. H., & Chiu, M. M. (1999). Building a culture of collaboration through hybrid language practices. *Theory Into Practice, 38*(2), 87–93. https://doi.org/10.1080/00405849909543837

Gutiérrez, K. D., Baquedano-López, P., & Tejeda, C. (1999). Rethinking diversity: Hybridity and hybrid language practices in the third space. *Mind, Culture & Activity, 6*(4), 286–303.

Gutiérrez, K. D., & Jurow, A. S. (2016). Social design experiments: Toward equity by design. *Journal of the Learning Sciences, 25*(4), 565–598.

Gynne, A., & Bagga-Gupta, S. (2015). Languaging in the twenty-first century: Exploring varieties and modalities in literacies inside and outside learning spaces. *Language & Education: An International Journal, 29*(6), 509–526.

Hagood, M. C., Leander, K. M., Luke, C., Mackey, M., & Nixon, H. (2003). Media and online literacy studies. *Reading Research Quarterly, 38*(3), 386–413. doi:10.1598/RRQ.38.3.4

Hirsh-Pasek, K., Golinkoff, R. M., & Eyer, D. E. (2003). *Einstein never used flash cards: How our children really learn and why they need to play more and memorize less.* Emmaus, PA.: Rodale Press.

Honeyford, M. A. (2014). From aquí and allá: Symbolic convergence in the multimodal literacy practices of adolescent immigrant students. *Journal of Literacy Research, 46*(2), 194–233.

Janks, H. (2001). Identity and conflict in the critical literacy classroom. In B. Comber & A. Simpson (Eds.), *Negotiating critical literacies in classrooms.* Mahwah, NJ: Erlbaum.

Knobel, M., & Lankshear, C. (2007). *A new literacies sampler.* New York, NY: P. Lang.

Kress, G. R. (2003). *Literacy in the new media age.* New York, NY: Routledge.

Kress, G. R., Jewitt, C., Bourne, J., Franks, A., Hardcastle, J., Jones, K., & Reid, E. (2005). *English in urban classrooms: A multimodal perspective on teaching and learning.* New York, NY: Routledge Falmer.

Kress, G. R., & Van Leeuwen, T. (2001). *Multimodal discourse: The modes and media of contemporary communication.* London, England: Oxford University Press.

Kruger, J., Epley, N., Parker, J., & Ng, Z.-W. (2005). Egocentrism over e-mail: Can we communicate as well as we think? *Journal of Personality and Social Psychology, 89*(6), 925–936.

Lam, W. S. E., & Rosario-Ramos, E. (2009). Multilingual literacies in transnational digitally mediated contexts: An exploratory study of immigrant teens in the United States. *Language and Education, 23*(2), 171–190.

Lam, W. S. E., & Warriner, D. S. (2012). Transnationalism and literacy: Investigating the mobility of people, languages, texts, and practices in contexts of migration. *Reading Research Quarterly, 47*(2), 191–215. doi:10.1002/rrq.016

Lankshear, C., & Knobel, M. (2006). *New literacies: Everyday practices and classroom learning* (2nd ed.). New York, NY: Open University Press.

Lewis, C., & Fabos, B. (2005). Instant messaging, literacies, and social identities. *Reading Research Quarterly, 40*(4), 470–501. doi:10.1598/RRQ.40.4.5

Martinez-Alvarez, P., Cuevas, I., & Torres-Guzman, M. (2017). Preparing bilingual teachers: Mediating belonging with multimodal explorations in language, identity, and culture. *Journal of Teacher Education, 68*(2), 155–178. doi:10.1177/00224871 16685752

Martínez-Roldán, C. M., & Smagorinsky, P. (2011). Computer-mediated learning and young Latino/a students' developing expertise. In P. R. Portes & S. Salas (Eds.), *Vygotsky in 21st century society: Advances in cultural historical theory and praxis with non-dominant communities* (pp. 162–179). New York, NY: Peter Lang.

McDougall, J. (2010). A crisis of professional identity: How primary teachers are coming to terms with changing views of literacy. *Teaching and Teacher Education, 26*(3), 679–687. doi:10.1016/j.tate.2009.10.003

Molle, D., Sato, E., Boals, T., & Hedgspeth, C. A. (Eds.). (2015). *Multilingual learners and academic literacies: Sociocultural contexts of literacy development in adolescents.* New York, NY: Routledge.

Ochs, E. (1993). Constructing social identity: A language socialization perspective. *Research on Language and Social Interaction, 26*(3), 287–306. doi:10.1207/s15327973rlsi2603_3

Ochs, E., & Schieffelin, B. (1989). Language has a heart. *Text, 9*(Special Issue), 7–25.

Orellana, M. F., Martínez, D. C., Lee, C. H., & Montaño, E. (2012). Language as a tool in diverse forms of learning. *Linguistics and Education, 23*(4), 373–387.

Sanchez, C., Plata, V., Grosso, L., & Leird, B. (2010). Encouraging Spanish-speaking families' involvement through dichos. *Journal of Latinos & Education, 9*(3), 239–248.

Sánchez, P., & Salazar, M. (2012). Transnational computer use in urban Latino immigrant communities: Implications for schooling. *Urban Education, 47*(1), 90–116.

Smith, H. L., & Riojas-Cortez, M. (2010). Cartitas de cariño: Little notes to say you care. *Language Arts, 88*(2), 125–133.

Street, B. (2001). The new literacy studies. In E. Cushman, E. R. Kintgen, B. M. Kroll, & M. Rose (Eds.), *Literacy: A critical sourcebook* (pp. 430–442). Boston, MA: Bedford/St. Martin's.

Téllez, K., & Varghese, M. (2013). Teachers as intellectuals and advocates: Professional development for bilingual education teachers. *Theory Into Practice, 52*(2), 128–135. doi:10.1080/00405841.2013.770330

Vásquez, O. A. (2003). *La clase mágica: Imagining optimal possibilities in a bilingual community of learners.* Mahwah, NJ: Erlbaum.

Wiemelt, J., & Welton, A. (2015). Challenging the dominant narrative: Critical bilingual leadership (liderazgo) for emergent bilingual Latin@ students. *International Journal of Multicultural Education, 17*(1), 82–101.

Zentella, A. C. (1997). *Growing up bilingual: Puerto Rican children in New York.* Malden, MA: Blackwell.

CHAPTER 13

THE PRACTICE OF *CARIÑO* FOR EMERGENT BILINGUAL STUDENTS

Latinx Students in the United States and Indigenous Guatemaltecos

P. Zitlali Morales
University of Illinois at Chicago

Lydia A. Saravia
University of Illinois at Chicago

ABSTRACT

This chapter reviews the literature on *cariño,* a term used to invoke cultural ideas included in *educación* and Spanish-speaking, bilingual classrooms (Bartolomé, 2008; Curry, 2016; Duncan-Andrade, 2006; Nieto, 2000). After describing scholars' use of the ethic of care, largely building on the work of Nel Noddings (1984), we explain our definition of *cariño* as a teacher's demonstrated understanding of students' sociopolitical and racialized realities through a demonstrated affection for students and their communities,

Transforming Schooling for Second Language Learners, pages 237–256
Copyright © 2019 by Information Age Publishing
All rights of reproduction in any form reserved.

evidenced through high academic expectations, and political advocacy. We provide two examples from qualitative studies in bilingual classrooms, the first conducted in the United States at the elementary level in a Spanish/English dual immersion school, and the second in a Latin American context at the secondary level where both Spanish and an indigenous Mayan language were used for instruction. Finally, we discuss implications of this work using *cariño* as a theoretical perspective.

One of the concepts invoked by scholars examining the schooling of Latinx emergent bilinguals is the idea of *cariño*. *Cariño* is the Spanish word for "care" or "affection." Thus, this idea of what is needed in the teaching of Latinx emergent bilinguals includes their socioemotional needs. We discuss how many scholars have highlighted this affective aspect of the teaching and learning interaction, particularly when examining the teaching of Latinx teachers working with emergent bilingual youth.

As the largest linguistic minority group in the geographic United States, it is relevant to look at pedagogical practices that are understood to be effective with Latinx students. This chapter looks at the literature focused on the notion of "*cariño*," an approximation in Spanish of the word "caring," but nuanced and linked to Latinx groups. *Cariño* indexes and draws from other ideas related to the cultural practices of families from Latin American descent, represented in the Spanish language, such as *educación*. The use of Spanish indexes the experiences of students of Latin American, Spanish-speaking heritage, even while acknowledging that not all Latinx students speak Spanish. We review how it has been used to look at teaching and learning with Latinx students, especially in bilingual teaching contexts.

While not all emergent bilinguals are Latinx and not all Latinx students are bilinguals, the majority of emergent bilinguals in the United States come from Spanish-speaking backgrounds or households. Therefore it is relevant to discuss the current state of schooling for Latinx students. Latinx students continue to lag behind their White counterparts in measures of academic achievement, literacy, and other school-based outcomes. Our perspective is that there is a significant inequity in the schooling of Latinx students that revolves around caring for them and understanding them sociopolitically. Some scholars argue that while issues of meeting the linguistic needs are legitimate, debates about bilingual education, for example, have served as a distraction from focusing on the myriad ways that access to schooling and resources have been inequitable for Latinxs from the inception of the United States (Gándara & Contreras, 2009). We agree with both the criticism that schools are not currently set up to leverage the cultural and linguistic assets of emergent bilinguals (Martinez, Morales, & Aldana, 2017), and that emergent bilinguals are highly concentrated in high-need areas in schools which are chronically underresourced (Gándara & Hopkins, 2010). The practice of *cariño* is difficult to assess, but it is also significant—because of its ideological basis and impact. It is in the practice of *cariño*, defined largely by Latina feminist scholars, that we see possibility in the improvement of schooling experiences and outcomes for Latinx students, including those who are emergent bilinguals.

Our purpose in this chapter is to look at how *cariño* has been discussed in the literature, including how the actions and practices of teachers may be illuminated when viewed through this lens. We trace the history of the term, reviewing studies that have used this concept to describe what they observe some teachers practice with students. We provide a few examples from our own empirical work, where we saw *cariño* being enacted by Latina pedagogues. Finally, we offer implications of the use of *cariño* as a theoretical frame.

REVIEW OF CARE AND *CARIÑO*

Scholars have long cited that experiencing care in the classroom significantly impacts the academic success of students of color or nondominant students (Antrop-González & De Jesus, 2006; Beauboef-Lafontant, 2008; Curry 2016; Nieto, 2000; Shevalier & McKenzie, 2012; Valenzuela, 2009). For example, drawing attention to an example from long ago, Nieto (2000) points to the 1984 National Commission on Secondary Education for Hispanics which found that Puerto Rican students' academic success or failure was related to having teachers that they feel care about who they are as people or experiencing rejection from their teachers. Students state, "'love' as the factor that can make or break their experience in school" (Nieto, 2000, p. 31). In research with African American students, Beauboeuf-Lafontant (2008) states that, "the academic success of students from subordinated backgrounds lies very much in the quality of the relationships which their teachers establish with them, and in the form of caring they demonstrate" (p. 252).

Research on the ethic of care is largely based on the work of Carol Gilligan and Nel Noddings. Gilligan's (1982, 1988) work describes care as essential to moral education, and Noddings (1984, 1988, 1992) has contributed to moral education in classroom practices. Other scholars have contributed to the scholarship on care, developing arguments for authentic care, critical care, and finally, *cariño*. We define *cariño* as a teacher's demonstrated understanding of students' political and racialized realities through an authentic love for the students and the students' communities, evidenced through high academic expectations, and advocacy on behalf of the students and the students' communities (Bartolomé, 2008; Curry, 2016; Morales, Vazquez, & Saravia, manuscript submitted for publication; Nieto, 2000; Saravia, 2017; Valenzuela, 1999).

AN ETHIC OF CARE

Nel Noddings' work on the ethic of care has been heralded as an important and compelling discussion "to understand curriculum as feminist" (Pinar, Reynolds, Slattery, & Taubman, 2008, p. 694). For Noddings (1984, 1992), caring is a moral act. In her definition of an ethic of care, the relationship between teacher and student is a reciprocal one where the teacher cares for the student, and the student responds. The scholarship on the ethic of care builds on Noddings' (1984) early definition of affection that involves dialogue and confirmation.

AUTHENTIC VERSUS AESTHETIC CARE

In her seminal work on Mexican and Mexican American students at a high school in Texas, Angela Valenzuela (1999) argued that teachers who are not aware of their students' home cultural practices can be dismissive of their students' behavior, misunderstanding their students as uncaring about doing well in school. This misunderstanding stems from a teacher misreading a student's attitude toward school, which is a result of the focus of caring being *aesthetic*. This aesthetic caring is typified by a teacher being "concerned first with form and nonpersonal content and only secondarily, if at all, with their students' subject reality" (Valenzuela, 1999, p. 22). Importantly, Valenzuela highlighted that when examining care in practice, the sociocultural context needs to be taken into account, as well as the sociohistorical and sociopolitical positioning of students. If not, misunderstandings may take place between teachers and students, each believing the other to be *uncaring*, whether about school or about themselves as individuals. Ultimately, Valenzuela (1999) evaluated these collective uncaring practices towards students at the school level as "subtractive" policies, designed to assimilate students into hegemonic, dominant structures and divest students of their cultural and linguistic practices.

Valenzuela's understanding of authentic care is informed by the idea of *educación*. The concept of *educación* is a cultural construct that provides instructions on how one should live in the world" (Valenzuela, 1999, p. 20). Reese, Balzano, Gallimore, and Goldenberg (1995) discussed their understanding of the key differences between education and its Spanish cognate:

> Although *educación* and the English term "education" overlap in important ways, *educacón* has a broader meaning. The term invokes additional, nonacademic dimensions, such as learning the difference between right and wrong, respect for parents and others, and correct behavior, which parents view as the base upon which all other learning lies. (p. 66)

Thus, there are particular cultural understandings embedded in the idea of *educación* that must be understood when looking at Latinx students in particular. Similarly, the idea of *cariño* must be understood to encompass broader understandings than the word "care." Scholars who have used the concept of *cariño* when describing teaching and learning are including cultural practices inclusive of the needs of Latinx students and their communities (Curry 2016; Duncan-Andrade, 2006; Nieto, 2000).

CRITICAL CARE AND "HARD" CARING

One of the areas where scholars depart from Noddings is on the aspect of high academic expectations. Noddings (1988) writes, "A high expectation can be a mark of respect, but so can a relatively low one" (p. 224). She offered the example of Rose, a student who is good at art, but not math. Noddings argued that the math instructor could lower the expectations in math, in a self-affirming process where the student is following her particular interests. However, there is no acknowledgment that often the stakes are higher in educational spaces for students of color.

In contrast, Nieto (2000) writes, "Care is demonstrated most powerfully through high expectations and rigorous standards, and in teachers' beliefs that students are worthy and capable" (p. 32). Similarly, Antrop-González and De Jesus (2006) explain that "critical care" captures the ways in which communities of color may care about and educate their own, and their intentions in doing so. Caring "must manifest itself as high academic expectations" (p. 426). Pedagogical practice of caring that lowers academic expectations of students is described as condescending (Antrop-González & De Jesus, 2006; Nieto, 2000). However well-intentioned, not expecting high academic achievement results in what Antrop-González and De Jesus (2006) refer to as "soft caring," where teachers pity students, and therefore, do not provide the rigorous curriculum they think students cannot handle. They contrast "soft" caring with "hard" caring, "a form of caring characterized by supportive instrumental relationships and high academic expectations" (p. 413). Thus, hard caring requires much of students, but acknowledges that schools must to be felt as supportive spaces by them, through vital relationships with others.

CULTURAL RELEVANCE AND SOCIOPOLITICAL
ORIENTATION

Demonstrating critical cariño means respecting and including students' cultures and languages in the curriculum (Nieto, 2000), as well as advocating on behalf of students. For either to happen, educators must understand the needs of their students' communities (the collective), as well as have a political orientation, in order to "recognize the unequal power relations among cultures that result in unequal status and treatment in society and in schools" (Bartolomé, 2008, p. 14). Nieto (2000) points out that research "has suggested that school policies and practices...negatively influence Latino students' academic performance, behavior, and decision to stay in or leave school" and that "Latinos expressed more negative feelings about their schools than did other students" (p. 26). Writing in regards to African American communities, Beauboef-Ladontant (2002) claims that loving children entails more than simply stating affection for them, but stems from a "a clear-sighted understanding of how and why society marginalizes some children while embracing others" (p. 80). To profess caring for children without understanding their social positioning is similar to holding a color-blind ideology.

In addition to providing academic rigor then, care consists of a recognition of the conditions affecting students. Bartolomé underscores that teachers need to have a clear understanding of the challenges Latinx students in a U.S. context face (Bartolomé, 2008). To care for students encompasses a knowledge of the historical struggles of the community (Valenzuela, 2009). Advocacy for students is one method of illustrating *cariño* beyond physical manifestations, such as a hug (Bartolomé, 2008). It can incorporate both structural and institutional (macro) changes, such as demanding bilingual education (Nieto, 2000), as well as encompass moment-to-moment (micro) interactions with children at a classroom level or improving home-school relations (Valenzuela, 1999).

In the education of Latinx student populations, scholars (Antrop-González & De Jesus, 2006; González, Moll, & Amanti, 2005) argue that the curriculum should tap into students' funds of knowledge. In other words, educators should acknowledge that students enter the classroom with a set of experiences and knowledge accumulated outside of the academic classroom. Curry (2016) refers to this pedagogical method of tapping into the students' fund of knowledge as critical cariño, defined as "caring undertaken with historical and political consciousness of students' communities and a desire to interrupt inequity" (p. 892). Feminist scholars of color, in particular, have argued for a critical feminist ethic of care which brings "a consciousness of collective responsibility to their craft wherein the survival and uplift of their own people hinge[s] on teaching with a sense of purpose beyond a mastery of content for mastery's sake" (Sosa-Provencio, 2016, p. 2). Through this lens, an ethic of care takes into consideration the political educational realities of nondominant students, and calls for the "need for an understanding of socioeconomic, cultural barriers that inhibit" historically marginalized students (Valenzuela, 1999, p. 109).

The following are two examples of how teachers practice the concept of *cariño* in the classroom. The first example is from a U.S. context at the elementary school level, and the second example is from a Latin American context at the secondary level where both Spanish and an indigenous Mayan language were spoken. Significantly, both of these examples are dual language contexts, that is, classrooms where the instruction takes place in two languages and the curricular program promotes multilingualism. In the first example, the practice of *cariño* produces the discursive concept of "regaño" [scolding]. In the second, an enactment of the curriculum of urgency is accompanied by the pedagogical practice of *cariño*. *Regaño* results from love and high academic expectations of the teacher, and the curriculum of urgency is a result from love of the community and fear of cultural loss.

CARIÑO ENACTED BY LATINA EDUCATORS

Regaño as *Cariño* in a Dual Immersion Classroom

This example comes from a qualitative study of a fifth grade classroom in a long-standing dual immersion program in southern California (Morales, 2010). Fifteen-year veteran teacher Maestra Segura (a pseudonym) instructed 50% of the day in Spanish and 50% in English. In this model, Spanish language arts (SLA) was taught separately from English language arts (ELA). By fifth grade, the level of Spanish vocabulary and grammatical constructions was rigorous—for both the "native" Spanish speakers as well as the population of students that had learned Spanish solely at school. To support students' engagement with language production at this level, Maestra Segura structured collaborative activities where dominant English- and dominant Spanish-speakers worked together to develop each language during both SLA and ELA.

As has been noted with teachers in other bilingual program examples (specifically in other dual immersion programs; Takahashi-Breines, 2002), Maestra Segura used affectionate language toward her students (e.g., "*vamos, amor*" ["let's go, love"]). But as Antrop-González and De Jesus (2006) describe, she also used language to hold them to a high standard. In particular, she verbalized repeatedly that the Spanish-speaking students had a lot of knowledge about their own language to share.

First Example: Holding High Standards
At "Back to School Night," Maestra Segura shared with the parents her expectations of their children in the fifth grade.

Maestra tells the parents that she and the students wrote a classroom constitution together. After reaching a compromise with them, she will assign students a "reasonable" amount of homework, which will mostly be language arts and math. There will be no homework in social studies or science unless there's a big project. Although she does expect students to read every day, and they must be chapter books. As far as what she wants to focus on in literature this year, she wants to take them from writing summaries to actually doing literary analysis. There will be monthly book reports due. This month the students chose to do them in English. So next month they will have to read a book in Spanish, which must be a chapter book (capitulos). A parent asks Maestra whether a book report will be expected in September (the present month). "Yes, a book report will be due," Maestra responds. She explains that they have to start right away with setting expectations. She suggests having a calendar at home to keep track of assignments. For the book report, she also wants an analysis, not a summary.

In this description of Maestra Segura's communication to the parents of her students, she describes clearly what she requires of students and what they have agreed to do (by way of writing a classroom "constitution"). She even explains how homework will be balanced, so that students can focus on reading chapter books every day. Most importantly, Maestra emphasizes to the parents that she is trying to push the students to engage literary analysis, rather than simple summaries. In this classroom, students will engage with both Spanish and English at high academic levels.

Second Example: Language of Affection

In Spanish language arts time, Maestra Segura has paired together students to review a list of vocabulary words that will be featured in the novel they will be reading in Spanish. She has ensured that each pair has one student stronger in Spanish, that is, speaks Spanish at home. In the pairing of Sarah and Rosita, Rosita is the stronger Spanish speaker, having been born in Mexico and attended kindergarten there. The vocabulary list features words relating to horses and horseback riding, as the novel is set in the 19th century United States. Maestra Segura has directed each pair to discuss the words together, trying to ascertain their meaning even if they are unsure.

01   Sarah: So. *Espadrilla es un . . . ¿Sabes que es?*

                    [So. 'Espadrilla' is a . . . Do you know what it is?]

                    (Rosita shakes her head slightly.)

02   Sarah: *¿No sabes?*

                    [You don't know?]

                    (Sarah looks disappointed. As Maestra approaches the large table, Sarah calls out to her.)

03	Sarah:	Ms. Segura! *Nosotros no sabemos,*
		[Ms. Segura! We don't know,]
04	Maestra:	*Tienes que pasar al cuaderno.* (to other students)
		[You have to transfer it to your notebook.)
05	Sarah:	*No sabemos lo que es esta palabra.*
		[We don't know what this word is.]
06	Maestra:	*Rosita, Rosita tiene un conocimiento MUY grande del idioma.*
		[Rosita. Rosita has a VERY vast knowledge of the language.]
07	Sarah:	*Ella, ella, deci... decid...* (mumbles)
		[She, she, sa... sai...]
08	Maestra:	*Ve a la proxima.*
		[Go to the next one.]

Rather than simply providing the students with the definition of the first word they get stuck on, Maestra Segura emphasizes the knowledge that Rosita has of Spanish. While she directs this comment to both Sarah and Rosita, she implicitly encourages Rosita to realize how much she knows and also reminding all of the students within earshot that they should be using each other as resources rather than immediately looking to her for the answers.

Sarah and Rosita take Maestra's advice and move on to the next vocabulary word, while Maestra Segura continues walking around the classroom. About three minutes later, Maestra returns to the pair.

01	Maestra:	Rosita, tú eres capaz de hacer casi todas esas palabras.
		[Rosita, you are capable of doing almost all of these words.]
02	Maestra:	Y si no, me dejas con el corazón roto.
		[And if not, you leave me with a broken heart.]
03	Maestra:	Vamos, amor.
		[Let's go, love.]

Upon her reappearance, Maestra Segura immediately addresses Rosita directly. Rather than provide more indirect encouragement, Maestra assures Rosita that she is a capable student, even without anyone's assistance. Maestra verbalizes her belief, understanding of Rosita's abilities, while making clear that she expects Rosita to be more forthcoming in this partner activity.

In this brief interaction, Maestra Segura simultaneously emphasizes the relationship and emotional connection between Rosita and herself. She invokes emotion, but refers to her own broken heart, or disappointment if Rosita does not rise to the task that Maestra has laid out for her students. In her parting comment, Maestra Segura uses the phrase of affection, "amor," to refer to Rosita while encouraging her to keep going ("Let's go").

Third Example: *Regaño ("Scolding") to Support High Standards for Academic Interaction*

During this same exercise, another student pair experiences a lack of participation by one of its members. Maestra Segura engages in the linguistic practice of *regaño*, in which she pushes her Spanish-fluent student, George, to rise to the expectations she has of him, and assume leadership in this activity where he is working with another student who does not speak Spanish at home. In Spanish, *regaño* means "to scold" or "reprimand." Maestra Segura did nurture her students, but also pushed and made demands of them. This discursive practice of *regaño* aligns with Antrop-González & De Jesus' notion of "hard caring," a form of caring "characterized by supportive instrumental relationships and high academic expectations" (Antrop-González & De Jesus, 2006, p. 413).

Melisa and George have been tasked with talking through the vocabulary words together, but Melisa has been the one doing most of the talking. As Maestra Segura approaches their table, Melisa asks this question out loud.

01	Melisa:	*¿Porque solo yo estoy hablando?*
		[Why am I the only one talking?]
02	Maestra:	*Exactamente Melisa. No lo entiendo.*
		[Exactly, Melisa. I don't understand it.]
		(Melisa smiles and looks down at her paper. George smiles as well.)
03	Maestra:	*Asumí que él iba tomar el liderazgo ahí.*
		[I assumed that he would take the leadership there.]
		(Maestra points her pencil in George's direction, shaking it multiple times.)
04	Maestra:	*Asumí que iba usar todo su capacidad del idioma.*
		[I assumed that he would use all of his capacity with the language.]
05	Maestra:	*Por favor George, no te me quedes. Por algo te puse aquí.*
		[Please, George, don't fall behind. I put you here for a reason.]
06	Maestra:	*Yo dije, 'No, George sí puede todas estas palabras'. Vamos.*
		[I said, 'No, George can do all of these words'. Let's go.

In responding to Melisa's rhetorical question, Maestra Segura feigns disbelief. Similar to the previous example with Sarah and Rosita, Maestra Segura has tasked George with making a significant contribution based on his linguistic abilities and providing some "leadership," as Maestra puts it. She reiterates her faith in George's capacity with the language, but also makes clear what she expects of him. Similar to the example with Rosita, Maestra verbalizes her belief that George has the ability to understand and define the words in Spanish before him. While Maestra Segura discursively supports George and his abilities as well as clearly articulates her high expectations, Maestra does not use any terms of endearment in this example. That makes this interaction an example of *regaño*, while still coming from a place of *cariño*.

THE CURRICULUM OF URGENCY—*CARIÑO* AS A PEDAGOGICAL PRACTICE TO AVOID CULTURAL LOSS

The second example we provide comes from a larger qualitative research study that examined the bilingual and intercultural curriculum of a teacher education institution in Guatemala predominantly serving the indigenous community of the Western Highlands. The faculty and administration of this school, called an *Escuela Normal Bilingüe Intercultural* (ENBI) were members of the indigenous community themselves and encouraged students to continue cultural traditions, including speaking the community language. Seño Aura[1] urged her students to take pride in their community's indigenous practices, in order for these cultural practices to remain alive. This section illustrates the ways in which Seño Aura, who taught psychology courses at the school site, practiced *cariño*. Her practice of *cariño* was one that was inclusive of the indigenous practices of the community as relevant knowledge to the content she taught.

For indigenous students in Guatemala, access to education continues to be perilous. The data is dismal for indigenous populations: 60% of the indigenous are illiterate (Patrinos & Velez, 2009), and among indigenous youth, girls have an average of 0.8 years of school while boys have an average of 1.8 years of school (Stavenhagen, 2008). Institutional systems of oppression, continued racism, marginalization, and poverty fuel the feeling of urgency to support student resiliency in the face of all these challenges. This feeling of urgency is then enacted in the everyday curriculum of this ENBI school.

ENBIs are a result of the 1996 Peace Agreements that ended a 36-year violent period in Guatemala, marred by acts of genocide primarily affecting indigenous populations. As a result of this period of genocide, the 1995 Agreement to Identity and Indigenous Rights and the 1996 Peace Accords were created in an attempt to restore human rights in Guatemala. One of the tenets of these documents ensured language rights and the inclusion of indigenous cultures, knowledge, and languages in educational institutions. Indigenous populations had been victims of genocide, where entire villages had been massacred or disappeared. In order to safeguard inclusion of indigenous identity in institutions of education, the creation of 22 ENBIs, one for each recognized ethnic group in Guatemala, was an institutionalized effort to recruit and train indigenous students as bilingual and intercultural primary school teachers. Presently, students at ENBIs are prepared to enter university and receive a curriculum that includes the teaching of English, in addition to continuing their language studies in Spanish and the indigenous language of the community.

Despite an attempt to address the demands of the Peace Accords, indigenous groups continue to be discriminated against by dominant groups and affected by Western influences to lead a cosmopolitan life. Similar to the Puerto Rican families Nieto (2000) highlights in her research, indigenous groups in Guatemala fear the power of dominant ideologies, including Western culture and media to teach their youth to "reject the values of their own communities, including language and culture" (Nieto, 2000, p. 20). Many youth do choose to assimilate to Ladino (non-indigenous, Spanish-speaking group) and Western cultures (Martinez Salazar, 2012). These realities also fed into a *curriculum of urgency* (Saravia, 2017). During the time Saravia spent at the school site, she often heard faculty warn the students that, "*En cincuenta años, tal vez ya no exista nuestro idioma.*" [In fifty years, our language might no longer exist.]

This curriculum of urgency was rooted in the political context and in the hopes by the faculty and administration for a continued collective and indigenous future. Because of the fear of cultural and linguistic loss, instructors such as Seño Aura brought in community practices and understandings into the classroom, attempting to value those knowledges students brought with them and insisting they value them as well.

While Seño Aura was not a language instructor, she used the indigenous community language as well as Spanish for instruction. Attention to the community's language and community practices was part of the national curriculum for ENBI. Seño Aura often asked the students to share what they knew about the subject being discussed. During one psychology class session discussing the gestation stages, Seño Aura invited students to share stories about their own family members and their childbirth practices. Students told stories of their 14-year-old family members who have had children. Seño Aura nodded in affirmation while students spoke. Being a member of the community, she was knowledgeable about how young some of the women were when they became mothers. She used storytelling to open a dialogue among the indigenous members of her classroom (Smith, 2012). When students were done sharing their stories, Seño Aura shifted to explain that 14-year-old bodies might not be fully developed to carry a child and give birth. While respecting the experiences of members of her community, Seño Aura added Western science to the conversation to explain the female anatomy and developmental stages. She listened to and validated students' experiences, while also adding to their understanding by teaching them the Western science knowledge she had acquired through her own studies. In a different academic space, students might not have felt comfortable sharing the childbirth stories for fear of stigmatization and further societal marginalization.

Students were reassured of their cultural identity in other areas of their education. As part of the national curriculum, the school held a series of health esteem workshops where students were separated by gender. This series consisted of four workshops, including one titled, *Identidad Personal* [Personal Identity]. The personal identity workshop involved some of the female faculty members providing female students lessons on self-acceptance and identifying as indigenous women. Seño Aura was one of the faculty members facilitating the workshop; some of the statements expressed towards the students including the following:

> "*No tenemos la capacidad de decir no a la identidad porque no podemos negar nuestra familia.*" [We cannot deny our identity because we cannot deny our family.]

> "*Yo soy indígena.*" [I am indigenous.]

> "*Somos mujeres; sabemos cómo nos vestimos; eso es identidad.*" [We are women; we know how we dress; that's identity.]

Seño Aura insisted that the female students should be proud of their identities as indigenous women, and that part of that visual expression of identity is the *traje*, the traditional woven dress of indigenous women in Guatemala.

Only female students received these lessons in regards to dress, but these lessons were tied to the older generation's fear of losing the community's youth to mainstream pressures of fitting into Ladino/Western culture. Certainly, the young women could pass as Ladinos if they chose to dress in mainstream ways and in Western styles; it is the indigenous style of dress and indigenous language(s) that marks them as something other than Ladino (Martínez Salazar, 2012). To the community elders, losing female students to Ladino styles of dress would be a loss of culture. *El traje* is a symbol of a culture alive and thriving. If young women do not wear the *traje*, the cultural practice of the traditional *traje* could cease to exist in a matter of a few generations, or 50 years. The lessons about dress and visual representation were tied to this sense of urgency and care for the larger indigenous community; they were a plea to the young people to protect the culture by continuing to live its practices. Further, the community elders passed on these sentiments to the youth out of a sense of love for their own community and culture. Seño Aura reminded the female students during the workshop,

> *Debo demostrar mis capacidades aunque haya discriminación y racismo. Somos mujeres; sabemos cómo nos vestimos; eso es identidad . . . Tengo que aceptarme a mí misma.*

[I must demonstrate my abilities (or knowledge) despite discrimination and racism. We are women; we know how we dress; that's identity...I have to accept myself.]

Seño Aura articulated her understanding of the racist reality students faced and the real pressure to assimilate; because of this understanding, she urged students to accept who they were as indigenous Guatemalans.

During an interview with Seño Aura, she described that she wanted to be seen as a *profésional, indígena* [professional and indigenous]. Further, she added that she would like for her students to see themselves as agents of change for their community.

A mi me gustaría que fueran maestros primero que entendieran nuestra realidad especialmente la sociocultural, la economía porque eso es la situación porque estamos. [I would like for the students to become teachers that understood our reality, especially our sociocultural and economic reality because that's the situation that we're in.]

As discussed by the examples highlighted here, Seño Aura used her understanding of students' political and racialized realities to teach students to take pride in who they were as indigenous youth. We argue that this is a powerful form of advocacy for indigenous cultural practices—teaching students to love who they are and where they come from. The inclusion of the local cultural and linguistic practice in an academic space helped validate the local community as knowledge producers. Her classroom was one that allowed students to share their knowledge and community experience without judgment or ridicule. Seño Aura exhibited *cariño* for her students through her deep understanding of the sociopolitical history and context of her students, and by holding them to the expectation that they also understand the community's sociopolitical context and will act on that knowledge for the benefit of the collective. Seño Aura enacted a *curriculum of urgency* (Saravia, 2017). Through pedagogical moves that highlighted and valued the community knowledge that students held, the instructor urged students to value and continue their indigenous cultural ways of living, or understand that they would be lost forever.

DISCUSSION

Scholars such as Nel Noddings have discussed the importance of care within educational spaces. The construct of care has been taken up and further theorized by scholars such as Valenzuela (1999) in particular sociocultural contexts and with specific students (i.e., Mexican-origin students in south Texas), conceptualizing authentic versus aesthetic care. Antrop-Gonzáles and De Jesús (2006) also theorized the notion of critical care and the difference between hard care and soft care. Latinx scholars examining bilingual contexts have used the term *cariño* (Bartolomé, 2008; Curry, 2016; Duncan-Andrade, 2006; Nieto, 2000), invoking the cultural ideas included in *educación* and Spanish-speaking contexts. To us, the idea has been useful to describe particular linguistic moves made by Latina educators in bilingual classroom spaces (Morales, Vasquez, & Saravia, manuscript submitted for publication; Saravia, 2017). The idea of *cariño* has explanatory power, and it could be further theorized and more widely applied. We propose future directions for research relevant to caring for students that takes into consideration issues of cultural practices and the political realities of particular students and their communities. We also discuss possible limitations for this way of looking at teachers' practices and interactions with students.

Based on the work of the scholars above, our definition of *cariño* includes holding students to high standards or providing academic rigor, a demonstration of affection (that necessarily implies a cultural component), and an understanding of the political positioning of the students one teaches that leads to a desire to improve the conditions of their students and their communities (Morales, Meza, & Maravilla-Cano, 2017). These three components are very similar to what Ladson-Billing (1995) includes in her description of culturally relevant pedagogy: academic success, cultural competence, and critical consciousness. Thus, we argue that the concept of *cariño* is an example of culturally relevant pedagogy. In describing how culturally relevant pedagogy differs from critical pedagogy, Ladson-Billings explains that the emphasis is on the collective: "I have defined culturally relevant teaching as a pedagogy of opposition (1992c) not unlike critical pedagogy but specifically committed to collective, not merely individual, empowerment" (p. 160). This emphasis on the collective was demonstrated in our own studies.

Seño Aura, for example, demonstrated *cariño* in a manner aligned with a commitment to a collective identity and not just individual empowerment. The "curriculum of urgency" resulted from a deep understanding of the positioning of the indigenous community as a whole in the historical and political context of Guatemala, and Seño Aura's commitment to the continuation of this community. Her pedagogical practices of storytelling, providing academic space for community experiences and knowledge, and demonstrating compassion for her community reflect this cariño. With Maestra Segura's practice of *regaño*, the teacher "demands" that students rise to the challenge of contributing to their dual language classroom, specifically as Spanish speakers. Her practice of *cariño* manifests through scolding and pushing her students to demonstrate their knowledge. Within these practices, both teachers show an understanding of the political climate and situation of their students because they are a part of these communities as well. In these cases, enactment of *cariño* comes from a sociocultural understanding of the specific community and a sociopolitical understanding of how students are positioned politically; this results in teacher advocacy for the students they teach.

Importantly, Latinx scholars have underscored the high demands that teachers must have, while understanding and supporting students' attainment of these standards (Antrop-González & De Jesús, 2006; Morales, Vasquez, & Saravia, manuscript submitted for publication; Nieto, 2000). In other words, the linguistic examples of displays of affection (e.g., using diminutives or words of endearment such as "mi amor"; Takahashi-Breines, 2002), are not the focus nor the pedagogical goal. What teachers should be in pursuit of, rather, are discursive or pedagogical tools to reach the goal of engaging students in their own learning and demonstrating the importance of established relationships among students, students' communities, and the teachers. As Nieto (2000) emphasized, taking into account the historical and political situation of students in one's classroom should not result in feeling bad for the students or limiting how one teaches, but rather it provides motivation for advocacy. This is a way to care not solely for the students, but also for the larger community. It is the difference between hard caring and soft caring (Antrop-Gonzáles & De Jesús, 2006) or exhibiting critical cariño (Curry, 2016).

IMPLICATIONS

We see three main implications stemming from this work around the practice of *cariño* at the institutional level. As Siddle Walker and Tompkins (2004) argue in regards to the education of African American children, there needs to be "larger institutional structures . . . to facilitate a message of caring consistent with the interpersonal message of caring" in order for the children to believe that they are being cared for (p. 92). The first implication regards funding. Investment in the education of students in marginalized communities is constantly being cut; there is a need to ensure equitable funding for high-need areas, which are communities where emergent bilinguals are often concentrated: Latinx ethnic enclaves and low-income neighborhoods.

Second, teacher education programs must ensure teachers are prepared to learn about the students they serve and the communities in which their schools are located. Educators "can either maintain the status quo, or they can work to transform the sociocultural reality in the classroom and in schools so that the culture at this micro-level does not reflect and reproduce macro-level inequalities" (Bartolomé, 2008, p. 14). To better support the education of emergent bilinguals, scholars recommend hiring qualified teachers from students' own communities (Gándara & Contreras, 2009;

Valenzuela, 2016). These teachers may better understand particular socio-historical and sociopolitical situations students are dealing with, while also recognizing the resources that do exist in these same communities, thus more likely to stay teaching there over time (Hanushek & Rivkin, 2006). Nondominant students need teachers who will prepare them academically but who also understand their families, cultural practices, and are familiar with the strengths of their communities, in order to bridge the distance between home and school.

The third implication is to continue to diversify the current teacher work-force, while also learning from teachers of color and multilingual teachers who are currently teaching. While the teaching force is still largely White, monolingual, and middle-class, institutional supports can be provided to increase the number of teachers coming from communities serving emergent bilingual students. Within schools that do contain teachers who are more reflective of the student body, more structured systems of teacher collaboration can be put into place, in order for teachers to learn together and learn from each other.

One potential limitation of this concept is that it risks essentializing practices that come from Latinx communities. Or overgeneralizing our understanding of a particular group of people.

Future Research

This concept of *cariño* is not limited to the education of Latinx students. These three tenets should be considered when working with all students of color or those who have been historically marginalized. For example, scholars have argued for a similar practice of prioritizing relationships and the sociopolitical positioning of students in the education of Black youth (Delpit, 2006; Jackson, Sealey-Ruiz, & Watson, 2014; Ladson Billings, 1995a; Ladson Billings, 1995b; Siddle Walker & Tompkins, 2004; St. John & Cadrey, 2004). In the realm of mentoring graduate students of color higher education, the idea of caring has been associated with ideas of "mothering" or "othermothering"; conceptually, scholars draw from the traditions of critical race theory (CRT), by way of providing testimonies for example.

CONCLUSION

While scholars have looked at advocacy at a macro level (Nieto, 2000) pointing to larger scale changes such as fighting for bilingual education, others have looked at advocacy in school and classroom spaces (Valenzuela, 1999). We argue that Maestra Segura and Seño Aura advocate for their students in daily interactions. In the current political climate in the United States and the persistent racial repression in Guatemala, the audacity to have high academic expectations and the teaching of ethnic pride is advocacy. Considering the current historical state of public education in the United States and in other spaces, "social justice work and education are necessary because of the high level of inequality that exists in the world" (Elenes, 2013, p. 140).

NOTE

1. "Seño" is short for *señora* or *señorita* and is a term of respect reserved for the elder women of the community. "Seño Aura" is a pseudonym for this instructor.

REFERENCES

Antrop-González, R., & De Jesús, A. (2006). Toward a theory of *critical care* in urban small school reform: Examining structures and pedagogies of caring in two Latino community-based schools. *International Journal of Qualitative Studies in Education, 19*(4), 409–433.

Bartolomé, L. I. (2008). Authentic cariño and respect in minority education: The political and ideological dimensions of love. *International Journal of Critical Pedagogy, 1*(1), 1–17.

Beauboeuf-Lafontant, T. (2002). A womanist experience of caring: Understanding the pedagogy of exemplary black women teachers. *The Urban Review, 34*(1), 71–86.

Beauboeuf-Lafontant, T. (2008). Politicized mothering: Authentic caring among African American women teachers. In L. I. Bartolomé (Ed.), *Ideologies in education: Unmasking the trap of teacher neutrality* (pp. 251–264). New York, NY: Peter Lang.

Curry, M. W. (2016). Will you stand for me? Authentic cariño and transformative rites of passage in an urban high school. *American Educational Research Journal, 53*(4), 883–918.

Delpit, L. (2006). *Other people's children: Cultural conflict in the classroom* (Rev. ed.). New York, NY: The New Press.

Duncan-Andrade, J. M. R. (2006). Utilizing cariño in the development of research methodologies. In J. L. Kincheloe, K. Hayes, K. Rose, & P. M. Anderson (Eds.), *The Praeger handbook of urban education* (Vol. 2; pp. 451–460). Westport, CT: Greenwood.

Elenes, C. (2013). Nepantla, spiritual activism, new tribalism: Chicana feminist transformative pedagogies and social justice education. *Journal of Latino/Latin American Studies, 5*(3), 132–141.

Gándara, P., & Contreras, F. (2009). *The Latino education crisis: The consequences of failed social policies.* Cambridge, MA: Harvard University Press.

Gándara, P., & Hopkins, M. (2010). The changing linguistic landscape of the United States. In P. Gándara & M. Hopkins (Eds.), *Forbidden language: English learners and restrictive languages policies* (pp. 7–19). New York, NY: Teachers College Press.

Gilligan, C. (1982). *In a different voice: Psychological theory and women's development.* Cambridge, MA: Harvard University Press.

Gilligan, C. (1988). The origins of morality in early childhood relationships. In C. Gilligan, J. V. Ward, & J. M. Taylor (Eds.), *Mapping the moral domain* (pp. 111–138). Cambridge, MA: Harvard University Press.

González, N., Moll, L. C., & Amanti, C. (Eds.). (2005). *Funds of knowledge: Theorizing practice in households, communities, and classrooms.* Mahwah, NJ: Erlbaum.

Hanushek, E. A., & Rivkin, S. G. (2006). Teacher quality. In E. A. Hanushek & F. Welch (Eds.), *Handbook of the Economics of Education* (Vol. 2, pp. 1051–1078). Amsterdam, Netherlands: Elsevier.

Jackson, I., Sealey-Ruiz, Y., & Watson, W. (2014). Reciprocal love: Mentoring Black and Latino males through an ethos of care. *Urban Education, 49*(4), 394–417.

Ladson-Billings, G. (1995a). But that's just good teaching! The case for culturally relevant pedagogy. *Theory into Practice, 34*(3), 159–165.

Ladson-Billings, G. (1995b). Toward a theory of culturally relevant pedagogy. *American Educational Research Journal, 32*(3), 465–491.

Martinez, D. C., Morales, P. Z., & Aldana, U. S. (2017). Leveraging students' communicative repertoires as a tool for equitable learning. *Review of Research in Education, 41*, 477–499.

Martinez Salazar, (2012). *Global coloniality of power in Guatemala: Racism, genocide, citizenship.* Lanham, MD: Lexington Books.

Morales, P. Z. (2010). *Examining the role of a dual language immersion program's language ideologies in scaffolding positive learner identities in dual language learners* (Unpublished doctoral dissertation). University of California, Los Angeles.

Morales, P. Z., Meza, R., & Maravilla-Cano, J. (2017, April). *Latin@ public school teachers in a changing Chicago:* Testimonios *from the classroom.* Paper presented as part of the symposium, Latin@ Educational Landscapes in Chicago: *Testimonios,* Resistance, and Praxis at the annual meeting of the American Educational Research Association, San Antonio, TX.

Morales, P. Z., Vazquez, V., & Saravia, L. A. (manuscript submitted for publication). Valuing Spanish and Spanish speakers: *Regaño* as caring in a dual immersion classroom.

Nieto, S. (2000). Puerto Rican students in U.S. schools: A brief history. In S. Nieto (Ed.), *Puerto Rican students in U.S. schools* (pp. 5–38). Mahwah, NJ: Erlbaum.

Noddings, N. (1984). *Caring: A feminine approach to ethics and moral education.* Berkeley, CA: University of California Press.

Noddings, N. (1988). An ethic of care and its implications for instructional arrangements. *American Journal of Education, 96*(2), 215–230.

Noddings, N. (1992). *The challenge to care in school.* New York, NY: Teachers College Press.

Patrinos, H. A., & Velez, E. (2009). Costs and benefits of bilingual education in Guatemala: A partial analysis. *International Journal of Education Development, 29*, 594–598.

Pinar, W., Reynolds, W. M., Slattery, P., & Taubman, P. M. (2008). *Understanding Curriculum: An introduction to the study of historical and contemporary discourses.* New York, NY: Peter Lang.

Reese, L., Balzano, S., Gallimore, R., & Goldenberg, C. (1995). The concept of *educación*: Latino family values and American schooling. *International Journal of Educational Research, 23*(1), 57–81.

Saravia, L. A. (2017). *Soy Indígena*: The Promise and Struggles of an *Escuela Normal Bilingüe Intercultural* in Guatemala. Unpublished doctoral dissertation. University of Illinois at Chicago. Chicago, IL.

Shevalier, R., & McKenzie, B. A. (2012). Culturally responsive teaching as an ethics- and care-based approach to urban education. *Urban Education, 47*(6), 1086–1105.

Siddle Walker, V., & Tompkins, R. H. (2004). Caring in the past: The case of a southern segregated African American school. In V. Siddle Walker & J. R. Snarey (Eds.), *Racing moral formation: African American perspectives on care and justice* (pp. 77–92). New York, NY: Teachers College Press.

Smith, L. T. (2012). *Decolonizing methodologies: Research and indigenous peoples* (2nd ed.). London, England: Zed Books.

Sosa-Provencio, M. A. (2016). Seeking a Mexicana/Mesitza critical feminist ethic of care: Diana's revolución of body and being. *Journal of Latinos and Education, 15*(4), 1–17.

St. John, E. P., & Cadrey, J. (2004). Justice and care in postsegregation urban schools: Rethinking the role of teacher education programs. In V. Siddle Walker & J. R. Snarey (Eds.), *Race-ing moral formation: African American perspectives on care and justice* (pp. 93–110). New York, NY: Teachers College Press.

Stavenhagen, R. (2008). Building intercultural citizenship through education: a human rights approach. *European Journal of Education, 43*(2), 161–179.

Takahashi-Breines, H. (2002). The role of teacher-talk in a dual language immersion third grade classroom. *Bilingual Research Journal, 26*(2), 461–483.

Valenzuela, A. (1999). *Subtractive schooling: U.S. Mexican youth and the politics of caring.* Albany: State University of New York Press.

Valenzuela, A. (2016). *Growing critically conscious teachers: A social justice curriculum for educators of Latino/a youth.* New York, NY: Teachers College Press.

SECTION V

CONCLUSION

CHAPTER 14

IMPLICATIONS AND FUTURE DIRECTIONS

Expanding Transformative Possibilities for Emergent Bilinguals in Contentious Times

Mariana Pacheco
University of Wisconsin-Madison

P. Zitlali Morales
University of Illinois at Chicago

Colleen Hamilton
University of Wisconsin-Madison

In this final chapter, we highlight the main themes growing out of the chapter contributions about how schooling is currently being and can *further* be transformed for emergent bilingual (EB) students. We put forward some key implications stemming from this work. This includes specific recommendations for policy makers, educators, researchers, families,

Transforming Schooling for Second Language Learners, pages 259–276
Copyright © 2019 by Information Age Publishing
All rights of reproduction in any form reserved.

communities, and critical allies who work with and serve EBs in educational settings. These recommendations could help realize the potential and the promise of equal *and* equitable educational opportunities regardless of students' racial/ethnic, sociocultural, socioeconomic, or linguistic background (August & Shanahan, 2008; Gándara & Contreras, 2009).

INSIGHTS: WHAT WE HAVE LEARNED

Despite the varied conditions, circumstances, and contexts the contributors have addressed in this volume, we highlight the broad themes that emerge from this research and scholarship. We emphasize as well the particular kinds of transformation that are necessary though not sufficient for EBs to benefit from equitable opportunities to learn and thrive in the short and long term.

Serving Emergent Bilinguals Remains Politicized

Many volume contributors emphasize the sociopolitical nature of teaching and learning, and the importance of taking this into account when examining the circumstances of EB students and their educational outcomes. Contributors centered on the extent to which contexts come to shape how particular approaches, programs, and models are instantiated, including the current cultural-historical and sociopolitical moment. In this view, teaching and learning are endeavors situated within particular sociopolitical contexts that have been described as xenophobic, anti-bilingualism, deficit-oriented, nationalist, and discriminatory based in racism and linguicism (Arce, 2004; Gutiérrez et al., 2002; Lippi-Green, 2012; Mitchell, 2013; Pacheco, 2010a). These contexts come to shape pedagogies, policies, programs, and practices for EBs such that their learning and development opportunities are amplified and/or constrained even as practitioners seek to reconcile these ideological and philosophical underpinnings. Thus, in theoretically and empirically exploring how we might transform schooling for EBs, it is important to first have a clear understanding about the political and ideological contexts that undergird our equity efforts.

The research and theoretical scholarship included in this volume attest to this reality. This work spanned national and international boundaries to argue that teaching EB and multilingual students remains highly politicized. The issues addressed reflect tensions and challenges pertaining to standardized assessments, curriculum and instruction, rights over school and community spaces, academic and linguistic tracking, access to postsecondary education, linguistic diversity in schools, and policymaking processes across school districts, communities, and states. Contributors emphasized the extent to which bilingual children and youths' languages and cultural backgrounds were devalued in schools and society and how this devaluing was reflected in classrooms, out-of-school programs, and the lived experiences of bilingual children and youth. Further, students and their language and cultural backgrounds were positioned as irrelevant to the processes of learning and academic work. English and the acquisition of English, however, remained unquestioned as a desirable outcome for nondominant EB students, particularly those from Chicano/a and Latina/o backgrounds.

Oftentimes, EB students and their families and communities were racialized, although their immigrant backgrounds, non-English languages, nondominant cultural experiences and knowledge, and newcomer statuses often functioned as proxies for their racial/ethnic backgrounds (Gutiérrez, Ali, & Henríquez, 2009). Hopkins and Brezicha (Chapter 4), for example, illustrate that Latina/o immigrants in the New Latino Diaspora (or nontraditional gateway regions; Hamann & Harklau, 2010) were perceived as an "invasion" by the majority White residents of Chesterfield, particularly in their local schools. City officials openly highlighted legality/illegality as a way to marginalize and surveil this growing Latina/o newcomer population, although it was clear that phenotype, appearance, lack of familiarity, and "accents" were also significant markers of difference. Unfortunately, the very presence of Latina/o students in the New Latino Diaspora creates a highly politicized context for serving EBs; for EB children and youth, their teaching and learning experiences are saturated with contentious nativist, nationalist, and racist ideologies and discourses.

Razfar (Chapter 2) notes that, on the one hand, the current political and cultural-historical moment is imbued with contentious discourses around who counts as *American* and the language varieties spoken in the United States, particularly by ethnolinguistic minoritized communities. On the other hand, he emphasizes that the increased visibility of our polylingualism and the language varieties we speak (e.g., Trump's discourse and rhetoric)—what he calls our *polyglot reality*—have come to create opportunities for processes such as affinities, affective alignments, and identities to take hold. He articulates a conceptual framework that shifts the focus from decontextualized analyses of language form and function typical of language researchers and educators to a focus on meaning, values, and hence ideology.

We are reminded by Bartolomé and Macedo (Chapter 3), however, that the meanings, values, and ideologies about nondominant communities and, specifically, the racism and xenophobia that have come to characterize our national discourse and practices have gone global. That is, the sociopolitical nature of teaching EBs, many of whom as immigrant Chicanos/as and Latinas/os are linguistically minoritized, reflects the teaching and learning contexts for nondominant children across the globe. As Gándara and Escamilla (2017) assert, "Ongoing and unresolved debates about immigration, testing and assessment, and teacher evaluation also constitute significant issues that might impede the future of bilingual education in the USA" (p. 11). Transforming schooling for EBs requires educators, researchers, and practitioners to confront the politicization from the outset across policies, pedagogies, programs, and practices.

Bi/Multilingual Spaces Are Contested

We are currently witnessing a visible and highly publicized increase in bilingual and dual language programs in the United States, including states and regions that are experiencing rapid growth in their Latina/o immigrant populations and are therefore increasingly serving EB students (e.g., Delaware, Oregon, Utah). A recent Department of Education (2015) report reveals that many states are actively increasing their bilingual program option, particularly dual-language or two-way immersion programs that, by design, serve English monolingual and EB students in the same classroom as they learn English and a non-English language (i.e., Mandarin Chinese, Spanish) and develop global awareness. Additionally, a growing number of states are developing policies to institute a Seal of Biliteracy that would confirm a student's bilingualism and biliteracy on their high school transcript. These increased offerings have been bolstered by research that demonstrates positive gains for EB students in terms of learning, academic achievement, and a positive sense of identity (Gómez, Freeman, & Freeman, 2005; González, 2005). Recall, of course, that California just reversed almost 20 years of Proposition 227.

While this trend portends a major shift in the valuing and status of bi/multilingualism in the United States, it is equally evident that bilingual and dual language programs also have the potential to exacerbate EBs' personal and academic vulnerability (Cervantes-Soon, 2014; de Jong & Howard, 2009; Valdés, 1997; Valdéz, Freire, & Delavan, 2016). Even popular media sources decry "the intrusion of White families into bilingual schools" and the extent to which increasing bilingual and dual language programs are ostensibly catering to the demands of White families who recognize the value of bi/multilingualism for their already-advantaged children (Williams, 2017). Thus, it is clear that the relationship between English monolingualism, bilingualism, and multilingualism in the United States remains contested as the intersection of languages and their speakers have been characterized historically by tolerance and repression (Gándara & Escamilla, 2017; Ovando, 2003).

This volume nonetheless demonstrates that shifting views of bilingualism and multilingualism means that discussions around policy, program, curriculum, assessment, and funding are more expansive in the sense that they speak to a more diverse set of issues. While we learn about some pointedly pernicious views on Latina/o immigrants and their school-aged children, we also learn about broader interests in equity- and social justice-oriented approaches, developing global citizens, preparing 21st century learners and teachers, and teaching and learning with heart, emotion, and *cariño* (Antrop-González & De Jesús, 2006; González, 2001; see Malsbary & Wolf, Chapter 9). Martínez, Hikida, and Durán (Chapter 10) illustrate that despite policies and practices that instantiate monolingual biases and ideologies, particularly in dual language programs, EB students and their teachers creatively enacted translanguaging practices that could potentially expand students' linguistic repertoires.

Across chapters, it is clear that bi/multilingual spaces are shaped by issues related to the place, status, and power of English; the racialization and racism experienced by EBs (or English Language Learners [ELLs]); educational policies and programs that minimally elevate the languages and cultural experiences of EBs; and standardized approaches to learning, teaching, curriculum, and assessment, for example. Contributors highlight the extent to which the promotion and sustainability of bi/multilingual spaces are inevitably forced to negotiate, navigate, and confront dominant forms of oppression and hegemonic structures. For example, we learn about the extent to which Latina/o bilingual youth creatively and actively design their own social and academic futures as they challenge, subvert, and defy teachers' low expectations of ELLs, academic and language tracking, and limited access to rigorous and high-quality instruction (in English). These Latina/o youth develop, as Hamilton and Pacheco (Chapter 11) demonstrate, strategies of resilience and networks of support (i.e., parents, siblings) to navigate their educational experiences, particularly around their language backgrounds, and create opportunities to secure entry into and funding for postsecondary opportunities. Cortéz and Gutiérrez (Chapter 7) examine translinguals participating in forms of everyday resistance (Pacheco, 2012) to reclaim community and neighborhood spaces and, in particular, employing their socio-spatial repertoires to enact and embody their "right to the city." The contributors suggest the implications of these repertoires for teacher education.

In sum, there are persistent ideologies and discourses underlying the promotion of bi/multilingual spaces, contexts, and educational settings as communities, children and youth, and parents and educators seek opportunities to reproduce the status quo or transform schooling for our most educationally vulnerable student populations. For example, bilingual children and youth in Arizona still contend with the oppressive teaching and learning circumstances that Proposition 203 has created and we cannot minimize that generations of bilingual students and teachers lived with the 1990s backlash in California schools. Along with a growing interest in bilingual and dual language programs, these spaces remain contested and therefore require vigilance so as to elevate and make visible lingering equity issues.

Transformation Requires Collective and Collaborative Efforts

Collective and collaborative efforts to significantly mediate and *re*-mediate the schooling experiences and school and classroom practices at the macro and micro levels are highlighted by contributors to this volume (Cole & Griffin, 1986; Gutiérrez, Morales, & Martinez, 2009). In short, transformation requires collective and collaborative efforts, or as hooks (1994) reminds us, to "collectively imagine ways to move beyond boundaries" (p. 207). We are struck by the numerous examples of individuals-acting-together to address educational issues, resist inequities and injustices, and demand equitable and transformative solutions for EBs. As many contributors drew on social theories of learning, language, and action, they demonstrated how individual parents, students, teachers, community members, after-school program staff, educational administrators, and government officials work collectively and collaboratively to transform schooling for EB children and youth.

Drawing on Engeström's (1986, 2009) conceptualization of collective activity as the unit of analysis (rather than individuals), Pacheco (2012) has theorized that collective engagement in *everyday resistance* against social and educational double binds has consequences for individual youths' learning, such as critical analyses, intertextual analyses, and historical analyses. Joint and collective activity—and hence activity systems—similarly become the objects of analysis in these chapters. The clearest examples pertain to the ways that individuals-acting-together mediate educational and language policy. For example, Hopkins and Brezicha (Chapter 4) highlight the importance of community-based boundary spanners who affected change by transforming and shifting local attitudes and perspectives about the Latina/o immigrant newcomer students that necessitate equitable policies, supports, and services.

Aldana and Martinez (Chapter 5) highlight the important roles that teachers, researchers, special interest groups, politicians, and citizens in California played in the political process and in effect as policy designers, makers, and shapers in and outside of schools. Even though Proposition 227 incited a major shift in schools and districts throughout the state, there was nevertheless a cadre of educators and bilingual educators in particular who resisted this anti-bilingual education initiative because it enhanced the vulnerability of EB students as well as the students' families and communities. That is, schools and educators who were committed to bilingual education programs prior to the passage of Proposition 227 were inclined to maintain them after its passage (Stritikus & Wiese, 2006; Valdéz, 2001). Thus, engaged researchers, practitioners, and administrators were actively making and shaping—and, in some cases, subverting—educational policy in their classrooms and schools as they relied on their knowledge and expertise about the most productive and powerful ways to serve EBs. In sum, as the recent passage of Proposition 58 demonstrates, educational policies can be overturned through collective and collaborative efforts to transform learning and educational opportunities for EB students. As Aldana and Martinez caution, however, Proposition 58 is not a panacea (Chapter 5): it is perhaps necessary but not sufficient to fully transform EBs' educational outcomes and experiences.

Teachers and students in classrooms and after-school programs have previously been conceptualized as collective activity systems (Gutiérrez, Baquedano-López, & Tejeda, 1999; Pacheco, 2010b). Additionally, the everyday practices of teachers and students in classrooms (and after-school programs) have been conceptualized as substantially and significantly shaping language policy—either critically or apolitically, overtly or covertly, and so forth (Menken & García, 2010; Ricento & Hornberger, 1996; Skilton-Sylvester, 2003). In this regard, the numerous chapters that focus on classrooms and after-school programs elevate the collectively accomplished interpersonal and interactional relations that come to affect learning, dynamic language practices, and collective identities. For example, Stillman's chapter (Chapter 6) demonstrates that collective and collaborative efforts among teachers, support staff, and administrators can attempt to integrate progressive pedagogies and social justice stances with ongoing efforts to standardize content standards and assessment. Given the unique environment of a dual language school in the borderlands, she shares the ongoing dialogues, struggles, and critical reflection in which they engage to undertake the indisputable challenge of expanding students' bilingualism and simultaneously facilitating rigorous and high-quality curriculum practices that realize social justice ideals.

As such, teachers and practitioners working collectively and collaboratively are understood as being "at the heart of language policy" (Ricento & Hornberger, 1996, p. 417). In being at the epicenter of policy making and policy shaping in ways that have the potential to transform educational opportunities, outcomes, and experiences for EB students and their families and communities, we learn about the particular discourses, strategies, tool kits, and approaches they develop to realize their goals and ideals. Additionally, to undertake critical teaching and advocacy work, educational researchers and practitioners who serve EBs require supportive colleagues and allies, particularly because they are often marginalized by mainstream educators and administrators who rarely take up issues and challenges that pertain to EBs in equitable ways (Grinberg & Saavedra, 2000; Valdéz, 2001). Professionals who serve EBs require collaborative and collegial relationships with mainstream teachers who can support their critical work and advocacy (Arce, 2004; Mitchell, 2013) and the development of their collective "political and ideological clarity" (Bartolomé, 1994, 2004). This criticality, advocacy, and clarity must stem from fundamental theoretical understandings about first and second language learning and development as well as ways to enact these principles in classrooms in ways that are equitable and honor EB students' identities and dignity.

RECOMMENDATIONS: *EQUITY FOR WHOM?*

We revisit our conceptualization of *transformation* as the practice of freedom to "think and rethink, so that we can create new visions" (hooks, 1994, p. 12) of radical, just, and equitable education and schooling for EB students. As Razfar argues (Chapter 2), it is a critical moment in the United States for reimagining and reenvisioning our work as researchers, educators, and practitioners who serve EB students. Demographic shifts are being felt across the country, with increases of communities of color and children of immigrants. Furthermore, bi/multilingualism is more widely accepted in some regions, as evidenced by an increased interest in and development of bilingual and dual language programs. The number of EBs continues to grow, but so does our understanding of how to support their learning and development through particular policies, pedagogies, and practices. As the potential for supporting and advocating for bi/multilingual students increases, our institutional capacity has not kept pace, resulting in school systems, teacher preparation, and understandings of language development that are out of sync, particularly given shifting technologies and communicative modalities.

Thus, vigilance is crucial as communities respond to demographic shifts and to varied legal and statutory requirements to address the needs of their changing immigrant, newcomer, and linguistically diverse student populations. We must pointedly address the question of *equity for whom?* As Macedo and Bartolomé (Chapter 3) urged, educators must provide both rigorous and high-quality instruction as well as abolish the harmful experiences and symbolic and material violence they experience in schools and their communities. To this end, Sung (2017) has cautioned against the extent to which White interest convergence can come to narrowly shape bilingual education policies and programs, while Flores (2013) has argued that bilingual education must be driven by political critique—rather than technocratic and cognitive understandings of language and learning—if it seeks to empower language minoritized students. Pacheco & Chávez-Moreno (manuscript submitted for publication) contend that a radical bilingual education must re-center nondominant bilingual youths' voices and insights about how the relationship between language, power, and schooling intersect in their everyday lives.

Regarding dual/two-way language education, Valdéz, Freire, and Delavan (2016) repudiate its gentrification as it increasingly accommodates "more privileged inhabitants into a ghettoized neighborhood while less privileged residents [i.e., EBs] are priced or pushed out" (p. 604). Instead, as Cervantes-Soon (2014) argues, dual/two-way language education must address the potential disempowerment of nondominant students by promoting critical consciousness and social justice goals wherein language and biculturalism are viewed as critical thinking tools to address "glocal" issues that acutely affect nondominant students.

Given that volume contributors have substantiated that serving EBs remains politicized, bi/multilingual spaces are contested, and the transformation of language and bilingual education requires collective and collaborative efforts, we conclude with the following recommendations. We believe these recommendations simultaneously build on the insights and political and ideological clarity (Bartolomé, 1994, 2004) we have deepened through the invaluable contributions to this volume, as well as critically and equitably transform learning opportunities, long-term educational outcomes, and schooling experiences for EB children and youth. We address considerations for policymakers, practitioners, teacher educators, critical allies, and researchers we believe are relevant to others who work with and serve EBs and their families and communities.

Recommendations for Policymakers

Educational and language-in-education policies and programs must continue to address the needs of EB students as well as equitably mitigate the low status of non-English languages and their speakers in schools so as to transform these students' vulnerabilities in and out of school. Even *multilingualism for all* approaches must remain vigilant so that EBs remain a central focus and concern. In this regard, bilingual education programs must be long-term, amplify the presence and use of minoritized languages, elevate the status of EBs and their families and communities, and institutionalize minoritized languages in assessment and accountability systems. For example, dual language 50–50 program models that ostensibly teach both languages roughly "equally" must deliberately and explicitly elevate minoritized languages, minoritized student populations, and minoritized parents and families in classrooms and throughout the physical and symbolic spaces of the school and district community. This increased awareness is especially necessary in nontraditional gateway regions and communities, or the New Latino Diaspora, where EBs comprise much smaller percentages of the overall population. Moreover, Seals of Biliteracy should be designed to benefit the EB student population that is increasingly being denied opportunities to take advantage of this opportunity to have their bilingualism and biliteracy acknowledged and celebrated (Davin & Heineke, 2017).

Policymakers must also ensure that assessment and accountability systems are available in as many non-English languages as possible to track EB students' growth in learning and academic outcomes and acquisition of bilingualism and biliteracy. Part of this effort includes a reliance on research and scholarship about effective policies, programs, and practices that challenge long-standing deficit views and approaches and hence value and build on the burgeoning linguistic diversity and resources in the United States. Policymakers must also invest in making language-in-education programs robust, rigorous, and high quality by exploring in particular how novel technologies could promote multimodalities that prepare students for success in the 21st century (Black, 2009; Lam, 2013). Finally, policymakers must remain vigilant that EB students from minoritized ethnolinguistic groups are graduating at proportionate rates and have full access to post-secondary education. In short, EB students must have social and academic supports and networks of support at critical transition points in their K–12 schooling (Callahan, 2005; Hamilton & Pacheco, Chapter 11).

Recommendations for Practitioners

First and foremost, we believe practitioners must strive to learn from their students and their students' parents, families, and communities about, namely, their linguistic repertoires—or their *hybrid language practices* (Gutiérrez, Baquedano-López, Alvarez, & Chiu, 1999; Gutiérrez, Baquedano-López, & Tejeda, 1999) and *translanguaging* (García, 2009; García & Wei, 2014). Given that recent research and scholarship has highlighted the ways that schools enact monolingual biases and approaches (May, 2014), practitioners must seek to learn about the discourses, varieties, dialects, and registers EB students develop in home-community contexts in both their home languages and English. Additionally, curriculum approaches have explored language minoritized students' funds of knowledge (González, Moll, & Amanti, 2006), translation practices (Orellana, 2009), political-historical knowledge (Pacheco, 2009, 2012), and socio-spatial repertoires (Cortéz & Gutiérrez, Chapter 7), for example. These insights could help practitioners' decision-making in the area of teaching, learning, and curriculum and, specifically, how to leverage EB students' linguistic repertoires and cultural knowledge to facilitate content area learning and to realize their academic potential. Practitioners' should share their growing knowledge of students' linguistic repertoires and of their students' parents, families, and communities with their colleagues, administrators, and support staff.

Further, as Orellana et al. (Chapter 8); Ek, Garza, and García (Chapter 12); and Morales and Saravia (Chapter 13) argue, it is essential to explore dominant frameworks of critical *cariño*, heart, and emotional practice that honor students' linguistic and cultural repertoires as well as affectively mediate the sociopolitical realities that characterize their life and schooling experiences. Similar to culturally relevant pedagogical approaches (Ladson-Billings, 1995), a *pedagogy of cariño* promotes rigorous and high-quality instruction, culturally appropriate affection, and a commitment to students' empowerment (Morales, Meza, & Maravilla-Cano, 2016). As Macedo and Bartolomé argue (Chapter 3), it is essential to engage in this work with political and ideological clarity and, specifically, consider how pedagogy and curriculum must help nondominant EB students to confront the xenophobic, racist, and vile circumstances that shape their—and their families and communities'—everyday lives and realities.

Given the ever-shifting policy landscape for EB students, practitioners must recognize the invaluable but powerful roles that they play in the implementation of educational policies and specifically, in language-in-education policies. As such, they could participate in critical dialogues about how to mediate policy, assessment, and accountability demands in ways that are equity- and social justice-oriented and serve EB students well. To this end, administrators like Mr. Ruiz (Stillman, Chapter 6) can play a powerful mediational role in that they can provide opportunities for their teaching and educational support staff to instantiate principles of critical pedagogy that promote dialogue and facilitate *conscientización* (Freire, 1996). Finally, practitioners must advocate for EB students by holding educational leaders and administrators accountable, ultimately, for ensuring that educational policies, programs, and practices ameliorate the overrepresentation of EBs in special education (Gándara, Rumberger, Maxwell-Jolly, & Callahan, 2003; González, Tefera, & Artiles, 2014) and the underrepresentation of EBs in gifted and talented education programs. Valdés (2003) has, for example, argued that bi/multilingualism should be considered as part of the criteria to expand conceptions of giftedness and for selection and placement into specialized programs that might increase EB students' educational opportunities.

Recommendations for Teacher Education

Institutions of higher education have major roles to play in preparing preservice and in-service teachers and educational leaders and administrators to substantially transform the educational outcomes and schooling experiences of EB children and youth, particularly in the areas of pedagogy, curriculum, teaching, and learning with nondominant linguistically diverse students. We emphasize that it is essential to prepare *all* teachers to serve linguistically diverse students and build on their strengths in their classrooms, rather than limit this targeted preparation to bilingual, world languages, or English as a second language (ESL) teachers. In particular, we believe that practitioners need to be prepared in the ways we discussed in the previous section. However, we believe teacher education programs must aggressively and strategically recruit racially, ethnically, linguistically, culturally, and religiously diverse preservice teachers who share some experiences and knowledge with EB student populations. To realize these possibilities, it will be necessary to create alternative pathway, accelerated, and grow-your-own programs that will institutionalize knowledge of EB parents, families, and communities as it pertains to serving EB students.

These alternative programs must be offered for educational leaders and administrators who will be well prepared to equitably work with and serve an EB student body and include an overview of language acquisition and development processes, knowledge of transformative pedagogy and curriculum, and awareness of bi/multilingualism and the resultant *hybrid language practices* and *translanguaging* (García, 2009; García & Wei, 2014; Gutiérrez, Baquedano-López, Alvarez et al., 1999; Gutiérrez, Baquedano-López, & Tejeda, 1999). Moreover, these leaders must be prepared to work collectively and collaboratively with their bilingual, world languages, and ESL teachers with regard to pedagogy and curriculum as well as the implementation of educational and language-in-education policies in ways that are responsive to student, parent, family, and community needs. For example, Athanases and De Oliveira (2008) demonstrated that most of their early career teacher participants found themselves advocating for EB students' equitable access to learning. Bilingual teachers who shared similar life experiences as EBs were acutely forthright in their advocacy: They routinely negotiated structures, systems, and key stakeholders and actively built coalitions and marshalled resources to advocate for equitable change in classroom, school, district, and community spaces. Leaders and administrators, therefore, must support this advocacy work. They must help facilitate and provide the institutional and professional support language teachers will need to learning about, from, and with their students, students' parents and families, and surrounding communities with heart, emotion, and *cariño* and to enact transformative pedagogies and practices.

Finally, teacher education programs must prepare practitioners to work collectively and collaboratively with disenfranchised community groups in particular so that pedagogical and curriculum approaches can leverage local knowledge, insights, and efforts at sociopolitical and socioeconomic self-determination. This engagement could lead to the kind of sustained and visible advocacy that researchers and scholars have promoted to challenge, subvert, and/or transform inequitable and unjust structures and systems that maintain the status quo and reproduce disproportionate participation in high-quality and rigorous schooling, graduation rates, and access to postsecondary education (Athanases & De Oliveira, 2008; Callahan, 2005; Gándara & Contreras, 2009). In this way, educators and school communities can become sanctuary spaces as nondominant children, youth, and families navigate the deleterious conditions and circumstances that characterize their lived realities.

Recommendations for Critical Allies

Across areas of education, there are numerous individuals who are not squarely charged with serving and working with EB students (i.e., mainstream teachers, administrators, support staff, parents, literacy coaches, researchers, clinicians, etc.). Oftentimes, however, the nonlanguage certification and title means that these individuals do not share the responsibility of ameliorating the inequitable outcomes and detrimental experiences of EB students. It seems essential that to reimagine, reenvision, and rearticulate educational policies, pedagogies, and programs for EB students, language educators will need the support of critical allies. These allies will need to take up the plight and struggles of EB students with regard to language and bilingualism but also with regard to broader forms of learning, growth, and access. Moreover, they will need to be willing to engage dominant group members in *decentering* their languages, cultural knowledges, literacies, educational merits, and entitlements in education to redistribute human resources (e.g., support staff) and material resources (e.g., funding, textbooks) and expand EB students' equitable access to rigorous and high-quality schooling and education.

Finally, these allies will need to consider ways that nonlanguage educators could design, plan, and implement pedagogical and curriculum approaches that promote language learning and development for all students but EB students in particular (García, Johnson, & Seltzer, 2016). This focus on expanding linguistic diversity might simultaneously address the plight and struggles of students who are constructed—through an intersection of racial, linguistic, cultural, and socioeconomic class categories—as deficient and hence speakers of English varieties that are "nonstandard" (Delpit, 2003; Flores & Rosa, 2015). Ultimately, truly collective and collaborative efforts to expand all students' linguistic repertoires might resonate in discussions about how to provide rigorous instruction that promotes learning and meaning making despite the current high-stakes accountability context that continues to fail EB students and their teachers (Menken, 2010; Pacheco, 2010b; Stillman & Anderson, 2017).

Recommendations for Researchers

We believe this volume has major implications for educational research-ers and scholars. First, it is imperative that we continue to deepen the knowl-edge base on EB students' language learning and development across con-texts and settings as well as to explore the implications of this knowledge for pedagogical and curriculum approaches. This work might continue to extend discussions related to how, for example, racist and anti-Chicano/ Latino rhetoric affect the language development of nondominant students (Hernández-Chávez, Cohen, & Beltramo, 1975; Peñalosa, 1980). For ex-ample, Chicano sociolinguist Peñalosa (1980) had previously observed that social science research had established the following:

> Chicano linguistic behavior is neither erratic nor the product of confused minds torn by culture conflict, nor do Chicanos suffer from congenital defi-ciencies of cognition and conceptualization, despite widespread stereotypes found in the social science and educational literature. (p. 6)

Yet, the "widespread stereotypes" that shaped the (mis)perception and (mis)interpretation of nondominant and Chicano students' linguistic rep-ertoires almost 45 years earlier seem to function in very similar ways today and, we contend, have been exacerbated in the Trump era. And while lan-guage education does not focus exclusively on EBs from Chicana/o and Latina/o backgrounds, we do believe the possibilities and challenges this student population faces has consequences for other nondominant EB stu-dents who are similarly racialized and minoritized.

Thus, the minimal gains we have made in social science research to repu-diate racist, anti-immigrant, anti-Brown, and anti-Black structures of social meaning perhaps demand reimagined and reenvisioned critical anti-racist approaches to bilingual, world languages, and ESL education that might include developing *with* students a language of critique and hope (Darder & Torres, 2003; Elenes, 2003; Leonardo, 2004). While researchers should continue to document the flexible and dynamic language practices of EB students (i.e., their linguistic repertoires), we believe this work is necessary but not sufficient for truly transforming the social meanings and educational structures that continue to constrain EBs long-term academic potential and trajectories. It is our hope that in terms of policies, pedagogies, and practic-es, this volume has demonstrated that educational research and scholarship might examine how instantiations of some of the principles, tenets, concep-tualizations, and practices can come to affect EBs' learning and schooling experiences. Finally, we believe that above all, we must elevate the voices and experiences of EB students as the sources of insight and knowing that could shape our way forward in education writ large and in language education in particular (Bartolomé, 1994, 2004; Darder, 1991; Freire, 1996).

REFERENCES

Antrop-González, R., & De Jesús, A. (2006). Toward a theory of critical care in urban small school reform: examining structures and pedagogies of caring in two Latino community-based schools. *International Journal of Qualitative Studies in Education, 19*(4), 409–433.

Arce, J. (2004). Latino bilingual teachers: The struggle to sustain an emancipatory pedagogy in public schools. *International Journal of Qualitative Studies in Education, 17*(2), 227–246.

Athanases, S. Z., & De Oliveira, L. C. (2008). Advocacy for equity in classrooms and beyond: New teachers' challenges and responses. *Teachers College Record, 110*(1), 64–104.

August, D., & Shanahan, T. (2008). *Developing reading and writing in second-language learners: Lessons from the report of the National Literacy Panel on language-minority children and youth.* New York, NY: Routledge.

Bartolomé, L. (1994). Beyond the methods fetish: Toward a humanizing pedagogy. *Harvard Educational Review, 64*(2), 173–194.

Bartolomé, L. (2004). Critical pedagogy and teacher education: Radicalizing prospective teachers. *Teacher Education Quarterly, 31*(1), 97–122.

Black, R. W. (2009). English-language learners, fan communities, and 21st-century skills. *Journal of Adolescent & Adult Literacy, 52*(8), 688–697.

Callahan, R. M. (2005). Tracking and high school English learners: Limiting opportunity to learn. *American Educational Research Journal, 42*(2), 305–328.

Cervantes-Soon, C. G. (2014). A critical look at dual language immersion in the new Latin@ diaspora. *Bilingual Research Journal, 37*(1), 64–82.

Cole, M., & Griffin, P. (1986). A sociohistorical approach to remediation. In S. de Castell, A. Luke, & K. Egan (Eds.), *Literacy, society, and schooling: A reader* (pp. 110–131). New York, NY: Cambridge University Press.

Darder, A. (1991). *Culture and power in the classroom: A critical foundation for bicultural education.* Santa Barbara, CA: Greenwood.

Darder, A., & Torres, R. D. (2003). Shattering the "race" lens: Toward a critical theory of racism. In A. Darder, M. Baltonado, & R. D. Torres (Eds.), *The critical pedagogy reader* (pp. 245–261). New York, NY: Routledge Falmer.

Davin, K. J., & Heineke, A. J. (2017). The seal of biliteracy: Variations in policy and outcomes. *Foreign Language Annals, 50*(3), 486–499.

de Jong, E., & Howard, E. (2009). Integration in two-way immersion education: Equalising linguistic benefits for all students. *International Journal of Bilingual Education and Bilingualism, 12*(1), 81–99.

Delpit, L. (2003). Language diversity and learning. In A. Darder, M. Baltonado, & R. D. Torres (Eds.), *The critical pedagogy reader* (pp. 388–403). New York, NY: Routledge Falmer.

Elenes, C. A. (2003). Reclaiming the borderlands: Chicana/o identity, difference, and critical pedagogy. In A. Darder, M. Baltonado, & R. D. Torres (Eds.), *The critical pedagogy reader* (pp. 191–210). New York, NY: Routledge Falmer.

Engeström, Y. (1986). The zone of proximal development as the basic category of educational psychology. *Quarterly Newsletter of the Laboratory of Comparative Human Cognition, 8*(1), 23–42.

Engeström, Y. (2009). Expansive learning: Toward an activity-theoretical reconceptualization. In K. Ileris (Ed.), *Contemporary theories of learning: Learning theorists in their own words* (pp. 53–73). New York, NY: Routledge.

Freire, P. (1996). *Pedagogy of the oppressed* (rev.). New York, NY: Continuum.

Flores, N. (2013). Silencing the subaltern: Nation-state/colonial governmentality and bilingual education in the United States. *Critical Inquiry in Language Studies, 10*(4), 263–287.

Flores, N., & Rosa, J. (2015). Undoing appropriateness: Raciolinguistic ideologies and language diversity in education. *Harvard Educational Review, 85*(2), 149–171.

Gándara, P. C., & Contreras, F. (2009). *The Latino education crisis: The consequences of failed social policies.* New York, NY: Harvard University Press.

Gándara, P. C., & Escamilla, K. (2017). Bilingual education in the United States. In O. García, A. Lin, & S. May (Eds.), *Bilingual and multilingual education* (pp. 1–14). New York, NY: Springer International.

Gándara, P., Rumberger, R., Maxwell-Jolly, J., & Callahan, R., (2003). English learners in California schools: Unequal resources, unequal outcomes. *Education Policy Analysis Archives, 11*(36). http://dx.doi.org/10.14507/epaa.v11n36.2003

García, O. (2009). *Bilingual education in the 21st century: A global perspective.* Malden, MA: Wiley-Blackwell.

García, O., Johnson, S. I., & Seltzer, K. (2016). *The translanguaging classroom: Leveraging student bilingualism for learning.* Philadelphia, PA: Caslon.

García, O., & Wei, L. (2014). Translanguaging: Language, bilingualism, and education. New York, NY: Palgrave MacMillan.

Gómez, L., Freeman, D., & Freeman, Y. (2005). Dual language education: A promising 50–50 model. *Bilingual Research Journal, 29*(1), 145–164.

González, N. (2005). Children in the eye of the storm: Language socialization and language ideologies in a dual-language school. In A. Zentella (Ed.), *Building on strength: Language and literacy in Latino families and communities* (pp. 162–174). New York, NY: Teachers College Press.

González, N. (2001). *I am my language: Discourses of women and children in the borderlands.* Tucson, AZ: University of Arizona Press.

González, N., Moll, L. C., & Amanti, C. (Eds.). (2006). *Funds of knowledge: Theorizing practices in households, communities, and classrooms.* New York, NY: Routledge.

González, T., Tefera, A., & Artiles, A. (2014). *The intersections of language differences and learning disabilities* (pp. 145–157). New York, NY: Routledge.

Grinberg, J., & Saavedra, E. R. (2000). The constitution of bilingual/ESL education as a disciplinary practice: Genealogical explorations. *Review of Educational Research, 70*(4), 419–441. https://doi.org/10.2307/1170777

Gutiérrez, K. D., Ali, A., & Henríquez, C. (2009). Syncretism and hybridity: Schooling, language, and race and students from non-dominant communities. In M.

W. Apple, S. J. Ball, & L. A. Gandin (Eds.), *The Routledge international handbook of the sociology of education* (pp. 358–369). New York, NY: Routledge.

Gutiérrez, K. D., Asato, J., Pacheco, M., Moll, L. C., Olson, K., Horng, E. L., . . . & McCarty, T. L. (2002). "Sounding American": The consequences of new reforms on English language learners. *Reading Research Quarterly, 37*(3), 328–343.

Gutiérrez, K. D., Baquedano-López, P., Alvarez, H. H., & Chiu, M. M. (1999). Building a culture of collaboration through hybrid language practices. *Theory Into Practice, 38*(2), 87–93.

Gutiérrez, K., Baquedano-López, P., & Tejeda, C. (1999). Rethinking diversity: Hybridity and hybrid language practices in the third space. *Mind, Culture, and Activity, 6*(4), 286–303.

Gutiérrez, K. D., Morales, P. Z., & Martinez, D. C. (2009). Re-mediating literacy: Culture, difference, and learning for students from nondominant communities. *Review of research in education, 33*(1), 212–245.

Hamann, E. T., & Harklau, L. (2010). Education in the new Latino diaspora. In E. G. Murillo, Jr., S. A. Villenas, R. T. Galván, J. S. Muñoz, C. Martinez, & M. Machado-Casas (Eds.), *Handbook of Latinos and education: Theory, research, and practice* (pp. 157–169). New York, NY: Routledge.

Hernández-Chávez, E., Cohen, A. D., & Beltramo, A. F. (1975). *El lenguaje de los Chicanos: Regional and social characteristics used by Mexican Americans.* Arlington, VA: Center for Applied Linguistics.

hooks, b. (1994). *Teaching to transgress: Education as the practice of freedom.* New York, NY: Routledge.

Ladson-Billings, G. (1995). *The dreamkeepers: Successful teachers of African American children.* San Francisco, CA: John Wiley & Sons.

Lam, W. S. E. (2013). Multilingual practices in transnational digital contexts. *TESOL Quarterly, 47*(4), 820–825.

Leonardo, Z. (2004). Critical social theory and transformative knowledge: The functions of criticism in quality education. *Educational Researcher, 33*(6), 11–18.

Lippi-Green, R. (2012). *English with an accent: Language, ideology and discrimination in the United States* (2nd ed.). New York, NY: Routledge.

May, S. (Ed.). (2014). *The multilingual turn: Implications for SLA, TESOL, and bilingual education.* New York, NY: Routledge.

Menken, K. (2010). NCLB and English language learners: Challenges and consequences. *Theory Into Practice, 49*(2), 121–128.

Menken, K., & García, O. (Eds.). (2010). *Negotiating language education policies: Educators as policymakers.* New York, NY: Routledge.

Mitchell, K. (2013). Race, difference, meritocracy, and English: Majoritarian stories in the education of secondary multilingual learners. *Race Ethnicity and Education, 16*(3), 339–364.

Morales, P. Z., Meza, R., & Maravilla-Cano, J. V. (2016). Latin@ students in a changing Chicago: Current disparities and opportunities within public schools. *Association of Mexican American Educators Journal, 10*(1), 107–129.

Orellana, M. F. (2009). *Translating childhoods: Immigrant youth, language, and culture.* Piscataway, NJ: Rutgers University Press.

Ovando, C. J. (2003). Bilingual education in the United States: Historical development and current issues. *Bilingual Research Journal, 27*(1), 1–24.

Pacheco, M. (2009). Expansive learning and Chicana/o and Latina/o students' political-historical knowledge. *Language Arts, 87*(1), 18–29.

Pacheco, M. (2010a). Performativity in the bilingual classroom: The plight of English learners in the current reform context. *Anthropology & Education Quarterly, 41*(1), 75–93.

Pacheco, M. (2010b). English-language learners' reading achievement: Dialectical relationships between policy and practices in meaning-making opportunities. *Reading Research Quarterly, 45*(3), 292–317.

Pacheco, M. (2012). Learning in/through everyday resistance: A cultural-historical perspective on community resources and curriculum. *Educational Researcher, 41*(4), 121–132.

Pacheco, M., & Chávez-Moreno, L. (manuscript submitted for publication). Recentering Chicano/Latino youth voices: Realizing empowering approaches to critical bilingual education.

Peñalosa, F. (1980). *Chicano sociolinguistics: A brief introduction.* Rowley, MA: Newbury.

Ricento, T. K., & Hornberger, N. H. (1996). Unpeeling the onion: Language planning and policy and the ELT professional. *TESOL Quarterly, 30*(3), 401–427.

Skilton-Sylvester, E. (2003). Legal discourse and decisions, teacher policymaking and the multilingual classroom: Constraining and supporting Khmer/English biliteracy in the United States. *International Journal of Bilingual Education and Bilingualism, 6*(3/4), 168–184.

Stillman, J., & Anderson, L. (2017). *Teaching for equity in complex times: Negotiating standards in a high-performing bilingual school.* New York, NY: Teachers College Press.

Stritikus, T. T., & Wiese, A. M. (2006). Reassessing the role of ethnographic methods in education policy research: Implementing bilingual education policy at local levels. *Teachers College Record, 108*(6), 1106–1131.

Sung, K. K. (2017) "Accentuate the positive; eliminate the negative": Hegemonic interest convergence, racialization of Latino poverty, and the 1968 Bilingual Education Act. *Peabody Journal of Education, 92*(3), 302–321.

U.S. Department of Education (2015). *Dual language education programs: Current state policies and practices,* Washington, DC.

Valdés, G. (1997). Dual-language immersion programs: A cautionary note concerning the education of language-minority students. *Harvard Educational Review, 67*(3), 391–430.

Valdés, G. (2003). Expanding definitions of giftedness. *The case of young interpreters from immigrant communities.* Mahwah, NJ: Erlbaum.

Valdéz, E. O. (2001). Winning the battle, losing the war: Bilingual teachers and post-proposition 227. *The Urban Review, 33*(3), 237–253.

Valdéz, V. E., Freire, J. A., & Delavan, M. G. (2016). The gentrification of dual language education. *The Urban Review, 48*(4), 601–627.

Williams, C. (2017, December 28). The intrusion of White families into bilingual schools. *The Atlantic.* Retrieved from https://www.theatlantic.com/education/archive/2017/12/the-middle-class-takeover-of-bilingual-schools/549278/

ABOUT THE CONTRIBUTORS

Ursula S. Aldana is an assistant professor in the School of Education at the University of San Francisco. Her research examines K–12 school culture with regard to issues of equity and access for racially/ethnically and linguistically diverse students. A former middle and high school teacher, she draws on her teaching experience in urban contexts as well as her personal experience with Catholic education to call on schools to better serve the whole child as a matter of social justice. Her work centers on the ways in which educators can leverage the cultural and linguistic assets of historically marginalized students in classroom and school contexts. Dr. Aldana's work has been published in the *Review of Research in Education, Anthropology, and Education Quarterly, Educational Administration Quarterly*, and others.

Lilia I. Bartolomé is a professor of applied linguistics at the University of Massachusetts in Boston. She previously taught at the Harvard Graduate School of Education, San Diego State University, and worked as an elementary school bilingual teacher and bilingual reading specialist before entering the academy. As a teacher educator, Bartolomé's research interests include the preparation of effective teachers of linguistic minority students in bi- and multilingual contexts as well as working with immigrant parents in order to better assist their children. Bartolomé has published extensively. Her publications include the following books: *Ideologies in Education: Unmasking the Trap of Teacher Neutrality* (2008, Peter Lang Publishing); *The Misteaching of Academic Discourses* (1998, Westview Press); *Immigrant Voices: In Search of Pedagogical Equity* (with Henry Trueba; 2000, Rowman & Little-

Transforming Schooling for Second Language Learners, pages 277–286
Copyright © 2019 by Information Age Publishing
All rights of reproduction in any form reserved.

field Publishers); and *Dancing with Bigotry: The Poisoning of Cultural Identities* (with Donaldo Macedo; 1999, St. Martin's Press).

Kristina Brezicha is an assistant professor of educational leadership at Georgia State University. She holds a dual-title PhD from The Pennsylvania State University in the Educational Theory and Policy and Comparative International Education. Her research interests focus on how education supports individuals' abilities to equitably participate in the democratic processes at both the local and national level domestically and internationally. Specifically, she has studied how immigrant students' experiences of in/exclusion has shaped their knowledge, attitudes, habits, and dispositions towards the political process. She also has examined how different actors and structures within the educational system including teachers, educational leaders, and school boards have facilitated the creation of inclusive and excellent educational opportunities. She has presented her work at numerous conferences such as the American Educational Research Association Convention, the University Council for Educational Administration Convention, and the Comparative and International Education Society Conference. Previously she has taught kindergarten through fifth grade special education students in New York City. She holds a Masters of Arts in Politics and Education from Teachers College, Columbia University and a Masters of Science in Urban Education from Mercy College.

Arturo Córtez is a doctoral candidate in the Graduate School of Education at the University of California, Berkeley. Broadly, his research examines how the everyday practices of nondominant youth can be leveraged toward transformative ends. In his dissertation, he explores how teachers build upon the resistance practices of youth experiencing the advances of gentrification in the San Francisco Bay Area. He holds a BA in the Biological Basis of Behavior from the University of Pennsylvania, an EdM from Harvard University, and an MAT from the University of San Francisco.

Leah Durán is an assistant professor in teaching, learning and sociocultural studies in the College of Education at the University of Arizona. She is a former elementary school teacher who worked in bilingual and ESL classrooms in Texas. Her research focuses on bilingualism and biliteracy in young children, with a focus on the design of literacy pedagogies for culturally and linguistically complex classrooms.

Lucila D. Ek is a professor in the Department of Bicultural-Bilingual Studies at the University of Texas at San Antonio. She received her PhD in Urban Schooling from the University of California at Los Angeles. She held a University of California president's postdoctoral position in the Ethnic Studies Department at the University of California in San Diego. Her research centers on bilingualism and biliteracy of Latinas/os and bilingual teacher education. Her articles have been published in the *International Multilingual Research Journal, Anthropology & Education Quarterly, Equity & Excellence in Education, Bilingual Research Journal,* and the *High School Journal.* She is associate editor for the *Association of Mexican American Educators Journal.*

Janelle Franco is a doctoral candidate in the Graduate School of Education and Information Studies (GSE&IS) at the University of California, Los Angeles (UCLA). Ms. Franco's dissertation research explores how young children living in multilingual communities use literacy and mathematical practices to represent their world through play. She has taught in multilingual communities throughout her career, in New York, Seattle, Argentina, and Mexico. Recently, she has worked with Dr. Marjorie Faulstich Orellana and her research team as a coordinator and researcher at B-Club, and as an instructional assistant supporting students in UCLA's Teacher Education Program.

Adriana García is currently a language support teacher at Northside ISD and provides Spanish and English support to students in kinder through fifth grade in reading and writing. She graduated with a double Bachelor of Arts in English and Spanish from Our Lady of the Lake University. She then continued and earned a Master of Arts in Spanish Literature from The University of Texas at San Antonio and earned a second Master of Arts in Early Childhood and Bilingual Education from Our Lady of the Lake University. She received her PhD in Culture Literacy & Language from The University of Texas at San Antonio. Her research centers on digital fotonovelas as a tool for biliteracy, digital literacy, and visual literacy development for Latino/a bilingual elementary students.

Armando Garza, PhD, is assistant professor in the Department of Elementary and Bilingual Education at California State University, Fullerton. In 2015, he received his PhD in Culture, Literacy, and Language from the University of Texas–San Antonio. As an immigrant himself, Dr. Garza's research interests are shaped by and focused on biliteracy and bilingualism of Latina and Latino students in U.S. schools, the success of emergent bilinguals in the areas of mathematics and science, bilingual teacher preparation programs, multicultural-multilingual education, Spanish literacies of Latino immigrant families, transnational educational experiences of Latina/o students, and issues of immigration and education on both sides of the U.S.–Mexico border. Using sociocultural theories of learning, he has conducted research in Mexico and the United States where he has explored language use in and out of school settings.

Kris D. Gutiérrez, Carol Liu professor, Graduate School of Education, University of California, Berkeley, is a learning scientist and qualitative methodologist whose research examines consequential learning in designed environments, with attention to students from nondominant communities, notably emergent bilinguals. Her work on *Third Spaces* examines the affordances of hybrid and syncretic approaches to literacy, new media literacies, and STEM learning and the remediation of functional systems of learning. Her work in social design experiments seeks to leverage students' everyday concepts and practices to ratchet up expansive forms of learning. Gutiérrez is a member of the National Academy of Education and past president of AERA and fellow of AERA and the Center for Advanced Study in the Behavioral Sciences. Gutiérrez was appointed by President Obama to the National Board for the Institute of Education Sciences. She has published widely in premier academic journals and is a coauthor of *Learning and Expanding with Activity Theory*.

Colleen Hamilton is a doctoral candidate in second language acquisition at the University of Wisconsin-Madison. Her research with Spanish–English bilingual youth in the United States explores their experiences of language and schooling on the path to college. In her dissertation, she analyzes how bilingual youth strategically position themselves for college by leveraging their bilingual experiences to identify systemic barriers, improvise spaces for translanguaging, and design their academic trajectories. She holds a BA in French and MA in Applied Linguistics and has taught English as a second language, French, and teacher preparation courses in language acquisition. Drawing on these experiences of teaching and learning, she focuses on contributing to more equitable, culturally-historically grounded, and dynamic understandings of language in academic contexts.

Michiko Hikida is assistant professor of reading and literacy for early and middle childhood in the Department of Teaching and Learning at The Ohio State University. Her research focuses on preservice teacher literacy education, and on the classroom literacy practices of students who are situated at the intersections of race, language, and ability profiling. Drawing on her experiences as a former elementary school teacher, she seeks to highlight students' and teachers' strengths in an effort to make schools more humane and loving spaces.

Megan Hopkins is an assistant professor of education studies at the University of California, San Diego (UCSD). Before joining UCSD, Dr. Hopkins held faculty appointments at The Pennsylvania State University and University of Illinois at Chicago. Her research explores how to organize schools and school systems for equity, particularly for English learners and immigrant students. Her current work uses mixed methods, including social network analysis, to examine how organizational structures, norms, and beliefs influence policy implementation and teachers' professional learning in bi/

multilingual contexts. Her research has been funded by the U.S. Department of Education's Office of English Language Acquisition, the Spencer Foundation, and the W.T. Grant Foundation. Her scholarship has appeared in several top-tier journals, including *American Educational Research Journal; Educational Policy, Educational Researcher,* and *Journal of Teacher Education;* and she is coeditor of the volumes *Forbidden Language: English Learners and Restrictive Language Policies* (with P. Gándara, Teachers College Press, 2010) and *School Integration Matters: Research-Based Strategies to Advance Equity* (with E. Frankenberg and L. M. Garces, Teachers College Press, 2016). In 2012, Hopkins received the Dissertation of the Year Award from the Bilingual Education Research Special Interest Group of the American Educational Research Association. In 2016, she was selected as a National Academy of Education/Spencer Foundation postdoctoral fellow. She is a member and fellow of the working group on ELL Policy (ellpolicy.org). Dr. Hopkins received her MEd in International Education Policy from Harvard University, and her PhD in Education at the University of California, Los Angeles.

Sarah Jean Johnson is a lecturer in social research methodology in education at the University of California, Los Angeles (UCLA) and a senior research associate at the enter of economic and social research at the University of Southern California (USC). In her research, she uses microanalysis of video methods to examine the moment-to-moment interactions of teachers and children as they engage with curriculum, so as to shed light on critical questions of how culture, language, and social structures influence learning. As a postdoctoral scholar at UCLA in the 2016–2017 academic year, Dr. Johnson worked with Dr. Marjorie Faulstich Orellana's research team examining the work of teacher education students and children in B-Club and the learning that occurs in such informal learning environments that promote play, language, and cultural learning. Sarah Jean's recent research has been published in *Linguistics and Education; Learning, Culture, and Social Interaction;* and *Teacher Education Quarterly.*

Donaldo Macedo is a professor of English and a distinguished professor of liberal arts and education at the University of Massachusetts, Boston. A critical theorist, linguist, and expert on literacy and education studies, Macedo is the founder and former chair of the Applied Linguistics Master of Arts program at the University of Massachusetts Boston. Donaldo Macedo has more than one hundred publications that include articles, books, and book chapters in the areas of linguistics, critical literacy, and multicultural education. His publications include *Literacy: Reading the Word and the World* (with Paulo Freire, Bergin and Garvey, 1987); *Literacies of Power: What Americans Are Not Allowed to Know* (Westview Press, 1994); *Dancing with Bigotry* (with Lilia Bartolomé, St. Martin's Press, 1999); *Critical Education in the New Information Age* (with Paulo Freire, Henry Giroux, & Paul Willis, Rowman &

Littlefield Publishers, 1999); *Chomsky on Miseducation* (with Noam Chomsky, Rowman & Littlefield Publishers, 2000); *Howard Zinn on Democratic Education* (with Howard Zinn, Paradigm Publishers, 2005); and *Imposed Democracy: Dialogues with Noam Chomsky and Paulo Freire* (2012).

Christine Brigid Malsbary is an anthropologist of education whose scholarship analyzes the complexities of social life in *hyper-diverse* cultural spaces—where youth of varying ethnonational and racial affiliations speaking upwards of ten languages collectively interact to produce new cultural forms and engage belonging across difference. Malsbary's most recent publication, the lead article for the *American Educational Research Journal's* December 2016 issue, catalogs the resources/assets of what she terms *hyper-diverse* spaces, promoting the possibilities of such spaces as resources for education and policy transformation. Malsbary has been honored for her work on diversity with a University of Michigan Exemplary Diversity Scholar award in 2012, and an award from the Association of American University Women in 2013. In 2014, Malsbary was awarded a NAEd Spencer postdoctoral fellowship. She is the author of 11 peer-reviewed articles, has given numerous national and international talks, and is currently appointed as visiting assistant professor at Vassar College where she teaches courses on the politics of language and teachers as cultural workers. She has been an active member of the American Anthropological Association and the Council on Anthropology and Education since 2010. Dr. Malsbary is also an activist and artist in New York City, where she engages in radical political education and collective self-organizing with local communities around issues of decolonization, anti-racism and anti-sexism. Her public, nonacademic writing can be found on her blog: https://cultureraceimmigration.com/

Krissia Martinez is a doctoral candidate at the Graduate School of Education & Information Studies (GSE&IS) at the University of California, Los Angeles (UCLA) in the Urban Schooling Division. Ms. Martinez's dissertation research examines the experiences of child language brokers in health care.

Danny C. Martinez is assistant professor of language, literacy and culture in the School of Education at the University of California, Davis. His research examines the language and literacy practices of Black and Latinx youth in urban secondary literacy classrooms. He is also interested in teacher learning as it relates to leveraging the communicative repertoires of youth in schools. Much of his research is informed by his own teaching in secondary schools in San Francisco and Los Angeles. His work has appeared in the *Review of Research in Education, Anthropology, and Education Quarterly, International Journal for the Sociology of Language,* among others.

Ramón Antonio Martínez is an assistant professor in the Graduate School of Education and the Center for Comparative Studies in Race and Ethnicity at Stanford University. His research explores the intersections of language, race, and ideology in the public schooling experiences of students of color, with a particular focus on bi/multilingual Chicanx and Latinx children and youth. Before entering academia, he was an elementary school teacher in the Los Angeles Unified School District.

P. Zitlali Morales is associate professor of curriculum and instruction in the College of Education, and affiliated faculty of the Latin American and Latino Studies (LALS) program at the University of Illinois at Chicago (UIC). Dr. Morales examines the language practices of Latinx youth and linguistic interactions of students and teachers in bilingual classrooms. Her work in teacher education prepares teachers to meet their multilingual students' needs by leveraging their linguistic skills and cultural knowledge. Her research interests include the education of emergent bilinguals, language ideologies, language and identity, and education policy. Dr. Morales is co-PI of a National Science Foundation funded project studying the digital literacy practices and transnational ties of immigrant youth.

Marjorie Faulstich Orellana began her career as a bilingual classroom teacher in Los Angeles Unified Schools, teaching second and third grade from 1983 to 1993. Now professor in the Graduate School of Education and Information Studies at UCLA, she serves as director of faculty for the Teacher Education Program and associate director of the International Program on Migration. The work of the first 6 years of B-Club (the program detailed in this chapter) is summarized in her 2016 book, *Immigrant Children in Transcultural Spaces: Language, Learning and* Love (Routledge). Her research on the work that the children of immigrants do as language and cultural brokers is summarized in her first book: *Translating Childhoods: Immigrant Youth and Cultures* (Rutgers University Press, 2009). She has also worked with a team of graduate students and teachers to design curriculum that connects language brokering to academic language skills (available at https://cxarchive. gseis.ucla.edu/xchange/repertoires-of-linguistic-practice/teachers-workroom). In addition to publishing in academic outlets such as the *American Anthropologist; Harvard Educational Review; Social Problems, Anthropology, and Education Quarterly; Reading Research Quarterly; and Linguistics in Education*, she maintains a blog (marjoriefaulstichorellana.com) and is a columnist for the *Huffington Post* and is past president of the Council of Anthropology and Education for the American Anthropological Association.

Mariana Pacheco's research focuses on meaningful opportunities for bi/multilingual and English learner students to use their full cultural, linguistic, and intellectual resources for learning and self-determination, particularly given the politically- and ideologically-charged macro contexts that affect their learning and development. She employs ethnographic and anthropological methods to understand sociopolitical and sociocultural processes related to language, teaching, learning, and curriculum. Her work contributes to theorizations and empirical knowledge of policies, programs, and practices that amplify what "counts" as knowledge and that enhance bi/multilingual students' academic potential through asset-based and strength-based educational practices, particularly for Chican@/Latin@, (im)migrant, and modest-income backgrounds. Currently, she has been collaborating and supporting bilingual teachers interested in ways to leverage these resources in the classroom, particularly the translanguaging practices that could enhance learning opportunities for bi(multi)lingual students. She is also involved in a collaborative project around immigrant inclusion & equity that focuses on the range of ways immigrant parents and youth seek—and assert their—inclusion in policy- and decision-making processes in education, particularly in the area of language education. Previously, she was an elementary bilingual (English–Spanish) teacher in Southern California and is a proud alumnus of the Migrant Education and Upward Bound Programs.

G. Beatríz Rodríguez received her PhD in 2016 from the Urban Schooling Division of the Graduate School of Education & Information Studies (GSE&IS) at the University of California, Los Angeles (UCLA). She also holds an MA in Multicultural Education from the University of San Francisco (USF) and a JD from The University of Pennsylvania. At the core of Dr. Rodriguez's scholarship and 20 years of experience teaching is her innovative, original research and writing on "Hip Hop Pedagogy" and transformative cultural, classroom practice(s). She currently teaches human geography for San Antonio Independent School District.

Aria Razfar is professor of literacy, language, and culture at the University of Illinois at Chicago and a faculty affiliate with Linguistics and the Learning Sciences Research Institute. Professor Razfar's research has been published widely in premier academic journals including *Mind, Culture, and Activity, Anthropology and Education Quarterly; Human Development;* and *Linguistics and Education.* He has edited and authored several books, including the best selling *Applying Linguistics in the Classroom: A Sociocultural Perspective* (Routledge Press, 2013). In 2013 he was awarded the University of Illinois at Chicago's *Researcher of the Year* for the social sciences. For nearly a decade he has directed several federally funded programs by the U.S. Department of Education and National Science Foundation aimed at developing researchers and teachers of English learners in urban schools. His expertise is grounded in sociocultural theories of language learning and STEM education. He currently directs English learning through mathematics, science, and action research (ELMSA).

Lilia Rodriguez is a doctoral student at the Graduate School of Education and Information Studies (GSE&IS) at the University of California, Los Angeles (UCLA), in the division of Urban Schooling. Ms. Rodriguez's dissertation work explores the power of play and imagination for children in urban schools.

Andréa C. Rodríguez-Minkoff, an alumna of the Graduate School of Education and Information Studies (GSE&IS) at the University of California, Los Angeles (UCLA), earned her PhD in Education with an emphasis in urban schooling. Her research interests include teachers' work and lives, children's understandings of race and gender, children's language ideologies, literacy as a social process, and intergroup relations and identity development in the context of schools. Dr. Rodríguez-Minkoff's interest in education and children's social worlds began when she worked at a preschool as an undergraduate student at Occidental College. In addition to her work in early childhood education, Dr. Rodríguez-Minkoff has also worked as a teacher educator at UCLA prior to joining the Donna Ford Attallah College of Educational Studies at Chapman University.

Lydia A. Saravia is a visiting lecturer in the English department at the University of Illinois at Chicago (UIC). She received her PhD in Curriculum and Instruction from the College of Education at UIC. Her dissertation focuses on the bilingual and intercultural curriculum of a school with a predominantly indigenous student population in the western highlands of Guatemala. She works on issues around the civic engagement of immigrant youth in the Development of Immigrant Youth in Action (DIYA) lab of Dr. Dalal Katsiaficas at UIC. Some of her research interests include language ideologies, language rights, indigenous rights, transnationalism, and international bilingual education. She has been published in *The Journal of Mujeres Activas en Letras y Cambio Social.*

Jamy Stillman is an associate professor of educational equity and cultural diversity in the University of Colorado, Boulder School of Education. A former bilingual elementary teacher, she now uses qualitative methods to explore intersections between education policy, teacher education, and K–12 classroom instruction, especially in the areas of language acquisition and literacy. Much of her research investigates how preservice and practicing teachers navigate the demands of high-stakes accountability policies and standards-based reforms, especially in high-poverty, under-resourced schools serving emergent bilingual students. She recently completed a study, funded by the Spencer Foundation, which explored teachers' interpretations and enactments of the Common Core State Standards in a high-performing dual-immersion school. In addition to the chapter featured in this book, findings from this study are reported in a coauthored book, *Teaching for Equity in Complex Times: Negotiating Standards in a high-Performing Bilingual School*, published in 2017 by Teachers College Press. Dr. Stillman's work has appeared in the *Review of Educational Research, Teachers College Record*, and *Journal of Teacher Education*, among other journals.

Jordan Wolf is a biology teacher on the 9th and 10th grade evolution/revolution team at Flushing International High School in New York. He has taught in New York City since 2005 and at Flushing High for eleven years. He serves immigrant students because he is the descendant of immigrants and believes everyone—no matter where they come from—should have the freedom to pursue their dreams. He has masters' degrees in environmental biology and education and has undertaken research studies on birds, reptiles, and insects in Upstate New York, Long Island's barrier islands, Maryland, Costa Rica, and Peru. Since 2013, Jordan has had a Master Teacher fellowship from Math for America as well as a fellow through the Fund for Teachers and Academy for Teachers. He continues to teach science because he believes the power to objectively understand the world around us gives us the power to improve it.

CPSIA information can be obtained
at www.ICGtesting.com
Printed in the USA
LVHW080327070921
697100LV00002B/18

9 781641 135078